Shakespeare, Bacon, Jonson and Greene

Shakespeare, Bacon, Jonson and Greene

A STUDY

BY

EDWARD JAMES CASTLE

Miracles are ceast:
And therefore we must needes admit the meanes,
How things are perfected.
Folio 1625.—*Hen. V. Act I. Sc.* 1.

KENNIKAT PRESS
Port Washington, N. Y./London

SHAKESPEARE, BACON, JONSON AND GREENE

First published in 1897
Reissued in 1970 by Kennikat Press
Library of Congress Catalog Card No: 77-113363
ISBN 0-8046-1010-X

Manufactured by Taylor Publishing Company   Dallas, Texas

Preface.

HAVE had some doubts whether I should publish this book.

The world does not like to have its established beliefs questioned; but so much has already been said and written on the "Bacon theory," and so many attempts have been made to unseat Shakespeare entirely, that I hope more good than harm may be done if we can ascertain the exact relations which existed between Shakespeare and Bacon.

The only question which is necessary to be decided in order to effect this purpose is, I think, whether or not my distinction between the "non-legal" and "legal plays" is well founded? For if Shakespeare personally had not the education of a lawyer, then I think it must be admitted he must have received assistance in some of his plays from one who had. There are a number of side issues which have been raised in the course of the inquiry, but this is really the only one we have to decide.

In these days of critical research, when from hour to hour our fund of information is being continually added to, it may be shown that I have made mistakes in collateral matters. I have discovered some such mistakes myself, which have been altered; others, no doubt, may still be found out. I however hope that, though the position I have taken up may not be accepted by all, I have at least given some novel and interesting facts concerning our great poet.

E. J. C.

TEMPLE,
February, 1897.

Contents.

Introduction.

THE LAW IN SHAKESPEARE'S WORKS (7). Collier and Lord Campbell's Opinion (8).

Chapter I.

KNOWLEDGE AND USE OF LAW (11).

Lord Campbell's Shakespeare's Legal Acquirements (13). The Sonnets (14). Poems (16). Colour (19).

Chapter II.

LEGAL PLAYS (28).

Measure for Measure (29). Pre-contract (29). Promos and Cassandra (34). Escalus (42). First Trial Scene (43). Observation thereon (52). Second Trial Scene (58). Henry VI. (60). First Part (61). Second Part (73). Hamlet (83). Lear (84).

Chapter III.

NON-LEGAL PLAYS (89).

Titus Andronicus (89). Macbeth (96). Cawdor (98). Twelfth Night (108). Othello (110). Leets and Lawdays (118). Misuse of Words — *Name* (126). *Doom* (127). *Enfranchise* (131). *Executor* (132).

Chapter IV.
Shakespeare—The Author (136).

Reasons alleged that he was not (139). Shakespeare's Early Life (140). Early Surroundings (142). His Father (143). Traditions (144). Reason for believing he joined the Stage as a Youth (149).

Chapter V.
Evidence that Shakespeare was a Writer of Plays (155).

Of Robert Greene (155). Groatsworth of Wit (159). Shakespeare's possible connection with Greene (162). Chettle (163). The Poems (166). Francis Meres (169).

Chapter VI.
Ben Jonson's Evidence that Shakespeare wrote Plays (171).

Jonson's Career (173). The Discoveries (175). Remarks to Drumond (177). Shakespeare's Plagiarism (178). The Poet Ape (179). John Shakespeare's Coat of Arms (182). Every Man in his Humour (186). Every Man out of his Humour (189). Poetaster (189). Return from Parnassus (191). Hamlet in reference to Jonson (192).

Chapter VII.
Bacon and Shakespeare (194).

Legal Friend not necessarily Bacon (194). Query, Coke (195). Resemblance between Bacon and Shakespeare's Writings (196). Identical Expressions, Metaphors, Opinions (196). Quotations and Errors (197). Mr. Donnelly's Cryptogram (198). Promus (199). Silence of Bacon (203). His Friendship for Jonson (204). The Position of the Stage in Elizabeth's Time (205). The Puritans (207). Bacon's concealed Authorship (208).

Chapter VIII.

BACON AND SHAKESPEARE, *continued* (210).

Gesta Grayorum (210). The Position of Gray's Inn (211). The Prince of Purpoole (212). The Entertainment at Greenwich (213). Mr. Spedding's Views as to Bacon assisting (214). Account of Gesta Grayorum (215). The Comedy of Errors (217). The Indictment of the Sorcerer (? Bacon) (219). The Speech of the First Councillor (223). Reasons for believing Bacon was the Prime Mover (225).

Chapter IX.

BACON AND THE FOLIO OF 1623 (229).

Henry VIII.: Reason for believing Work of Bacon and Jonson (230). A Legal Play (230). Distinction between Canon and Civil Law (234). Wolsey's Fall distinguished from Bacon's (237). Campeggio's Letters (238). Cavendish's Account of Wolsey (240). Henry VIII.'s Friendship for Wolsey (242). Wolsey's Arrest, Cause of (243). Wolsey in the Play (244). Bacon's Position (246). The attention given to Wolsey as Chancellor (248). The Eulogy on More (254). The Coronation Procession (255).

Chapter X.

THE HISTORY OF THE PLAY OF HENRY VIII. (258).

Wolsey's Entertainment at York House (259). Burning of the Globe Theatre, 1613 (260). Dr. Johnson's View as to the Authorship (261). Halliwell's Objection (261). Knight's (262). The Poverty of the Language (263). The Stage Directions (264). Jonson's Masques (265). The Prologue of Henry VIII. (266). Jonson's Lines to Himself (269).

Chapter XI.
Circumstances connecting Bacon with the Folio of 1623 (272).

His Fall and Sentence (273). His Letter to the King about Henry VII. (274). Spedding's View (275). First mention of Henry VIII. (276). Bacon's Application for the State Papers (276). His Excuse for not continuing Henry VIII. (278). Conclusion (280).

SUPPLEMENTARY CHAPTERS (283).

Chapter I.
The Actor-Author (284).

Knowledge of Stage Life (285). References to Acting (285). Knowledge of Stage Business (286). Measure for Measure (287). Lear (287). Hamlet (288). The Position of the Stage (293). Female Characters played by Boys (295). Malone's History of the Stage (297). View of the Puritans (299). Hamlet (301). Two Gentlemen of Verona (302). Merchant of Venice (304). As You Like It (306). Twelfth Night (307). Devil is an Ass (308). The New Inn (310). Shakespeare and Greene (311). The Character of Adam (312). The Three Parts of Henry VI. (314). Bacon's Secret Compositions (318). The Northumberland Manuscript (319). The Gray's Inn Masque (323). Essex's Device (327). The Masque of Mountebankes (329). Entertainment of Bacon at Gray's Inn (336).

Chapter II.
Bacon & Shakespeare's respective Contributions (304).

Collaboration, how effected (341). Henry VII., when Written (341). Sejanus, did Bacon assist (346). The Folio of 1623 (348). How Printed (349). The Origin of the Manuscripts (351). Jonson's Contributions (352).

INTRODUCTION.

It is perhaps necessary to offer some explanation for giving this Study to the world. For though what is called the Shakespeare-Bacon question has attracted a considerable amount of attention since it was first raised by Mrs. Delia Bacon in January, 1856, yet the general opinion seems to be that there is either nothing in the suggestion, or there is not sufficient data to settle the matter one way or the other.

But from Shakespeare, as out of Africa, there is always something new, and as I think I have arrived at evidence which, if true, gives a solution of the problem, I have ventured to bring what I have discovered before that jury which must ultimately decide all questions—namely, educated public opinion. I was led to take some trouble about the matter through coming across Halliwell's Life of Shakespeare, which embraces, it is believed, all the documentary evidence known to exist relating to Shakespeare's career. I thought

I would study it and see whether there was any light to be discovered. It was the middle of a rather dull Long Vacation, when " Time stands still with the Lawyer," and the intellectual exercise was some substitute for the out-door amusements which the weather did not always permit. The work grew more and more interesting, and was at intervals followed up. I had by no means a theory to support; was not even an advocate, but one desirous of ascertaining the facts, and I think this is shown by my various changes of opinion as I got more and more into the subject. Originally I, no doubt, leaned to the Bacon theory; it is, as I believe Burke says, more pleasing to exercise our ingenuity in proving that which is not accepted than to merely support what is. But, after some consideration, I came to the conclusion that Shakespeare was the sole author of the two Poems Venus and Adonis and Lucrece, the Sonnets and the Plays, and that there was no evidence that Bacon had anything to do with them, nor any necessity for imagining that he had.

This view was arrived at by a very simple process of reasoning: the great peculiarity, as so many lawyers—Malone, Lord Campbell, and others—have noticed, is the extraordinary knowledge of law to be found in Shakespeare's works.

This "law" is to be found equally in the two Poems as it is in the Sonnets or Plays, and as by common consent it has been admitted, even by the Baconians, that these Poems were Shakespeare's; therefore it seemed clear if Shakespeare could find the law for the Poems, why not for his other works? There were, no doubt, many ways by which he might have acquired a knowledge of law; he might have shared the rooms with a Templar, and while the one studied the other might have written and insensibly have worked in some of his friend's knowledge; but however acquired, if Shakespeare was the sole and undoubted author of the Poems, then I could find no reason why he should not be the author of the Plays.

This reasoning, however, depended upon the fact that Shakespeare was the sole author of the two Poems; if the world had carelessly and perhaps contemptuously allowed him to retain these as his property, it did not prove that they were entirely his work. However, I do not think I should have changed my opinion if I had not almost by accident, and in a way that will be explained hereafter, made a discovery, which is, that the law, the peculiar feature of Shakespeare's works, is not universally to be found in his Plays —there are many which contain no law; and this, I think, is my discovery (for the other fact has been noticed by others, Lord Campbell giving a list of fourteen plays which have no law); there are some plays which show not only absence of law, but ignorance of it. That is to say, there are plays which it might be presumed were written wholly or in part by one who had a legal training, there are others which raise no such presumption, and there is a third class which, from the ignorance of law displayed and the misuse of well-known legal terms and phrases, raise a strong presumption that no one with a legal education could have written them. These plays I shall speak of as non-legal plays, and the others as legal plays. I also discovered that the non-legal plays are so mixed up in point of time with the legal plays, that it cannot be said the former were written before Shakespeare acquired his law or after he had forgotten it. It seems, if these data be true, that only one conclusion could be drawn, *i. e.*, Shakespeare had a legal friend who assisted him, whether this was Bacon or not at present is immaterial. We have in some plays a Poet and a Lawyer, and in others a Poet working alone, who when he does use legal phrases, makes mistakes in his law.

I do not think any one can quarrel with this. Law is a comparatively dry subject, only to be acquired by a large amount of experience and trouble; there is no intuitive knowledge of the forms of pleading and the use of technical words and phrases, and therefore if these are to be found in some of the Plays, we have a knowledge that must have been acquired; and this is inconsistent with ignorance of the use of these phrases, &c., which I think I shall show clearly exists in some of the other Plays; if so, the argument is, as schoolmen say, irresistible, or, as lawyers say, conclusive,—the Poet must have been aided by a Lawyer. I did not rest here, but I examined what evidence there was to show that Shakespeare was the Poet and that Bacon was probably the Lawyer.

In my investigation I found it was like an explorer going up a river in a new country, there were so many branches to be followed up to see what they contained; and for some time past my work has been to separate the side issues from the principal one. I have therefore reserved a great deal of what I think is interesting and explanatory and kept this apart from the main argument, which is this,—that a person acquainted with law and the life of a lawyer and the practice of our courts, who examined the Poems, Sonnets and Plays which we know as Shakespeare's, would, if the name of the author had not come down to him, find a remarkable acquaintance not only with law, but with the habits and thoughts of a lawyer, in a great number of these works; but he would also find in others a want, and more than that, a positive ignorance, of this knowledge. And when he came to examine contemporaneous history, he would find evidence that Shakespeare was the Poet and Bacon the person who probably assisted him in some of the plays, &c.; for I at once admit, so carefully was the relationship between Shakespeare and the lawyer who I believe assisted him concealed, that it is by indirect rather than direct evidence, inference rather than proof, we can bring it home to Bacon.

I propose, first to show the nature of the legal knowledge in the plays; then to establish that the Poet was himself ignorant of law, and next to trace the evidence which proves Shakespeare to be the Poet, and that which points to Bacon as being his legal friend. And afterward I propose to deal with the matters which I have discovered in the course of this investigation, which I think may prove of interest to the Shakesperian student, as throwing some light upon the question.

The Law in Shakespeare's Works.

If one reads the Prefaces which were written by Johnson, Warburton and others, in the early part of last century, the question which seemed most discussed by those commentators was whether Shakespeare was or was not a learned man. Great difference of opinion arose, and the disputants, in wrangling over their bone of contention, often indulged in personal abuse. In the present century, the learning of Shakespeare is taken to be above suspicion. He is, especially by the Germans, supposed to have known all things, both in his present and past, and to have foreseen what was likely to happen in the future; he is supposed to have been everywhere, seen everything, and read all books; but amidst this general admiration there is the one subject of law which has been a puzzle to his editors and commentators of this century who have not been able to satisfy themselves as to how or where he acquired that intimate knowledge of Law of which we find evidence scattered through his works. He could not know a science like Law by intuition; he did know it, therefore he must have acquired it: the question was, how. This has been the problem of this century. I do not know who first suggested that he might have been as a boy in an attorney's office at Stratford; but it was a straw to catch at; it was a solution of the difficulty, such as it was. Collier appeared, however, determined to take an opinion on the subject, and he wrote to Lord Campbell to ask him to look into Shakespeare and see whether there was any evidence that justified this belief. As Lord Campbell puts it in his answer: "You demand rather peremptorily my opinion on the question, keenly agitated of late years, whether Shakespeare was a clerk in an attorney's office before he joined the players in London?" What the learned judge's views on this question are I shall discuss hereafter; but in the course of his inquiry, he tells us that he has examined Shakespeare's writings for "expressions and allusions that must be supposed to come from one who has been a *professional lawyer*." He says, that in fourteen out of the thirty-seven plays generally attributed to Shakespeare, he finds nothing that fairly bears upon the controversy. These fourteen plays are—

The Two Gentlemen of Verona.
Twelfth Night.
Julius Cæsar.
Cymbeline.
Timon of Athens.
The Tempest.

Richard II.
Henry V.
Henry VI., Part I.
Henry VI., Part III.
Richard III.
Henry VIII.
Pericles.

Titus Andronicus.

I do not agree with this list. I find in nearly all the historical plays a large amount of law. I think that there are several plays that should be added to the list, Macbeth, Othello, &c.; but for the present we have, in Lord Campbell's opinion, fourteen plays which show no legal knowledge, and twenty-three plays that do.

This in itself is a very remarkable fact. For we have an author who in about three out of five of his plays saturates them, if I may use the word, with his legal knowledge, and in the other two out of the five makes no use of it. It is curious that this of itself has not attracted anybody's attention to what I believe to be the real truth, viz., that Shakespeare was himself ignorant of law, and that he received help where the law is to be found. But apparently this distinction between the two descriptions of plays has hitherto escaped notice. In order, however, that the comparison may be properly understood, it is necessary to examine what is the legal knowledge shown in the legal plays, and how far, as Lord Campbell puts it, it consists of expressions and allusions that must be supposed to come from one who has been a professional lawyer. If, then, on examination of the other description of plays we find not only this knowledge wanting, but expressions and allusions which could not be supposed to come from a professional or any other kind of lawyer; in other words, if we find instead of knowledge ignorance, then I think the conclusion that must be drawn is pretty obvious.

CHAPTER I.

KNOWLEDGE AND USE OF LAW.

I PROPOSE before considering those Plays of Shakespeare which I term Legal Plays, to inquire shortly into the general knowledge and use of legal terms which are to be found in Shakespeare's works. I do not lay so much stress upon their presence in the Plays, &c., as other persons have done, because I believe they are capable of being learned from books, and are, therefore, not so valuable a test, to my mind, as the familiarity with the habits and thoughts of counsel learned in the law, which I think is the peculiar characteristic of the legal plays. Still, they no doubt are worth consideration, as showing the vast range of legal subjects known to, or affected to be known by, the writer of these works.

In making this investigation I must, to a certain extent, go over the same ground as Lord Campbell in his "Shakespeare's Legal Acquirements." But there are many matters which I think he has overlooked; indeed, with all respect to his memory, I think he has done his work in a somewhat perfunctory manner. It seems that he, or someone for him, has marked the legal phrases in Shakespeare's works, which he has afterwards explained, in many cases only repeating what Malone had said before him. The consequence of confining his attention to legal expressions is, that he has missed entirely the more subtle evidence which points to the life and habits of a lawyer which may not happen to be clothed in legal language. I think this will be seen more clearly hereafter; at present I propose to adopt the effect of what he has written, adding to it where I consider it necessary, so that I may make this study complete in itself, and at the same time I may not repeat at too great length what is already before the world.

The biographer of Malone tells us that he took great pains in studying black letter law for the purpose of explaining the legal allusions to be found in Shakespeare's plays, and, as I have said, Lord Campbell has, for the most part, taken Malone's information and worked it up into his agreeable, but perfunctory, book. But both these authors, I think, have taken too narrow a view of the subject, and have therefore failed, as I have said, to recognize the evidence of the social and professional life of an English barrister, which is to be found by those who look for it.

There are, no doubt, several ways in which a person may work his professional knowledge into his writings. Judge Halliburton, the author of Sam Slick, has given us a series of letters supposed to be written by different persons on board the *Great Western*.[1] In one that is supposed to be from a lawyer's clerk, he has worked in a series of legal phrases, of which the following is an extract:—

"There are several ladies on board 'femes soles,' and 'femes couvertes;' but as I have no intention to be 'unques

---

[1] The Letter Bag of the *Great Western*, p. 123.

accouplé' for at least 'infra sex annos,' my master will have no occasion to be alarmed at it, as an act 'per quod servitium amisit.' They are, however, a very agreeable 'set-off' of a 'dies non' on shipboard to the 'prolixity' of our proceedings. My 'prochaine amie' is a girl of eighteen years of age, beautiful as an houri; but alas, she has not only 'nulla bona' of which I could have an immediate 'habere facias possessionem,' but unfortunately 'Nil habuit in tenementis,'[1] or I do not know that I would not perpetrate marriage with her 'nunc pro tunc.'"

This is a mere tour de force, an effort of ingenuity to work in as many legal phrases as possible, and is like sticking pins into a pin-cushion, and is quite different from the way the law is introduced into the Plays. Any lawyer no doubt could string together these phrases, but when the judge tried his hand at writing a letter from a cadet to his mother, he seems not to have displayed the proper professional learning; for I find a note to this letter, written by a midshipman I suppose, of H.M.S. *Conqueror*, to the effect that it is "Quite absurd, and written by no cadet or midshipman, whether in the Royal Navy or merchant nav*e*y;" an opinion which I have no doubt is quite correct, notwithstanding the shaky spelling.

No one can express an adverse opinion on the legal part of the "legal plays." Lord Campbell has passed the highest encomium upon the accurate knowledge displayed.

In his letter to Mr. Collier, he says[2]—

"Whilst Novelists and Dramatists are constantly making mistakes in the law of marriage, of wills, and of inheritance,

---

[1] Query *in futuro*.
[2] Shakespeare's Legal Acquirements, p. 108.

to Shakespeare's law, lavishly as he propounds it, there can be neither demurrer, nor bill of exception, nor writ of error.

"He is no doubt equally accurate in references to some other professions, but these references are rare and comparatively slight."

Again, speaking of Henry IV., Part 2[1]—

"Therefore, if Lord Eldon" [one of the greatest lawyers of his time] "could be supposed to have written the play, I do not see how he could be chargeable with having forgotten any of his law while writing it."

This is the opinion of one who was himself a great lawyer, and with it no one would, I suppose, disagree, so far as it refers to legal plays; but in the non-legal plays I shall, I think, show this language is inapplicable, for in them we have not the accurate law which he so praises, but the laughable mistakes of the novelist and dramatist he previously mentioned.

I have already said that Lord Campbell's inquiry into the law in these plays is by no means an exhaustive one; but even the subjects which Lord Campbell has collected cover a large area: the rights of a freeholder, special pleading, the conduct of one judge to another, fine and recovery, arrest on mesne process, action on the case, deed polls, writ of extent, præmunire, legal memory, criminal law, conveyancing, Crown Office practice, the court leet, trial by battle, tenure in chivalry, wardship, marriage of minors, and many others, too long to enumerate. Still he has omitted a great many.

Sonnets.

I propose now to mention shortly some of the legal allusions to be found in Shakespeare's works which I

---

[1] Page 73.

think Lord Campbell has either overlooked or not treated fully. And first as to the Sonnets, where we find a rule of law that is well established as very good law now; it is that payment of a debt by a surety releases the debtor as far as the creditor is concerned, though in one sense the debtor personally has paid him nothing. The surety who has paid has his remedy to compel the debtor to repay the debt; but the original creditor, being satisfied, can no longer claim anything against him.

In the Sonnets we find this clearly alluded to. The author is referring to some old love of his who has attracted the affections of a common friend, whereby he is deprived of his love and friend, and yet is not himself set free.

In Sonnet CXXXIII., the author complains the lady has captured both himself and his friend, and continues in CXXXIV. thus:

> "So now I have confessed that he is thine,
> And I myself am mortgaged to thy will;
> Myself I'll forfeit, so that other mine
> Thou wilt restore, to be my comfort still;
> But thou wilt not, nor he will not be free,
> For thou art covetous, and he is kind;
> He learn'd but, surety-like, to write for me,
> Under that bond that him as fast doth bind.
> The *statute*[1] of thy beauty thou wilt take,
> Thou usurer, that putt'st forth all to use,
> And sue a friend, came debtor for my sake;
> So him I lose through my unkind abuse.
>   Him have I lost; thou hast both him and me;
>   *He pays the whole, and yet am I not free.*"

---

[1] An old form of bond, whereby a man's body and lands were made liable to be taken in satisfaction of a debt incurred either as a merchant or in the staple market.

The Sonnets are full of legal allusions, Lord Campbell particularly notices No. XLVI., and says,—

"I need not go further than this Sonnet, which is so intensely legal in its language and imagery, that without a considerable knowledge of English forensic procedure, it cannot be fully understood."

The eye and the heart being joint tenants of a lady, have a contest as to how she is to be partitioned between them; there are regular pleadings, the heart being represented as plaintiff, the eye as defendant, and the jury decide for the eye in respect of the lady's outward form, for the heart in respect of her inward love.

I do not wish to weary the reader with too many examples. I have only to show that here, as in the other works of our author, there is that special legal knowledge, and use and abuse of such knowledge, which, as far as I know, we find in no other writer.

Poems.

In Venus and Adonis we have a subject which one would think an unlikely one to lend itself to the use of law terms. Yet there are two very distinct references in it to legal ideas. The one of some poetical beauty, the other grotesque and commonplace; in the first, speaking of concealed sorrow, we have—

> But when the heart's attorney[1] once is mute,
> The client breaks, as desperate in his suit.

The second refers to the terms of a common money bond, as it is called, which was a contrivance by the

---

[1] The tongue.

KNOWLEDGE AND USE OF LAW.

English lawyers to enforce payment of a debt, or the fulfilment of some other obligation on a fixed day. Time was not considered by the law an element of the contract in many cases. Thus, if a debtor promised to repay a loan at a certain date, if he failed to do so the creditor, though he might be put to great inconvenience by the non-receipt of the money on the day named, could not recover any damages for the non-fulfilment of the promise beyond interest in certain cases. This might be a very inadequate remedy for the damage the creditor might suffer in being thus disappointed in his money at the proper time. He would have to proceed by action to recover, and might be delayed by the different proceedings in law. To remedy this the English lawyers contrived the plan of making the debtor enter into a bond in which he acknowledged that he was indebted to the creditor in a sum generally twice the original loan. This bond being under seal was binding though not true; but there was a condition attached to it, viz., that if the debtor paid or otherwise fulfilled his obligation on the day named the bond should become null and void. So that the creditor had the sanction of the penalty of a double payment to enforce the return of the sum due on the day named. This penalty, as it was called, being a penalty was very strictly construed by the Courts, and was not always a money one. It may be remembered in the "Merchant of Venice" it was a pound of flesh, and Portia, well knowing the law, or rather, having the author's knowledge, saved Antonio's life by noticing the fact that flesh only was mentioned, so that not one drop of blood was to be taken, and a pound to a hair's weight, neither more nor less, was to be cut off. In "Venus and Adonis" the author, with his fondness for law, brings this money bond into use. He makes Venus, in the midst of her passion, being an Italian goddess, play upon the terms and conditions to be found in a bond, even to its sealing with wax:

> Pure lips! sweet seals in my soft lips imprinted,
> What bargains may I make, still to be sealing?
> To sell myself I can be well contented,
> So wilt thou buy, and pay, and use good dealing;
>   Which purchase, if thou make, for fear of slips
>   Set thy seal-manual on my wax-red lips.
>
> A thousand kisses buys my heart from me;
> And pay them at thy leisure, one by one.
> What is ten hundred touches unto thee?
> Are they not quickly told, and quickly gone?
>   *Say, for non-payment that the debt should double,*
>   *Is twenty hundred kisses such a trouble?*

This allusion by Venus to an English common money bond is so incongruous that it is almost burlesque, and is one of the examples that seem to me to point to dual authorship; the Master not taking the matter seriously, the pupil accepting what is given to him, like the old story of, I believe, Sir Joshua Reynolds persuading a citizen at a public dinner to take fish sauce with his pudding. I believe no one knowing the commonplace and sordid ideas connected with a money bond could have made the goddess of love, in the height of her baffled passion, stoop to use such low imagery.

Some of the most remarkable references to law are to be found in the "Rape of Lucrece," where the author shows that he is familiar with a very technical and intricate form of pleading, happily long obsolete, which for some time has ceased to be any part of modern practice. An ordinary writer might have known the conditions of a money bond, though I doubt if he would have thought of introducing it into a passionate poem like "Venus and Adonis"; but I doubt if any one but a lawyer would have been familiar with the example I am now about to refer to.

The word "colour" as used in legal pleadings has a very specialized meaning. In ordinary language besides its first meaning of hue or tint, it, like its sister word complexion, has, no doubt, a secondary meaning of appearance, as, "acting under the colour or complexion of justice." But the old English lawyer used it as something beyond an appearance, viz., a pretended title, and it has been thus defined:—

"Colour in pleading is a feigned matter which the defendant or tenant uses in his bar, when an action of trespass, or an assize, or entry sur disseisin for rent or forcible entry is brought against him in which he gives the plaintiff or demandant some colourable pretence which seems at first sight to intimate that he hath good cause of defence, the intent whereof is to bring the action from the jury's giving their verdict upon it to be determined by the judges, and, therefore, it always consists of matter in law, and that which may be doubtful to the *lay people*."[1]

Now this put into ordinary comprehensible language, as far as I can gather, appears to mean that a defendant who had entered upon certain lands for which act he was being sued, and wished to justify his doing so, had not only to state his own title, but had to give a false title to the plaintiff. And very difficult questions arose, because if the defendant set out a good title in the plaintiff he put himself out of court, because he admitted the plaintiff was right; and if he

---

[1] Viner's Abridgment.

set out no title at all he was wrong, as his plea simply meant a denial of the plaintiff's right altogether. So that he had to steer his false allegation between Scylla and Charybdis. An example given in Reeve's "History of the English Law," illustrates the defendant's difficulty. The defendant alleged that a lease to a man and his wife had been granted by a certain Abbot. One died, the other married the plaintiff and then died, leaving the plaintiff in possession of the property, and the defendant alleged that the original lease had been extended to the plaintiff; the courts held this was bad colour because a lease for lives could not be extended to a third person, and, therefore, the plea simply alleged that the plaintiff had no title.

In other words, it appears that the defendant could not set out his own title under which he justified, without, for some reason which now seems impossible to understand, setting out a fictitious title for his adversary. I do not propose to attempt to explain why this was so, because I do not know, for luckily these things have all passed away. But, apparently, this doctrine of colour was one of the quagmires into which the legal mind of the Norman—who had for the first few centuries after the conquest been trying to graft the law of Justinian upon the English "common law"—had led or driven the judges. Phillimore speaking of this period says [1]:—

"At the same time the language and decisions of our judges, on questions of real property and special pleadings were more like the whimsical extravagance of a goblin allowed by some mysterious dispensation to apply to human

---

[1] Maxims of Jurisprudence, p. 1.

affairs the morbid weakness of a perverted intellect, than the errors and mistakes of beings possessing the usual faculties and invested with the outward appearance of humanity."

Of this nature, in my opinion, was colour as understood by the lawyers of old "very doubtful to the lay gents," probably meaning jury. And it is now still more doubtful and unknown to the modern lawyer, and so might it rest were it not for the fact that, whoever wrote the Plays and Poems, at least that of Lucrece, was at home in this very abstruse manner of pleading. It may, therefore, be necessary to say one or two words more in explanation of the use of this word, before giving the occasions on which it is used. I think it will, however, be sufficient to say that colour sets out a title which, though probable, is really false, or as it is said—

"Colour ought to be such a thing which is good colour of title and yet is no title, *e.g.*, as a deed of lease for life without livery, because the title, though apparently good, was really bad because it had not the necessary formality of actual putting in possession which was called ' livery.'"

In the Plays we find "colour" used in the strict legal sense as I have explained it as well as in its more colloquial manner of pretence or appearance. The latter I need not refer to, but I think the following examples show that the author knew the legal meaning and use of the word as representing a title or justification. Thus in "Cymbeline" that king refuses to continue the tribute to Rome, and says:—

> Cæsar's ambition,
> (Which swelled so much that it did almost stretch
> The sides o'the world,) *against all colour*, here
> Did put the yoke upon us ; which to shake off,
> Becomes a warlike people, whom we reckon
> Ourselves to be.

The only interpretation to give to the word colour here seems to me to be that which the law attaches to it, *i. e.*, title or justification.

In a "Winter's Tale," where Florizel is persuaded by Camillo to fly with his love to Leontes, who is, unknown to all, her father, he says—

> Worthy Camillo,
> What *colour* for my visitation shall I
> Hold up before him ?

Here the technical use of the word is perhaps not quite so certain, but I think a stronger meaning is given to the language if we use it in the legal sense of title or justification. However, in the next example, the word is used in its strict legal sense.

Henry IV., pointing out to his son the folly of his conduct and the opportunity it gives the Percys to attack the Crown as he formerly attacked Richard II., says[1]—

> And even as I was then is Percy now.
> Now by my sceptre, and my soul to boot,
> He hath more worthy interest in the state,
> Than thou, the shadow of succession :
> For, of no right, nor *colour* like to right,
> He doth fill fields with harness in the realm ;
> Turns head against the lion's armed jaws.

In the Second Part, "Henry VI.," where Gloster's death is determined on, Beaufort says[2]—

> That he should die is worthy policy :
> But yet we want a *colour* for his death :
> 'Tis *meet he be condemn'd by course of law.*

The Cardinal does not here seek a pretext, but a

---

[1] 1 Henry IV., Act. III. Scene 2.
[2] Act III. Scene 1.

justification or title for the act as he is to be condemned by law.

Other examples no doubt might be found, but there is sufficient, I think, to show that the author was fully alive to the use of the word in its technical sense. I do not find in any of the examples given in the dictionaries this technical use of the word, nor do I think it will be found elsewhere except in purely legal works. In the rape of Lucrece, this special use of "colour" is very marked, we find the author using this word in its strict legal sense on two occasions. First, as we are told, when Tarquin is in his chamber arguing with himself—

> Thus, graceless, holds he disputation,
> 'Tween frozen conscience and hot burning will.

He forces himself to action, saying—

> Why hunt I then for *colour* or excuses?

Again, when she is trembling at the sight of the intruder, where she—

> Who, o'er the white sheets, peers her whiter chin,
> The reason of this rash alarm to know,
> Which he by dumb demeanour seeks to shew;
> But she with vehement prayers urgeth still,
> *Under what colour he commits this ill.*

In other words, under what title or justification he commits this trespass. If this intrusion were by a husband, the answer would be by colour of a husband's rights. If a favoured lover had to reply, his answer would be by colour of leave and licence. Tarquin has no colour—he is a trespasser pure and simple. He therefore plays upon the word as we so often find in our author's works.

> Thus he replies: "The colour in thy face
> (That even for anger makes the lily pale,
> And the red rose blush at her own disgrace)
> Shall *plead* for me, and tell my loving tale."

He immediately reverts to the legal sense of the word, for he continues—

> "Under that colour am I come to scale
> Thy never-conquered fort."

It seems, therefore, that our author's works show us familiarity with this abstruse and happily now obsolete form of special pleading as they appear to do of all other legal knowledge.

There are a good many more uses of legal phraseology in this poem. Lord Campbell gives the following:—

> Dim *register* and *notary* of shame!

> For me, I force not argument a straw,
> Since that my case is past the help of law.

> No rightful plea might plead for justice there.

> Hath served a dumb arrest upon his tongue.

To these may be added—

> I will not poison thee with my *attaint*,

alluding to the corruption of blood hereafter explained which follows attaint.

Lucrece also sets out her will—

> This brief abridgement of my will I make:
> My soul and body to the skies and ground;
> My resolution, husband, do thou take;
> Mine honour be the knife's that makes my wound;
> My shame be his that did my fame confound;
> And all my fame that lives, disbursed be
> To those that live, and think no shame of me.
> * * * * *
> Thou Collatine shalt *oversee* this will.

An overseer was sometimes the executor, sometimes a friend, appointed to see the provisions of the will carried out by the executors.

I have thus far dealt with the mere legal expressions as we find them in the Plays, Sonnets and Poems. I have, as far as I may be allowed to say, tried to be accurate in my law, but it must be remembered that I am not writing a legal treatise, but endeavouring to ascertain what law a lawyer would know some 300 years ago, say, between the years 1590 and 1610. If I had been writing a modern law book, I should have confined myself in a great measure to decided cases, which would have been so decided by a judge after hearing what could be said on either side. But in trying to ascertain how far some of the plays have worked into them the law of Elizabeth and James, I have had no such assistance, and therefore mistakes may have crept in. If this should be proved to be so, of course I should regret it; but I think in any case there must be enough proved to show that the law in Shakespeare's works is not the law of a country solicitor's boy, as some suggest Shakespeare may have been; and when we come to the plays, I think it will be seen it could not be gathered from books as in Chaucer's time, French was learned *atte le Bow*, but is the knowledge of a person who must have lived on terms of intimacy with barristers, judges, &c.

I have already noticed, that the suggestion that Shakespeare learned his law in an attorney's office when a boy at Stratford is one that has been often made, and on it Collier asked Lord Campbell's opinion, which gave him the opportunity of replying in the letter which he afterwards published. If my view of the facts be correct, that Shakespeare never knew any law, there can be no reason for the supposition; but, apart from this, I think any one who has considered even the small part of the law in the plays, which I shall refer to, must be satisfied that the knowledge of law there shown is not that of an attorney, still less of an attorney's clerk, and a great deal less of an attorney's office boy, which is almost all Shakespeare could have been. Shakespeare nowhere displays the learning and knowledge to be picked up in an attorney's office, but, on the contrary, it will be seen his ideas are illustrated by expressions that could only have been learned by an actual attendance in the courts, at a pleader's chambers, going circuit, or by associating in terms of the closest intimacy with those who had lived the lives of the Bench and Bar.

When lawyers are spoken of in the Plays the old and correct meaning is given to the word, *i.e.*, members of the Bar, and though on a very few occasions an attorney is spoken of, this word is used in its original and historical meaning of "an agent." I think there are but two or three references to an attorney-at-law in all Shakespeare's works. In the practice of that branch of the legal profession an observer, such as Shakespeare must have been, would have seen a great deal of life. Matters of strong dramatic interest must have come under his notice, causes won, causes lost, matters of practice, and many other things must have attracted his attention. Yet whilst we find innumerable references made to judges, law courts, members of the Bar, &c., in fact something from the lives of all manners and conditions of men is found in his Plays; there is nowhere the slightest example of an illustration or expression being taken from a working attorney's life. In those days the distinction between the Bar and the attorney was, perhaps, more clearly drawn than it is in these, where one brother becomes a solicitor, and another a member of the Bar; and the former very often becomes the more successful man. And if Shakespeare was the lawyer of his Plays, and he acquired his law at Stratford in his youth, he must have resolved to forget the ladder up which he had climbed. If Bacon supplied the law, from what we know of his vanity and pretension, it is easy to understand how he might be too big a man to remember anything about attorneys-at-law.

CHAPTER II.

LEGAL PLAYS: MEASURE FOR MEASURE—HENRY VI. (PARTS 1 AND 2)—KING LEAR—HAMLET, &C.

IN examining some of the plays, which for the sake of distinction I have termed "Legal Plays," I have not attempted to make an exhaustive study. It is a work of some labour to read a play so attentively as is necessary in order to discriminate between legal knowledge and legal ignorance. One has to read and re-read to be sure that there has been no overlooking of the indications of the one or the other. I have, therefore, limited my inquiry to ascertaining sufficient evidence to prove, on the one hand, the knowledge, on the other, the ignorance, of both law and lawyers which we find in my opinion in Shakespeare's works.

We must always remember that the law we find is the law of England at the end of the Sixteenth Century, regardless of the particular period or country in which the scene is laid. And the play which, perhaps, best of all shows an acquaintance with the study and practice of our law in Shakespeare's time, and of the manners, habits, and customs of the English judge, is "Measure for Measure," where I think we shall find the latter described by one who knew him well, and was not afraid to draw him as he was.

"*Measure for Measure.*"

This play which is, I think, the one that contains most legal information, &c., has on many occasions been associated with Bacon's name, because Toby Matthew, writing to him in an undated letter, says, " I will not promise to return you weight for weight, but *measure for measure.*" This, of course, may refer to other things besides this play; but it is one of the many curious matters which we shall come across which are capable of more than one explanation, it is true; but one of these explanations points to Bacon, and it may be that Bacon did send this play to Matthew to read; but this is only conjecture—not evidence.

This play is not one which one would choose were it not for the very strong evidence of legal knowledge and training we find in it. It turns upon the legal effect of a pre-contract, and it may not, therefore, be out of place to give a short sketch of the changes that had taken place in the law upon this subject. In Shakespeare's time it was in a transitive state, at least I think so, though in the absence of the records of the ecclesiastical court one can only hazard an opinion. But as far as I have been able to trace the changes in the law they appear to be as follows:

The Pre-contract.—Before the Reformation, the Pope claimed the right to set aside marriages where either of the parties had entered into a pre-contract, or where the parties were related to one another within certain degrees. From a recital in a statute of Henry VIII. it appears all that was necessary to set aside a marriage which had been regularly solemnized, and the parties had lived together perhaps for years, children born, &c., was the evidence of two witnesses of a pre-contract, or of relationship within the degrees not allowed by Rome; the marriage was dissolved, the innocent party divorced, and the children made bastards. Although the pre-contract had not been followed by intimacy, the Pope held there was a contract of marriage which had to be enforced, and that the question of intimacy did not arise. This position taken up by the ecclesiastical courts at Rome no doubt was a great difficulty in their way when the divorce between Henry and Catherine had to be considered. Catherine claimed to have been but a wife in name to Henry's brother Arthur. But this was immaterial from the Catholic point of view. There had been a binding marriage with Arthur, and that being so, a subsequent marriage with his brother Henry was so impossible that it was contended no dispensing power possessed by the Pope was able to make it possible. Mr. Froude in his history seems to have missed this point. I only refer to it here as showing the effect of a contract of marriage before the Reformation. Henry the VIII., in the Act already referred to,[1] enacted that, unless intimacy had followed the pre-contract, no subsequent marriages were to be defeated by it, and the pre-contract was not to be considered binding.

The effect of this Act was twofold. It preserved existing marriages from being defeated by a mere pre-contract which no doubt was the primary intention of the statute, which by using the word *pre-contract* seems to show what was under consideration was not

---

[1] 32 Hen. VIII. c. 38.

the first or original contract, but the second one, which was sought to be avoided on the ground of the first or pre-contract. Secondly, it prevented the courts from enforcing the original contract unless intimacy had taken place, even where there had been no subsequent marriage. This was thought to be a great defect, and when Henry died, one of the first Acts passed by his successor's advisers was to re-create the power to enforce, that is to compel specific performance of a mere contract of marriage. The 2 & 3 Edw. VI. c. 23, apparently contemplated only the evils arising from the want of power to enforce a contract of marriage and took no notice of the larger evils that might arise by the dissolution of existing marriages in consequence of the mere pre-contract being enforced. For the Act only refers to the fact that persons who had contracted marriage with others broke that contract, "even at the very church-door or marriage feast, the man to take another spouse, and the espouse to take another husband, &c." For these reasons the Act of Henry was from the 1st May, 1549, so far as regards the pre-contract, repealed, and "was reduced to the estate and order of the king's ecclesiastical laws of the realm which, immediately before the making of the said statute, in this case were used in this realm." This Act of Edward was extended by one of Mary, but Elizabeth revived the statute as passed by Edward.

By sect. 2 of the Act of Edward VI. "the King's Ecclesiastical Judge, having the pre-contract sufficiently and carefully proved before him, is to give sentence for matrimony commanding solemnization, cohabitation, consummation and tractation as becometh man and wife to have." And that this might affect subsequent marriage was clearly present to the legislature for a proviso is inserted "that no marriage contract before the first of May then next (1549) should be dissolved for a mere pre-contract." Probably a good many people got married in a hurry in that year. This was apparently the effect of the law as it appeared by statute. But one of the advantages of having the tribunals of a country situated in the country and not at the Court of a foreign Pope, or Prince, is that their decisions are more liable to be controlled by local views, public opinion, &c. And, no doubt, this power of enforcing a mere first contract at the expense of a second one and thus destroying the status of an innocent wife and family was felt to be the cause of great injustice to the parties to second contracts, and to produce no great happiness to those of the first. And now, since the Marriage Act of George II., the Ecclesiastical Courts are not allowed to compel specific performance of a pre-contract, the injured party being left to recover damages by an action at law for breach of a promise. But before this Act, there can be little doubt that the power of enforcing specific performance of a mere contract to marry had gradually fallen into disuse, the process by which this was accomplished no doubt would be very interesting to trace, but it does not lie within the scope of this study, and it would be one of some difficulty, owing to the absence of reports in the Ecclesiastical Courts. In the *Duchess of Kingston's Case*,[1] where the opinion of the judges was, in 1776, given to the House of Lords, a reference is made to suits having been brought in the

---

[1] Smith's Leading Cases.

Ecclesiastical Court upon a promise of marriage, presumably to enforce it *in facie ecclesiæ*. But whether the judges were referring to what was in their time an existing practice or as seems more probable to ancient law, it is difficult to say. But we have not to trace what is the law now, but to show that there has been a gradual transition, arising from the necessity of protecting the second and existing marriage. In Shakespeare's time, the ecclesiastical authorities required a bond, in the case of licences, to be entered into with sureties, that no pre-contract, &c., existed. It was the difficulty of reconciling the date of Shakespeare's own bond with the birth of his first child that has given rise to some scandal; and in the case of ordinary marriages, they relied upon the almost terrible exhortation to come forward and speak or for ever after to hold the tongue as some protection for parties marrying. But, however that may be, the mere recovery of the penalty upon a bond was no effectual recompense for the great injury that was done by breaking up a home, dissolving a marriage, &c., because some love-making with vows of eternal constancy could be twisted into a pre-contract. The result, no doubt, was that the good sense of mankind made the judges at first exercise their power of enforcing the mere contract with great discretion, then difficulties were no doubt thrown in the way. The proof was made more difficult until the law died by disuse. In, perhaps, the same way that in modern days the action for breach of promise can only, with effect, be brought by a woman, the juries being told not to allow a male plaintiff to succeed.

I have taken some pains to show that there has been this gradual change in the law, because, as I have pointed out, the law in the Plays is the English law of Shakespeare's time, and if we apply this rule to the view of the law of the pre-contract as given in "Measure for Measure," we have, as it were, a photograph of the law in a transition state, passing through changes of which we have no accurate record.

If we can trust the law as Lord Campbell says we can, it would seem that, at the end of the sixteenth century, there had already been a re-action in favour of the view taken by Henry VIII., that a mere pre-contract was not enforceable where there had been no intimacy; but directly the parties had lived as man and wife, the Court would compel them to sanctify their contract by the ecclesiastical ceremony. This seems to me the conclusion to be drawn from the Duke sending Mariana to the man who had contracted to marry her, and then, and not till then, requiring him to do so, before the church. With these preliminary observations on the pre-contract, which I trust will not be considered out of place, I will proceed to the examination of the Play.

Promos and Cassandra.—" Measure for Measure " is founded upon a comedy written by George Whetstone which was dedicated by him to his worshipful friend and kinsman William Fleetwood, Recorder of London, on the 29th July, 1578, so that it was a comparatively old play when Shakespeare began to write, which we may suppose to have been about 1592—4. The plot of Whetstone's play turns upon the idea of a woman sacrificing her honour, to save her lover's or relation's life, but doing so in vain as her only reward is to receive his dead body. The story is one of those root stories that make their appearance in so many forms, and are sometimes to be traced back into remote antiquity. At times the woman surrenders herself without marriage, and sometimes the exigencies of morality are satisfied and she consents to become the wife, as in "Trovatore," where the heroine marries the Count to save her lover, and then takes poison. Whetstone works up this idea by supposing the King (of Hungary) to have sent one Promos to be in the commission to look after a place called Julio. The stage directions for reading his letters patent show some care (they must be fair written on parchment with some great counterfeit seal). Promos finds one Andrugio has been guilty of incontinence with Polina; he is condemned to death. His sister Cassandra pleads with Promos, who offers to pardon her brother if she will yield herself to him; to this she consents, and yet he orders the brother's head to be given to her. Another prisoner dying, the gaoler cuts off the latter's head as being Andrugio's. Cassandra, not knowing the difference, tells the whole story to the king, who makes Promos marry Cassandra, and then is about to have him executed when he is moved to forgive him by the appearance of Andrugio and all ends happily. Promos, however, has a man called Phallax, who is made a kind of inferior judge or officer, before whom a certain lady called Lamia is brought as one having a very doubtful character. He dismisses the informers and falls in love with her, and in the end loses his wealth and office, and the lady gets whipped. There are some allusions to legal practices in the play, but they are written in a hostile spirit, not in the way references are made in Shakespeare's Plays; thus, when complaints are made of the extortion of Phallax who holds a charge over a debtor's house, who has paid nearly all his debt and is ready to pay the remainder, but Phallax says it is forfeited. Ulrico, whom the king has commissioned to see these things righted, says:—

> *Summum jus*, I see, is *Summa injuria*,
> So these wrongs must be salved some other way.

Thus Phallax, when he seeks to gain over Lamia whom he ought to punish, and she warns him of the risk he runs, he says—

To 'scape such pain wise men without suspect can measure,
Furthermore, I have been (my girl) a lawyer to, too long
If, at a pinch, I cannot wrest the law from right to wrong.

And when the charges are brought home to Phallax by the king, and he asks, what all prisoners or accused persons have generally granted to them, time to answer the accusation,—

> I humbly crave
> Of your grace, for answer, respite to have,

the king says,—

> Why! to devise a cloke to hide a knave,
> Friend, "*Veritas non quærit Angulos*"
> And if yourself, you on your truth repose,
> You may be bold these faults for to deny,
> Some little care upon their oaths to lie,
> See if any on your behalf will swear.

Phallax can get none, so he confesses and is, therefore, only condemned to lose his office and effects without bodily punishment. An English judge would, I think, have granted him the time, but would not have given much effect to the fact that he confessed when he could do nothing else.

Now, when we see in the Play of "Measure for Measure" how this is altered, I think it must be admitted that the later play could only have been written with the assistance of one learned in the law.

The Play of "Measure for Measure" is a good example of the refinement and elevation of idea with which the very difficult subject is treated. In fact, this is overdone; for, as I shall show, from a desire not to dishonour the two guilty lovers, their liason is sanctified by a pre-contract, which really takes all point out of the story. In this the old play is better constructed, for the sister there laments that her brother's fault cannot be cured by marriage.

> The law is so severe in scourging fleshly sin,
> As marriage to work aftermends doth seldom favour win.

Polina, addressing herself (Act. V. Scene 3), says—

> And he for to repair thy fame, to marry thee that vowed,
> Is done to death for first offence.

Here there is no question of any pre-contract, but in "Measure for Measure," Act I. Scene 3, Claudio distinctly tells Lucio—

> Thus stands it with me:—Upon a true contract,
> I got possession of Julietta's bed;
> You know the lady; she is fast my wife,
> Save that we do the denunciation lack
> Of outward order: &c.

So that in reality there is no motive left for the play.

It is not only, however, on this point that "Measure for Measure" is a refinement on "Promos and Cassandra." The heroine is saved from even a temporary degradation by having Mariana to take her place, and though some of the low life of the old play is reproduced, it is toned down and put rather as low comedy than the mere villany it is in the original. But particularly the rapacious and dishonest pettifogger Phallax is replaced by a grave and learned judge, Escalus. And it is to this character I shall have more particularly to refer, as I think he is a sketch from life of such a judge as Bacon himself might have been, where his natural manners were not modified by the private interest of himself or others. Before discussing, however, the peculiar character of Escalus, I propose to take the play as a whole, and show what evidence there is of its having been written wholly or in part by some one who was well acquainted with English law.

I have already pointed out the changes that had taken place in our marriage law. Now "Measure for Measure" turns upon the view that where there had been a contract to marry, the Church, or rather, the Ecclesiastical Courts would, where intimacy had followed, compel the parties to perform the contract. There are many forms of plot where the husband leaves the wife at the church door, and afterwards by some trick she gains possession of her husband. This is the plot of "All's Well that ends Well." But this is the only story as far as I know, that turns upon the effect of such a trick upon the pre-contract. The play opens, as may be remembered, of a Duke, whose city we learn incidentally is Vienna, leaving his government to a man of austere piety, joining with him in the commission the venerable judge, Escalus, because he thinks he has not been severe enough in the execution of the Laws. It appears that a certain Claudio has entered into this pre-contract with a lady and lived with her until she was almost about to become a mother; the contract has been concealed in order to get settlements out of the lady's friends. And the first thing that Angelo does is to seize this Claudio and condemn him under an old law to be executed. It seems, and this is the point upon which I think the play has been too much refined, that Claudio had only to confess the real facts, as he states them to his friend Lucio, to be acquitted, but this is ignored, and he is to be executed; in the meantime the Duke returns in the garb of a friar, and revisits his city to see how Claudio is getting on. He rather expects, and, I fancy, hopes he will show himself in different colour; he is evidently too good to please the Duke,

"Lord Angelo is precise:
Stands at guard with envy; scarce confesses,
That his blood flows, or that his appetite
Is more to bread than stone: Hence shall we see
If power change purpose, what our seemers be."

Amongst other things, he goes to the prison and there learns that Isabella, the prisoner Claudio's sister, has been to see Angelo to ask for her brother's life. Angelo has been struck with her beauty and has promised his pardon if she will come to him that night. The brother wishes it. But she refuses. The Duke solves the difficulty by happily remembering the English law, and the convenient fact that the austere Angelo had promised one Mariana marriage, and because she had lost her money had not carried out his promise. And he thus states the facts with due *legal precision* :—

"She should this Angelo have married; was affianced to her by oath, and the nuptial appointed: between which time of the contract and the limit of the solemnity, her brother Frederick was wrecked at sea, having in that perished vessel the dowry of his sister."

Mariana is persuaded by the Duke to take Isabella's place and to go to Angelo, but she only consents if the Duke, who is disguised as a friar, will advise her to do it, which he does, saying,—

> He is your husband on a pre-contract:
> To bring you thus together, 'tis no sin;
> Sith that the justice of your title to him
> Doth flourish the deceit.

The next day, before the Duke, Mariana is asked to unveil, but she claims the position of a married woman:—

> Pardon me, my Lord; I will not show my face,
> Until my husband bid me.

Then follows one of those plays between question and answer which we so often find in Shakespeare's works:—

> What! are you married?
> No, my Lord: &c.

To return to our law.

Angelo pooh-poohs the pre-contract and denies the intimacy and all goes well with him till the Duke is discovered under his guise of a friar, when Angelo acknowledges his guilt as a lawyer would.

> Then, good prince,
> No longer session hold upon my shame,
> But let my trial be my own confession;
> Immediate sentence then, and sequent death,
> Is all the grace I beg.

But the Duke has another duty to perform, to complete the marriage of Mariana; he takes no notice of Angelo's confession, except to say,—

> Come hither, Mariana:—
> Say, wast thou e'er contracted to this woman?
> *Angelo.* I was, my lord.

Upon this admission, the Duke then does what the Ecclesiastical Courts always then could do, viz., require the religious ceremony to be performed.

> Go, take her hence, and marry her, instantly.
> Do you the office, friar.

And when they return, the Duke speaks of him—

> For this new married man, approaching here.

It is not necessary to speak of the curious effect of that which was a sin legalising, or rather purifying, itself, because apparently they were not man and wife until they acted as such, though, as I have stated, the letter of the statute was that the contract itself was sufficient; but this is not the way the law apparently was understood then, for, as I think, the reasons already given; differing from the Scotch law, which only required the subsequent act to give effect to a contract *in futuro*. The Scotch case which went to the House of Lords was that of a man who was living with a person not his wife, and, under pressure of her relations went in and said, addressing her by name, "I marry you;" upon this she rose and bowed. He then went out and immediately shot himself. The Lords held that the words being present words and not a promise in the future, there was a binding marriage.

Throughout the whole play we find traces of its being the work of one thoroughly acquainted with legal proceedings. It is hard to explain how a man recognizes certain facts, as, for instance, that a person who is speaking is thoroughly acquainted with the language he is using. If it be the language of the hearer, he can at once recognize whether he is or is not listening to a foreigner who is not at home in the language. So it is with the use of legal phraseology in this play.

We have a scene in a court which seems drawn from life. At first Escalus, who is the ordinary judge, sits with Angelo, who has been joined in the commission.

Now, Escalus is described in the first Act by the Duke, who addresses him—

>   Since I am put to know, that your own science
>   Exceeds, in that, the lists of all advice
>   My strength can give you . . .
>   The nature of our people,
>   *Our city's institutions*, and the *terms*
>   For common justice, you are as pregnant in,
>   As art and practice hath enriched any
>   That we may remember.

This language is not at all well-expressed, but there is sufficient to show that the Duke intended to speak very highly of Escalus's legal attainments. I was very much struck with the peculiar name of Escalus which is given to this distinguished judge. The meaning of the word *esca* is "food," but Escalus itself has no meaning in Latin or Greek, and was not, as far as I could see, an anagram on the name of any well-known judge. In looking, however, through Lord Campbell's Lives of the Chief Justices, I could find no clue to the name at first. And yet it did not seem to be one which was chosen without a reason. But I found that, up to the close of the seventeenth century, the two principal Chief Justices who were likely to be taken as examples were, omitting Glanville, Gascoigne who has been worked up into the Plays of Henry the Fourth and Fifth, and Sir John Fortescue, who had earned a world-wide reputation for his judicial integrity and as the author of (as Lord Campbell terms it) "the immortal treatise" "De laudibus legum Angliæ." Now, it seems to me, that Escalus may have been derived from the second half of this judge's names, "Fort escue" being strong-shield, "escue" put into a classical form of Esculus or Esc*a*lus, so as to avoid any confusion with "esculus," eatable. If so, I think we shall have a clearer idea of the play if we suppose the part of Escalus to be played by Sir John Fortescue.

With him, as the play tells us, we have Angelo joined in the commission, the austere man of virtue, who insists upon sending Claudio to execution, whilst Escalus, the old judge who has learned to treat human offences with some consideration, pleads for him; but Angelo is a hanging judge. The late Sir John Karslake, one of the best *raconteurs* at the Bar, used to tell a tale of a judge such as Angelo, who was getting old and weak, being terrified into letting a prisoner be acquitted, by the counsel for the defence saying: "And then, gentlemen of the jury, we hear of a judge being a hanging judge: if such monsters exist, I do not envy them their reputation in this world, nor their punishment in the next." This scene is such a remarkable picture of our law courts that I have set it out in full, so that the reader may appreciate more easily the various points that arise:—

Enter ANGELO, ESCALUS, *a* JUSTICE, *and* SERVANTS.

Ang. We must not make a scare-crow of the law,
Setting it up to fear the birds of prey,
And let it keep one shape, till custom make it
Their perch, and not their terror.
    Esc.   Ay, but yet
Let us be keen, and rather cut a little,

Than fall, and bruise to death: alas! this gentleman,
Whom I would save, had a most noble father.
Let but your honour know,
(Whom I believe to be most strait in virtue,)
That, in the working of your own affections,
Had time cohered with place, or place with wishing,
Or that the resolute acting of your blood
Could have attained th' effect of your own purpose,
Whether you had not, sometime in your life,
Err'd in this point, which now you censure him,
And pull'd the law upon you.

Ang. 'Tis one thing to be tempted, Escalus,
Another thing to fall.   I not deny,
The jury, passing on the prisoner's life,
May in the sworn twelve, have a thief or two
Guiltier than him they try: what's open made to justice,
That justice seizes.   What knows the laws,
That thieves do pass on thieves?   'Tis very pregnant,
The jewel that we find, we stoop and take 't
Because we see 't; but what we do not see,
We tread upon, and never think of it.
You may not so extenuate his offence,
For I have had such faults; but rather tell me,
When I, that censure him, do so offend,
Let mine own judgment pattern out my death,
And nothing come in partial.   Sir, he must die.

Enter Provost.

Esc.   Be it as your wisdom will.
Ang.   Where is the provost?
Prov.   Here, if it like your honour.
Ang.   See that Claudio
Be executed by nine to-morrow morning:
Bring him his confessor, let him be prepared;
For that's the utmost of his pilgrimage.   [*Exit* Provost.

Esc.   Well, heaven forgive him! and forgive us all!
Some rise by sin, and some by virtue fall;
Some run from brakes of vice, and answer none;
And some condemned for a fault alone.

Enter ELBOW, FROTH, Clown, Officers.

Elb. Come, bring them away; if these be good people in a commonweal, that do nothing but use their abuses in common houses, I know no law; bring them away.

Ang. How now, sir! what's your name? and what's the matter?

Elb. If it please your honour, I am the poor Duke's constable, and my name is Elbow; I do lean upon justice, sir, and do bring in here before your good honour two notorious benefactors.

Ang. Benefactors? Well; what benefactors are they? are they not malefactors?

Elb. If it please your honour, I know not well what they are: but precise villains they are, that I am sure of; and void of all profanation in the world, that good Christians ought to have.

Esc. This comes off well; here's a wise officer.

Ang. Go to: what quality are they of? Elbow is your name? Why dost thou not speak, Elbow?

Clo. He cannot, sir; he's out at elbow.

Ang. What are you, sir?

Elb. He, sir? a tapster, sir; parcel-bawd; one that serves a bad woman; whose house, sir, was (as they say) plucked down in the suburbs; and now she professes a hot-house, which, I think, is a very ill house too.

Esc. How know you that?

Elb. My wife, sir, whom I detest before heaven and your honour.

Esc. How, thy wife?

Elb. Ay, sir, whom I thank heaven is an honest woman.

Esc. Dost thou detest her therefore?

Elb. I say, sir, I will detest myself also, as well as she, that this house, if it be not a bawd's house, it is a pity of her life, for it is a naughty house.

Esc. How dost thou know that, constable?

Elb. Marry, sir, by my wife, who, if she had been a woman cardinally given, might have been accused in fornication, adultery and all uncleanliness there.

Esc. By the woman's means?

Elb. Ay, sir, by Mistress Overdone's means: but as she spit in his face, so she defied him.

Clo. Sir, if it please your honour, this is not so.

Elb. Prove it before these varlets here, thou honourable man, prove it.

Esc. Do you hear how he misplaces?

Clo. Sir, she came in great with child; and longing (saving your honour's reverence) for stewed prunes; sir, we had but two in the house, which at that very distant time stood, as it were, in a fruit dish (a dish of some three-pence; your honours have seen such dishes); they are not china dishes; but very good dishes.

Esc. Go to, go to; no matter for the dish, sir.

Clo. No, indeed, sir, not of a pin; you are therein in the right; but, to the point: as I say, this mistress Elbow being (as I say) with child, and being great bellied and longing, as I say, for prunes; and having but two in the dish (as I said), master Froth here, this very man, having eaten the rest (as I said), and (as I say) paying for them very honestly; for, as you know, master Froth, I could not give you three-pence again.

Fro. No, indeed.

Clo. Very well; you being then (if you be remembered) cracking the stones of the foresaid prunes.

Fro. Ay, so I did, indeed.

Clo. Why, very well; I telling you then (if you be remembered) that such a one, and such a one, were past cure of the thing you wot of, unless they kept very good diet, as I told you.

Fro. All this is true.

Clo. Why, very well then.

Esc. Come, you are a tedious fool; to the purpose—what was done to Elbow's wife that he hath cause to complain of? Come me to what was done to her.

Clo. Sir, your honour cannot come to that yet.

Esc. No, sir, nor I mean it not.

Clo. Sir, but you shall come to it, by your honour's leave, and I beseech you look into master Froth here, sir; a man of fourscore pound a year, whose father died at Hallowmas. Was it not at Hallowmas, master Froth?

Fro. All-hollond eve.

Clo. Why, very well; I hope here be truths; he, sir, sitting (as I say) in a lower chair, sir; 'twas in the *Bunch of Grapes*, where, indeed, you have a delight to sit; have you not?

Fro. I have so; because it is an open room, and good for winter.

Clo. Why, very well then; I hope here be truths.

Ang. This will last out a night in Russia,
When nights are longest there; I'll take my leave,
And leave you to the hearing of the cause;
Hoping you'll find good cause to whip them all.

Esc. I think no less; good morrow to your lordship.
[*Exit.*
Now, sir, come on; what was done to Elbow's wife, once more?

Clo. Once, sir? there was nothing done to her once.

Elb. I beseech you, sir, ask him what this man did to my wife?

Clo. I beseech your honour, ask me.

Esc. Well, sir; what did this gentleman to her?

Clo. I beseech you, sir, look in this gentleman's face. Good master Froth, look upon his honour; 'tis for a good purpose; does your honour mark his face?

Esc. Ay, sir, very well.

Clo. Nay, I beseech you, mark it well.

Esc. Well, I do so.

Clo. Does your honour see any harm in his face?

Esc. Why, no.

Clo. I'll be supposed upon a book, his face is the worst thing about him; good then; if his face be the worst thing about him, how could master Froth do the constable's wife any harm? I would know that of your honour.

Esc. He is in the right (constable); what say you to it?

Elb. First, an it like you, the house is a respected house; next, this is a respected fellow, and his mistress is a respected woman.

Clo. By this hand, sir, his wife is a more respected person than any of us all.

Elb. Varlet, thou liest; thou liest, wicked varlet; the time is yet to come that she was ever respected with man, woman, or child.

Clo. Sir, she was respected with him before he married with her.

Esc. Which is the wiser here, Justice, or Iniquity? Is this true?

Elb. Oh thou caitiff! Oh thou varlet! Oh thou wicked Hannibal! I respected with her before I was married to her? If ever I was respected with her, or she with me, let not your worship think me the poor duke's officer; prove this, thou wicked Hannibal, or I'll have mine action of battery on thee.

Esc. If he took you a box o' th' ear, you might have your action of slander too.

Elb. Marry, I thank your good worship for it; what is't your worship's pleasure I should do with this wicked caitiff?

Esc. Truly officer, because he hath some offences in him that thou wouldst discover if thou couldst, let him continue in his courses, till thou knowest what they are.

Elb. Marry, I thank your worship for it. Thou seest, thou wicked varlet now, what's come upon thee. Thou art to continue, now, thou varlet, thou art to continue.

Esc. Where were you born, friend?

Fro. Here in Vienna, sir.

Esc. Are you of fourscore pounds a year?

Fro. Yes, an't please you, sir.

Esc. So; what trade are you of, sir?

Clo. A tapster; a poor widow's tapster.

Esc. Your mistress's name?

Clo. Mistress Overdone.

Esc. Hath she had any more than one husband?

Clo. Nine, sir; Overdone by the last.

Esc. Nine? Come hither to me, master Froth. Master Froth, I would not have you acquainted with tapsters; they will draw you, master Froth, and you will hang them; get you gone and let me hear no more of you.

Fro. I thank your worship; for my own part I never come into any room in a taphouse but I am drawn in.

Esc. Well, no more of it, master Froth: farewell. Come you hither to me, Mr. Tapster. What is your name, Mr. Tapster?

Clo. Pompey.

Esc. What else?

Clo. Bum, sir.

Esc. 'Troth, and your bum is the greatest thing about you; so that, in the beastliest sense, you are Pompey the great; Pompey, you are partly a bawd, Pompey, howsoever you colour it in being a tapster. Are you not? Come, tell me true; it shall be the better for you.

Clo. Truly, sir, I am a poor fellow, that would live.

Esc. How would you live, Pompey, by being a bawd? What do you think of the trade, Pompey? Is it a lawful trade?

Clo. If the law would allow it, sir.

Esc. But the law will not allow it; nor it shall not be allowed in Vienna.

Clo. Does your worship mean to geld and splay all the youth of the city?

Esc. No, Pompey.

Clo. Truly, sir, in my poor opinion, they will to't then. If your worship will take order for the drabs and the knaves, you need not fear the bawds.

Esc. There are pretty orders beginning, I can tell you. It is but heading and hanging.

Clo. If you head and hang all that offend that way but for ten year together, you'll be glad to give out a commission for more heads. If this law hold in Vienna ten year, I'll rent the fairest house in it after threepence a bay. If you live to see this come to pass, say Pompey told you so.

Esc. Thank you, good Pompey; and in requital of your prophecy, hark you,—I advise you, let me not find you before me again upon any complaint whatsoever; no, not for dwelling where you do. If I do, Pompey, I shall beat you to your tent, and prove a shrewd Cæsar to you; in plain dealing, Pompey, I shall have you whipt; so for this time, Pompey, fare you well.

Clo. I thank your worship for your good counsel; but I shall follow it, as the flesh and fortune shall better determine.

Whip me? No, no; let carman whip his jade;
The valiant heart's not whipped out of his trade. [*Exit.*

Esc. Come hither to me, master Elbow; come hither, master Constable. How long have you been in this place of constable?

Elb. Seven year and a half, sir.

Esc. I thought by the readiness in the office you had continued in it some time. You say seven years together?

Elb. And a half, sir.

Esc. Alas! it hath been great pains to you. They do you wrong to put you so oft upon't; are there not men in your ward sufficient to serve it?

Elb. Faith, sir, few of any wit in such matters; as they are chosen, they are glad to choose me for them. I do it for some piece of money, and go through with all.

Esc. Look you, bring me in the names of some six or seven, the most sufficient of your parish.

Elb. To your worship's house, sir?

Esc. To my house; fare you well. What's o'clock, think you?

Just. Eleven, sir.

Esc. I pray you home to dinner with me.

Just. I humbly thank you.

Esc. It grieves me for the death of Claudio. But there's no remedy.

Just. Lord Angelo is severe.

Esc. It is but needful;
Mercy is not itself, that oft looks so;
Pardon is still the nurse of second woe:
But yet,—poor Claudio!—there's no remedy.
Come, sir.

If any lawyer reads this scene, every line of which requires, I think, careful study, he must admit it has been written either by one who has drawn the scene from life, or has been assisted by one well versed in the every-day life of the English law courts. And when we come to consider the bye-play between Angelo and Escalus, I think there is reason to adopt the latter view. In the first place the court is constituted not only, of the two judges Angelo and Escalus with their servants, who in the modern edition are termed officers, but a magistrate attends. I believe this to be a purely English custom for the magistrates to sit, as they sometimes do, upon the bench with the judges, though taking no part in the proceedings. The judges then begin discussing the sentence to be passed on Claudio.

This discussion our author, however, gives us as being in open court, in order that we may more fully appreciate Angelo's fall hereafter. In the same way that the unspoken thought of real life is given as an *aside* on the stage. The discussion shows Angelo determined to carry out an obsolete and cruel law, and Escalus, as one more acquainted with the causes of human infirmity, pleading for a lesser punishment than death, and telling Angelo if he had been tempted he might have fallen, &c., dramatically foreshadowing what was to be. To which Angelo makes reference to a jury, who might have a thief or two amongst their number, "*passing* on the prisoner's life"; and shortly after returns to his own conduct and says even if he had such faults it would not extenuate Claudio's offence, &c. And finally he gives his decision:—

"Sir, he must die."

Escalus acquiesces, and then follows the order for his execution specifying the time and day.

The practice at the present day is for the judge to pass sentence of death, leaving the day for the execution to be fixed by the sheriffs. But formerly it was not so and the course followed in "Measure for Measure" seems to have been the old practice.

Thus in the report of the case of Holloway[1] who had been outlawed for treason he refused to stand a trial, and having confessed his crime being without any defence, we find the following dialogue between the too well known Chief Justice Jeffreys and the governor of Newgate.

L. C. J. Captain Richardson, I think Wednesday and Friday are your usual execution days, are they not?
Richardson. Yes, my Lord. Either of them.
L. C. J. Then Wednesday, seven night.
Richardson. Does your Lordship appoint Wednesday next?
L. C. J. No, that will be too quick. Wednesday week.

So in the judicial murder of Sir Thomas Armstrong who was also outlawed; but having within one year claimed a trial which Jeffreys refused with the acquiescence of the attorney-general, Sir Robert Sawyer, for which he was afterwards expelled from Parliament; we have Jeffreys brutally answering Armstrong, who said :—

I ought to have the benefit of the law, I demand no more.
L. C. J. That you shall have by the grace of God. See that the execution be done on Friday next according to law. You shall have the full benefit of the law.

The serious business of the court being disposed of, that is the issuing the order for Claudio's execution, there is introduced to us by way of relief, one of those incidents that so often come before our courts. The subject-matter was no doubt suggested by the scenes of debauched life to be found in the original play; but the incident is sketched in with the humour of a Fielding; I think our author has insensibly changed

---

[1] State Trials, vol. 10, p. 6.

the scene, and we are no longer in the high court of Vienna if we ever were there, but on circuit in an English assize town; and into this court comes the constable, one Elbow, who has some cause of suspicion that his wife has been introduced to a certain Mr. Froth by a hanger on to loose women, called throughout the play Clown, who, as we have seen, admits under cross-examination that his name is Pompey Bum. It appears that the lady has cleared herself in her husband's eyes, but it is a significant fact that she the principal witness, and person said to be injured, is not called.

Now the bye-play of the scene is wonderfully well treated; we have Angelo, the bad-tempered judge, treating the whole matter with impatience, asking a question or two, and then relapsing into moody silence until he can stand it no longer, and breaking out into blank verse:—

> This will last out a night in Russia,
> When the nights are longest there; I'll take my leave,
> And leave you to the hearing of this cause;
> Hoping you'll find good cause to whip them all.

With this spiteful remark he leaves the court, Escalus addressing him as a puisne judge would the chief—

> Good morrow to your lordship.

It may be noticed that Escalus, not being the chief, is not addressed as my lord, but as "your worship."

Now comes a wonderful change over the scene: "when the cat is away the mice will play." Hitherto Escalus has been repressed by "the presence of Angelo." He has listened to the parties squabbling and avoiding the point, namely, what was supposed to be done to the wife, and only asked a question or two; but, as soon as Angelo leaves him alone, he unbends. He soon gets to the real merits by saying:

Now, sir, come on: what was done to Elbow's wife, once more?

The clown evades, as he always does, a direct reply; but a happy thought strikes him; he asks the judge to look at Froth and Froth to look at the judge; and then asks the judge if he sees any harm in Froth, or if he thinks he was likely to do the constable's wife any harm. On the view, Escalus readily acquits him, and says clown is in the right. As the judge, at once looking at Froth practically dismisses what might be a serious charge, and as the audience to appreciate the position must see why he does so, I think we must assume that Froth is a young simpleton who, whatever his latent powers of vice may be, was for the time one who was more likely to be tempted that to attempt. He has told us before that his father died at all Hollond eve, and probably having come into his money, he had fallen into the clown's hands. But to proceed. The charge being practically dismissed, nothing follows but a cut and thrust dialogue between all the parties in which the judge joins. Finally, he dismisses Froth with a very professional joke.

Come hither to me, master Froth. Master Froth, I would not have you acquainted with tapsters. [*Clown had called himself a tapster.*] They will *draw* you, master *froth*, and you will *hang* them. Get you gone, and let me hear no more of you.

To Clown his dismissal is not quite so friendly.

Hark you: I advise you, let me not find you before me again upon any complaint whatsoever, no, not for dwelling where you do. If I do, Pompey, I shall beat you to your tent, and prove a shrewd Cæsar to you; in plain dealing, Pompey, I shall have you whipt; so for this time, Pompey, fare you well.

The learned judge, in dismissing the two prisoners, has not done. We have a sketch of what no doubt from time to time often occurred on circuit when the judges attempted to restrain the practice of one man being chosen year after year to fill the office of constable. Now, nations make their customs as they do their paths—by continually treading the way they find most convenient; they may be stopped or restrained by individual authority for a time, but that dies, and the nation perseveres. We have, in modern days, long recognized that it is a good thing to have a permanent filling of the position of constable, and not to change the individual every year. Our ancestors saw the expediency of this in Shakespeare's time. But the law said no. The office of constable like that of sheriff, churchwarden, overseer, &c., was one that each citizen was supposed to serve when called upon, and however inconvenient the constant change might be, the law desired to see its own views carried out.

The office of parish constable was one that any inhabitant had to serve if elected to it by the jury at the court leet; but these courts were not always held, and the office was often filled year after year by the same person who was paid by the parish generally for undertaking the somewhat invidious duty. But that there should be, as it were, a professional constable was not the idea of the law, which rather looked to each inhabitant taking it in turn, and no doubt the practice led sometimes to abuse, especially where the person who from year to year acted was of the Dogberry or Elbow type, and we find long after Shakespeare's time, an Act was passed in the 13 & 14 Car. II. giving two justices the power of electing a constable when there was none, and of removing any one who had been more than a year in office. Now inferentially we see Escalus as it were the judge on circuit claiming this power, for he says, as a mere incident in the play, no subsequent action apparently being taken—

Esc. Come hither to me, master Elbow; come hither, master Constable. How long have you been in this place of constable?

Elb. Seven year and a half, sir.

Esc. Alas! it has been great pains to you. They do you wrong to put you so oft upon't. [*The playful chaff of the Lord Chief Justice.*] Are there not men in your ward sufficient to serve it?

Elb. Faith, sir, few of any wit in such matters; as they are chosen, they are glad to choose me for them. I do it for some piece of money, and go through with all.

To this Escalus, as one can well imagine many a hard-headed judge has done, determines to use the man for his own destruction.

Look you, bring me in the names of some six or seven, the most sufficient of your parish.

To this Elbow obsequiously says (suspecting nothing, half or all, according to the wit of the man)—

To your worship's house,[1] sir?

To my house. Fare you well,

says Escalus, polite to the last, and there the incident

---

[1] Probably referring to the judge's lodgings, which would be well known to Elbow.

drops; but all this savours of the judge on circuit, where the judge's lodgings would be well known to the constable, and does not, to my mind, tell of the experience gained on the stool in a country attorney's office, or behind the scenes of a London theatre. The scene is brought to a conclusion by the interval there is, at what is known as the rising of the court. It often happens that the arrangement of the business is done at the time when the judge rises from his seat and remains standing. It is said that when the late Mr. Pelligrini, the artist for "Vanity Fair," attended the Tichborne trial to make a sketch of the late Chief Justice Bovill, he could get no attitude that pleased him until when the work was over, the judge rose and remained standing for a few minutes arranging some matter. A rapid sketch was made of the chief, which was the origin of the well-known cartoon. So Escalus, when his work was over, turns to the justice who has been in attendance, but taking, of course, no part in the business, and addresses a few words to him, expressing regret for Claudio's death, showing what has been weighing in his mind during all the fooling with the constable, and finally, after asking what time it is, invites him, as judges so often do the justices, or members of the Bar, to dine with him.

When we look at the range of subjects connected with English legal and judicial life which have been introduced into this scene which is laid itself in Vienna, I think we have a very good example of the legal acquirements to be found in these plays.

It has been suggested to me that this scene shows no higher legal training than the trial scene in

Pickwick. But Dickens had some legal learning in Doctors' Commons. I believe he was properly qualified to practise, and he may and probably had help in arranging his scene. It is, however, more of a burlesque, the incidents were introduced to amuse not as here, mere matters of passing interest, *i.e.*, the appointment of constable, &c. Besides, Pickwick's trial scene stands alone. This is only one amongst many examples of legal training. And I think, that if Shakespeare was assisted by some legal friend, that this scene can hardly have been touched by Shakespeare, except where blank verse is used. The sharp dialogue between the judge, the prisoners, and the constable seem to me to be the work of one mind, and that a touch by another hand would have spoilt it. I look upon it as Bacon's unassisted work. I say Bacon's, because it so resembles his style of writing when he was unbending. It was the kind of low comedy wit he was so fond of when he could indulge in it, at least, if the examples to which I shall hereafter have occasion to refer are his. At present, all that I think can be said is that in this scene we have a sketch of a day in court in the time of Elizabeth drawn by a master's hand.

There is another trial scene in the play. In the first one, after the sentence on Claudio which is not meant by the author to be enforced; the subject is, as we have seen, treated lightly. But in the second trial we have a more serious view. In this scene we find the Duke has left Angelo and Escalus to deal with the accusations against the former. He has to retire for the purpose of appearing as the friar, and, before going, he has thrown Angelo off his guard by pretending to disbelieve the witnesses. Angelo asks the Duke—

> Now, good my lord, give me the scope of justice.

The Duke says—

> Ay, with my heart;
> And punish them unto your height of pleasure.
> * * * * *
> You, lord Escalus,
> Sit with my cousin; lend him your kind pains
> To find out this abuse.

Having thus formed the Court, he goes to re-appear immediately as the Friar Lodowick. In the trial that follows, Angelo, no doubt, knowing that he is guilty as he believes with Isabella, takes little part. But Escalus is shown acting as a judge does who is moved by partizanship, and has lost his judicial impartiality. It is as different a picture from the judge playing the fool with Elbow, as a rough sea is from a calm one. He starts with laying a trap for the friar, and, let us hope, unconsciously stating an untruth. Of course, he does not know that the friar is the Duke who had been present.

Esc. Come, sir! Did you set these women on to slander lord Angelo? *They have confessed you did.*
Duke. 'Tis false.

Escalus is startled; he does not venture to re-assert it, but says—

> How! know you where you are?

The Duke, in his indignation, says—

> Respect to your great place! and let the devil
> Be sometime honoured for his burning throne.

And then asks for himself—

> Where's the Duke? 'tis he should hear me speak.

Then follows the scene which speaks for itself, showing as it does how Escalus catches at everything to justify his preconceived opinion that there has been a conspiracy between the friar and the women against his friend Angelo. The latter, like the rabbit, lies low. But when he sees that Escalus is losing sight of the main question, and is generally losing his head, Angelo calls up the talkative Lucio to say what he can vouch against him.

Lucio with charming but Baconian or Shakesperian impudence, says that all the abuse of the Duke, which he had before imputed to the Duke when he was the friar, the friar had said, and ultimately unmasks the Duke, who, being discovered, makes Escalus resume his seat and then presides, and Angelo becomes the prisoner. Escalus is silenced, he has been led away, and at last, when everything is confessed, gives a lame apology.

> My Lord, I am more amazed at his dishonour,
> Than at the strangeness of it.

No one takes any notice, and the poor old judge steps into the back-ground and, except for a short side-remark to Angelo, says no more.

First and Second Parts of Henry VI.

In "Measure for Measure" we have a sketch of what one might almost call a day on the bench; in the first part of "Henry VI." we have a glimpse of the life of a law student. It is true Part I. of "Henry VI." was considered by Malone not to be Shakespeare, principally because there were certain contradictions about Henry's age, *i. e.*, when his father died he was only nine months old, but he is made to say of Talbot,[1]—

> I do remember how my father said,
> A stouter champion never handled sword.

An argument founded upon any such inaccuracies does not now meet with approval. It may, however, be because Malone threw this doubt upon "Henry VI.," Part I., that Lord Campbell passed it over as a play not containing any of the expressions or allusions of a professional lawyer. Whereas, I think, it is full of reference to legal life and manners.

Henry VI., Part I.

In this play the dates are all hopelessly confused and the incidents piled together as it suited the author to place them, irrespective of their true position in history. The play, for instance, opens with the funeral of Henry V. in Westminster Abbey. Now this king died in France on the 31st August, 1422, and his brother Bedford continued his wars in that country against the Dauphin, whose father, Charles VI., died in Paris in October of the same year, when the Dauphin became by right Charles VII., but was not yet crowned. Bedford had great success for six years or so, till the Maid of Orleans appeared on the scene in 1429, when she raised the siege of Orleans, carried Charles off to Rheims, where he was crowned May, 1429. Henry V. had a magnificent funeral. It commenced in Paris, and continued with great ceremony through France. His funeral services were

---

[1] Act III. Scene 4.

performed in England at St. Paul's, and finally his body was taken to Westminster Abbey for interment. During the short time it remained there above ground, we have the first scene of the play, in which enter several messengers stating that all the French towns are lost, the French king crowned at Rheims, &c., all of which were not true at that date, but are part of the later action of the piece. This scene also refers to the commencement of the quarrel between Gloster, the young king's uncle, and Beaufort, his great uncle. But we have not to deal with these historical inaccuracies, but with the expressions and allusions of a lawyer, which are so numerous that it seems impossible to understand their being entirely overlooked by Lord Campbell.

The first of these occurs when the partizans of Gloster and Winchester (Beaufort) come to blows.[1] The Lord Mayor enters and reproves them in vain; they continue their quarrel and the stage direction is (*Here they skirmish again*), upon which the Lord Mayor says—

> Nought rests for me, in this tumultuous strife,
> But to make open proclamation :—
> Come, officer, as loud as e'er thou canst cry.

Officer. All manner of men assembled here in arms this day, against God's peace and the king's, we charge and command you, in his highness's name, to repair to your several dwelling-places; and not to wear, handle, or use, any sword, weapon, or dagger, henceforward, *upon pain of death.*

This quiets the combatants, for Gloster says,—

> Cardinal, I'll be no breaker of the law :
> But we shall meet, and break our minds at large.

---

[1] Scene 3.

In the use of this proclamation, I find that the law of the author was, as is often to be found in the plays correctly stated as regards the law, as it existed in Shakespeare's time, and it is no doubt in the proper form; but the occasion was not one, in my opinion, in which it would or should have been used.

In the early days of English history the law was always ready to put down riotous assemblies; and by an Act of Henry the Fourth, the duty of the civil magistrate was to suppress and disperse by force persons unlawfully and riotously assembling; and such persons were liable at common law to be fined and imprisoned. But this appeal to the strong arm of the law did not make the remaining, after notice to disperse, a special crime. It was the assembling and the tumult which were punishable, not the being on the ground after proclamation, though this was so at the time when the play was written, *i.e.*, towards the close of Elizabeth's reign, but was not the law at the period of the play, *i.e.*, in Henry the Sixth's reign. It is evident where a tumult is going on, the presence of mere passive spectators is a danger; and when Edward the Sixth came to the throne, it was made high treason for twelve persons or above being assembled together to attempt to kill or imprison any of the king's council or to alter any laws, and to continue together by the space of an hour after being commanded by the justices of the peace to retire. This Act was altered by Mary making it *felony*. The words of the Act are: "If any persons of the number of twelve or more being assembled together shall intend, go about, practise, or put in use with force and arms unlawfully and of their own authority, to change any laws made for religion by authority of

Parliament, the same number of twelve or above being commanded by the sheriffs, &c., by proclamation in the Queen's name, to retire and repair to their house or whence they came, shall be adjudged felons and suffer death." But the same Act, where the number was under twelve, made it a misdemeanor not punishable by death, but by fine and imprisonment.

The proclamation of the Lord Mayor was, therefore, wrong, historically speaking, because it was of no effect in Henry VI.'s time, and was out of place and irregular because it was not clear that the rioters were twelve in number, and it is clear that their meeting by chance and fighting was not one of the objects of meeting, against which the Act of Mary was directed. This Act was continued by Elizabeth for her life, and then dropped by the Stuarts and not revived until the first of George the First, when it was re-modelled, and made perpetual as the Riot Act. The power of the justice to suppress the assembly was the *posse comitatus*, which was held to be all persons, noblemen and others, except, if need be, women, clergymen, persons decrepit, and infants under fifteen.

I think, therefore, that the proclamation as here given was the work of a lawyer, but in this particular case it was an anachronism and also inapplicable to the particular form of riot. Although the proclamation of the mayor arrested the combatants, and they fell to words not blows, yet they do not show any disposition to obey the order to retire until the mayor threatens to call out the *posse comitatus*—

> I will call for clubs, if you will not away.

Malone says this refers to peace officers armed with clubs, but it is rather the well-known call for the assembling of the apprentices. It is not probable there were sufficient peace officers in the city; but the apprentices were always ready to leave the work at this call and suppress riots, if not make them. However, the disputants leave, and the mayor still fulfilling his duty, says:—

> See the coast cleared, and then we will depart.

It subsequently appears they obey the letter of the law and disarm, but fill their pockets with stones and commence again breaking each other's pates, and the Mayor of London, as he was entitled to do, petitions Parliament, or rather the Lords, where Henry is sitting.[1]

> Oh, my good Lords,—and virtuous Henry,—
> Pity the city of London, pity us!

In this first part of "Henry VI." occur two scenes,—one in the Temple Gardens, which shows that the author was well acquainted with the habits and life of the members of the Temple, and the other in Parliament, where he shows an equally accurate knowledge of the law and practice of Parliament.

In the Temple Gardens, we have an adjournment from the hall, where the parties have been disputing, and have adjourned to the gardens, where, as often is the case, the cool air may have helped them to keep their tempers.[2]

---

[1] Act III. Scene 1.

[2] This reference to the Temple Gardens, not saying whether the Inner or the Middle Temple is meant, curiously enough points to the writer being a member of Gray's Inn. This will be seen better when we discuss the *Gesta Grayorum* in 1594-5. At present I shall only point out that there was a strong alliance between Gray's Inn and the Inner Temple. The former speaking of the latter as the Temple; an Inner or a Middle Temple man would have given his Inn its proper title.

We have five noblemen and *another lawyer* brought on to the stage as if they had all been in the hall and were all lawyers. Now a great number of noblemen did join the Temple in those days, but as the records only go to 1547, the accession of Edward VI., we have no means of knowing whether these had so joined. But as they had been in the hall, where, except on rare occasions, guests are not admitted, it seems to me, the author is only referring to what might have been the case. At all events, they enter the gardens, Richard Plantagenet, heated and excited with an argument he has had, evidently with Somerset, and the rest apparently have no wish to keep up the dispute. But Plantagenet will not be quiet, he insists on having the opinion of his friends.

Plant. Great lords and gentlemen, what means this silence?
Dare no man answer in a case of truth?
Suffolk. Within the Temple hall we were too loud;
The garden here is more convenient.
Plant. Then say at once, if I maintain'd the truth.

They attempt to put him off, but he insists and plucks the white rose. Somerset plucks a red, and so on each one siding with Plantagenet or Somerset until the unnamed lawyer says—

Unless my study and my books be false,
The argument you held, was wrong in you;
[*To Somerset.*
In sign whereof, I pluck a white rose too.

It seems to me, however, that in point of law Somerset was right and the unnamed gentleman of the long robe wrong, for when Somerset begins to state his argument, it is, that as Plantagenet's father had been executed for treason in the late king's days, he, as his son, stood attainted, corrupted, and exempt from ancient gentry, the father's trespass yet being guilty in the son's blood.

> And, till thou be restored, thou art a yeoman.

This seems to me unanswerable law. In vain Plantagenet says—

> My father was attached, not attainted;
> Condemn'd to die for treason, but no traitor.

His friend Warwick tells him of the only true means of getting over the difficulty:—

> This blot, that they object against your house,
> Shall be wiped out in the next Parliament.

Now this is all correct law. A person executed for treason had his blood attainted; no one, upwards or downwards, could inherit through him, and therefore the title and estates of the Duke of York, which would have been his as heir to his paternal grandfather, Edward of Langley, Duke of York, were stopped by the attainted blood of his father. This could only be removed by the reversal of the attainder by an Act of Parliament, or by a re-grant of the lands and titles by the Crown, in other words a fresh creation. And we see subsequently this done in both ways. For the king in Parliament says,[1]—

> My loving lords, our pleasure is,
> That Richard be restored to his blood.

Upon this apparently the Lords vote,—for Warwick says,—

> Let Richard be restored to his blood;
> So shall his father's wrongs be recompensed,

and Winchester,—

> As will the rest, so willeth Winchester.

---

[1] Act III. Scene I.

The king, upon his swearing fealty, gives him back his inheritance and says,—

> I girt thee with the valiant sword of York:
> Rise, Richard, like a true Plantagenet:
> And rise *created* princely Duke of York.

Previous to this being done, Plantagenet had himself recognized that Somerset's argument was right, for he says, when the lords are disputing—

> Plantagenet, I see, must hold his tongue;
> Lest it be said, Speak, sirrah, when you should;
> Must your bold verdict enter talk with lords?

I may say, as far as I can discover, all this is pure imagination of the author. For at the first Parliament held in Henry VI.'s reign Plantagenet attended as the Duke of York, and no questions were raised. Most probably he had been restored to his father's estates and titles by Henry V. It is evident in the play that Richard Plantagenet is meant to be a member of the Temple; for as we have seen not only is he described as coming from the Hall, but in the second act, scene 5, we have Edmund Mortimer as a prisoner in the Tower dying of old age sending for Plantagenet, his nephew.

> But tell me, keeper, will my nephew come?
> *Keeper.* Richard Plantagenet, my lord, will come,
> We sent unto the Temple, to his chamber;
> And answer was returned, that he will come.

(In fact Mortimer was a friend of Henry V., attended his funeral, and died some two years afterwards quite a young man.) The only reason I can conceive for this scene is, that the author, having taken the trouble to work out Plantagenet's title as Duke of York, and to the Crown, did not like to waste his trouble, so brings in Mortimer to tell it all over to Plantagenet, who must have known it before.

The lawyers called their rooms chambers, and always have; but the matter, I think, is put at rest by the closing lines of the scene in the Temple Gardens, already referred to, where Plantagenet, Warwick, Vernon and the other lawyer being left together, Plantagenet, after thanking them for plucking a white rose with him, says—

> Thanks, gentle sir.
> Come, let us four to dinner; I daresay,
> This quarrel will drink blood another day.

And thus makes up the set of four, which is the number who dine in a mess together.

It may not be known generally, but it is assumed, that the destruction of the records of the members of the Bar by Jack Cade in this very reign has prevented modern investigation from tracing very clearly in what way they came into occupation of the Temple. It is supposed that certain serving brethren affiliated themselves to the Templars, some of whom went into the courts and acted as protectors to suitors, &c., whilst others attended the sick. In some way the large body of the Bar, the successors of the apprentices or counters, became possessed of the Temple, whilst the *servientes ad legem* or serjeants-at-law had their own Inn or Inns; but one practice survived which, I suppose, came down from the old Knight-Templars, *i.e.*, that the barristers and students dined together in sets of four, this number being chosen for a general and mutual espionage. To those who care for these matters the following extracts from the Rules of the Knight-Templars [1] may not be without interest as showing the origin of this custom, which still prevails.

---

[1] Addison's "Knight Templars," p. 19.

Rule VIII. In one common hall or refectory we will that you take your meat together, where, if your wants cannot be made known by signs, ye are softly and privately to ask for what you want.

No wonder that the disputants in the garden scene found—

> Within the Temple hall we were too loud.

Rule IX. At dinner and at supper let there be always some sacred reading. If we love the Lord we ought anxiously to long for, and we ought to hear with most earnest attention, his wholesome words and precepts.

The Templars, until recent times, preserved this practice of reading but during dinner only. They read some disputed law matter instead of religion. And though the practice has now ceased, except for a short revival a few years back, in the Inner Temple a Bencher is still called *lector* the year before he serves as treasurer. And it as *lector* that his arms are placed in the Hall.

Rule XI. Two and two ought in general to eat together that one may have an eye upon the other.

This rule is ambiguous: it might refer to messes of two or of four. The latter is, as we have seen, the practice of the Inns of Court which exists now, and the passage from "Henry VI.," Part I., given above, to my mind shows it so existed in the time of Shakespeare.

It is also to be remarked, that during the quarrel between Plantagenet, Duke of York, and Somerset in the Temple Gardens, the latter calls the former a yeoman—

> We grace the yeoman by conversing with him.

As we have seen, Warwick tries to explain and misstates York's pedigree.

Then Plantagenet says—

> He bears him on the place's privilege,
> Or durst not, for his craven heart, say thus.

Johnson, it appears, explains this by saying the Temple was a religious house, and as such exempt from violence, revenge, and bloodshed. It is, however, shown by others, as was the case, that the Temple had long ceased to be such; and Robson suggests[1] blows might have been prohibited by the regulations of the Society. I have not been able to find any such regulation; but that the Templars wanted keeping in order, the following description of a town and gown row on rather an extravagant scale, which I have found in Hollinshed, seems to prove. In this year, 20 Hen. VI., the year in which the wife of Gloster was accused of witchcraft and treason:—

There was a great fray in Fleet Street between gentlemen of Courts and inhabitants of London, insomuch that much blood was spilt, divers slain outright, and some mortally wounded, besides great harm otherwise done and suffered.

In the scene between Gloster and Winchester in Parliament, we have another illustration of its practice. Gloster offers to follow the usual course to exhibit a bill against Winchester, but the latter snatches it and tears it, saying—

> Comest thou with deep premeditated lines,
> With written pamphlets studiously devised,
> Humphrey of Gloster? If thou canst accuse,
> Or aught intend'st to lay unto my charge,
> Do it without invention suddenly;
> As I, with sudden and extemporal speech,
> Purpose to answer what thou canst object.

---

[1] Page 65.

To which Gloster says—

> Think not, although in writing I preferr'd
> The manner of thy vile outrageous crimes, &c.

This, although hashed up into a dramatic squabble, is based upon the usual way in which articles of impeachment are preferred against a peer. Blackstone says these are a kind of bill or indictment. Had the dispute not been arranged for the time, probably a Lord High Steward would have been appointed and proceedings continued in the ordinary way.[1]

Again where Vernon strikes Bassett in pursuance of the old dispute between York and Somerset, Bassett refers to the law making it death to draw a sword in the king's garden (Henry the Sixth was then in his French Palace where he went to be crowned), and says,—

> Villain, thou know'st the law of arms.

There is a further reference to law made by La Pucelle just as she is going to execution, which refers to a cruel charge made against her in Hollinshed, to which respect for her memory prevents me from further alluding.

The principal action in this play is laid in France, consequently the opportunities for the display of legal phraseology is not of such frequent occurrence.

---

[1] Now this is all imagination, for Hollinshed gives the actual Bill preferred by Gloster, accuser of Winchester, at a Parliament specially held by Bedford, who came to England for this purpose. The Lords were to arbitrate between the two; their award was duly given, and is set out in Hollinshed. A feast followed, at which the king was knighted by Bedford; but the peace was a hollow one, for the quarrel soon broke out again.

LEGAL PLAYS. 73

Henry VI., Part. II.

Lord Campbell tells us that, in the speeches of Jack Cade and his coadjutors in the play, we find a familiarity with the law and its proceedings which thoroughly indicate that the author must have had some professional practice and education as a lawyer, and he takes as an example in "Henry VI.," Part II. Act IV. Sc. 2.

Dick. Let's kill all the lawyers.

Cade. Nay, that I mean to do. Is not this a lamentable thing, that of the skin of an innocent lamb should be made parchment? that parchment being scribbled o'er should undo a man? Some say the bee stings, but I say, 'tis the bees' wax, for I did but seal once to a thing, and I was never mine own man since.

In the Quarto it is only verbally different, Dick says,—

I have a suit unto your lordship.

Cade. Be it a lordship, Dick, and thou shalt have it for that word.

Dick. That we may go[1] and burn all records,
And that all writing may be down,
And nothing used but the sign and tally.

Cade. Dick, it shall be so, and henceforward all things shall be in common.

And in Cheapside my palfrey shall go to grass.

Why is't not a miserable thing that of the skin of an innocent lambe parchment should be made, and then with a little blotting over with ink a man should undo himself? Some say 'tis the bees that sting, but I say, 'tis their wax, for I am sure I never sealed to any thing but once, and I was never my own man since.

So, as to the indictment on which Lord Saye was

---

[1] To the Inns of Court.

arraigned,[1] Lord Campbell says it is certain that the drawer of the indictment must have had some acquaintance with the Crown Circuit Companion and must have had a full and accurate knowledge of that rather obscure and intricate subject—Felony and benefit of Clergy. As this indictment is found almost in the same words, and identical as to the *material points* in the quarto, the same remarks necessarily apply to its author also. And in the same way the clerk of Chatham is hanged with his pen and penhorn about his neck for being able to read.

So in Jack Cade's proclamation which Lord Campbell says deals with still more recondite heads of jurisprudence. Where he refers to the *Droits du Seigneur*, and concludes :—

Men shall hold of me *in capite*, and we charge and command that their wives be as *free* as heart can wish, or tongue can tell.

In the Quarto these last words are slightly altered.

And that their wives shall be as free as heart can *think* or tongue can tell.

Now these words have, as Malone tells us, received a judicial interpretation, and Campbell follows him. See Year Book, Hil. Term, 10 Hen. VII., folio 13, pt. 6. In Scotland a deed oftens runs " as long as grass can grow or water flow." But it requires a law of some study to be able to quote from the Year Books, and we find the author of both Quarto and Folio doing this.

These examples are by no means all the law that is to be found in both the quarto and folio plays. We have an apprentice accusing his master of high

---

[1] Act IV. Scene 7.

treason. The master says he does it out of malice, and that he has a witness to prove this malice. The king thereupon asks the Protector Gloster—

In the Quarto:

> Uncle Gloster, what do you think of this?

In "Henry VI.," Part II.—

> Uncle, what shall we say to this in law?

In both Quarto and Folio Gloster gives the correct judicial answer.

In the Quarto:

> My lord, the law is this, by case it rest suspicious,
> That a day of combat be appointed.

The master accepts, the prentice declines, upon which Suffolk says—

> You must either fight, sirrah, or else be hanged.

In "Henry VI.," Part II., Gloster says—

> Let these have a day appointed them
> For single combat in convenient place;
> For he hath witness of his servant's malice.

The master accepts, the prentice, as in the Quarto play, declines, and is told he must fight or be hanged. All this correctly states the appeal by combat, the essential part of which is, there must be a doubt; for if there were anything like certain evidence, the plaintiff was not called upon to prove in this extraordinary manner what there was reason to suppose he could prove by ordinary legal methods. Here it was evident it was one man's word against another, and a witness of malice was vouched to, on the part of the defendant, therefore the procedure was correctly laid down by Gloster.[1]

One more example. In the first part of "Henry VI.," Gloster, as we have seen, charges the Bishop of Winchester. In these two plays the position is reversed. A parliament is held at Bury to which Gloster is summoned, and on his appearance there is charged by the Bishop of Winchester, now cardinal in both plays, in almost the same words: that in his Protectorship—

> You did devise
> Strange torments (*tortures*) for offenders by which means
> England hath been defamed by tyranny;

to which Gloster admits—

> That murder he did torture.

In the Quarto, he adds—

> "above the rate of common law."

These words are altered in "Henry VI."—

> "Murder, indeed, that bloody sin; I tortured
> *Above the felon*, or what trespass else;"

the meaning of which is not quite clear. Now this omission of the reference to the common law in the later play is very curious, because, although the torture of suspected persons was often done, the English lawyers were always opposed to it. As one

---

[1] The result of the battle as told by Hollinshed is, that the Master was so fortified with liquor by his friends that he proved an easy victim, but the servant did not live long unpunished, as he was convicted of theft and executed shortly afterwards. I think it is clear that during Henry VI. reign there was going on one of those preliminary skirmishes against the church which led the way to the Reformation, represented by Gloster who opposed, and Winchester, who defended the church; and the chronicler's sympathies were with Gloster, the good Duke Humphrey.

report says: "Trial by rack" is unknown to English law; finally, the judges who met to consult before the trial of Felton, the murderer of the Duke of Buckingham in James I.'s reign, declared unanimously, as Blackstone tells us, to their own honour and the honour of English law, no that such proceedings were allowable by the laws of England. Since then it has never been used here. Now, if Bacon had anything to do with these two plays he may, before he became Lord Chancellor, have followed his old instincts as a common law lawyer, and stated in the earlier play that torture was above (or outside) the common law; but as he had been attorney-general and had to attend examinations under torture, and lord chancellor, and member of the king's council, before the second play, he may have often had to be a consenting party to its use, and so thought it advisable to omit the reference to its being opposed to the common law.[1]

I have read over this second part of "Henry VI." several times to ascertain if I have omitted any traces of legal knowledge, and each time it seems to me something fresh is discovered. Since writing the above, I have discovered two more traces of the author being acquainted with a lawyer's training. In Act II. Scene 1,

---

[1] Lord Campbell says, in his "Lives of the Chief Justices," speaking of Coke, who, as attorney-general, often attended the examination of prisoners under torture, although afterwards in his old age making the rack illegal. He laid down in the most peremptory manner that torture was contrary to the law of England, and showed how the rack, or rake, in the Tower was first introduced in this reign of Henry VI. by the Duke of Exeter, and ever afterwards called the Duke of Exeter's daughter. Like his predecessor Egerton, and his successor, Bacon, he thought that the Crown was not bound by this law, and a warrant for administering torture being granted by the council, he unscrupulously attended to see the proper degree of pain inflicted.

at Bury, there is the discovery of an impostor who pretends to have been miraculously restored to sight. Gloster who is described in Hall's Chronicle as being well acquainted with the civil law, cross-examines the man with the skill of a defender of prisoners at the Old Bailey. The man is evidently prepared to tell any amount of lies, and his wife is ready to support him. After eliciting that though blind from his birth, he has, as he says, become lame from a fall from a plum-tree which he had climbed in his youth, Gloster throws him off his guard by pretending to disbelieve him when he is really speaking the truth, when he says he can see now.

Gloster says :—

> Let me see thy eyes;—wink now: now open them :—
> In my opinion yet thou see'st not well.

The man, knowing he can see well, is eager to convince Gloster he is speaking the truth on this point, and insists that he can see. Gloster, apparently to test his sight, asks him the colour of the different cloaks around, which he correctly gives as red, black, coal-black, &c. He then says he has never seen a cloak before. Gloster then asks him the names of the different persons, which, of course, he does not know, upon which Gloster says :—

> If thou hadst been born blind,
> Thou mightst as well have known all our names, as thus
> To name the several colours we do wear.
> Sight may distinguish of colours ; but suddenly
> To nominate them all it is impossible.

And so has him flogged through all the towns till he returns to Berwick whence he came. We are not here considering whether counsel are justified in laying traps for a witness. This will depend on whether he is a witness of truth or the reverse; but the example given shows an aptitude for, and appreciation of, cross-examination which, as I have said, smacks of actual practice in the courts. This incident is to be found in the Folio and the Quarto.

One more example, and I hope it is the last I shall discover of legal knowledge, with which the whole part or play seems saturated. It arises on the trial of Eleanor, wife of the Duke of Gloster for conjuring, for which she was sentenced by the king to two or three days' penance (the Folio and Quarto vary), and then to banishment for life to the Isle of Man. This is also historical, and taken from Hall and Hollinshed's Chronicles; but the details of the punishment of her accomplices are, I believe, the work of the author. It is suggested by the chronicler that Sir John Han was employed to lead Eleanor, Gloster's wife, into a trap, taking her to the witch, and then arranging for her to be caught in the act. This idea is worked out in the play.

Hall, in his Chronicles, commences the twentieth year of King Henry VI. with a description of the articles preferred by Gloster against the Bishop of Winchester, principally for accepting a Cardinal's hat, &c. This was referred by the king to his council, who, Hall says, were for the most part spiritual persons.

So, what for fear and what for favour, the matter was winked at, and backed out, and nothing said to it; and fair countenance was made to the duke as though no displeasure had been taken, nor no malice borne either in heart or remembrance against him. But venom will once break out and inward grudge will soon appear, which was this year to all men apparent, for divers secret attempts were advanced forward this season against the noble Duke, Humphrey of Gloster, which, in conclusion, came so near that they bereft him both of life and land as you shall hereafter more manifestly perceive. For first this year Dame Eleanor Cobham, wife to the said Duke, was accused of treason, that she by sorcery and enchantment intended to destroy the king to the intent to advance and promote her husband to the Crown. Upon this she was examined in Saint Stephen's Chappell before the Bishop of Canterbury, and there by examination convict and judged to do open penance in three open places within the city of London, and after that adjudged to perpetual prison on the Isle of Man."

Margaret Jourdain, surnamed the Witch of Eye, was burnt in Smithfield. One of the servants was hanged at Tyburn, protesting his innocence, another died in the Tower, and the rascal, Sir John Han, received a pardon, which supports the idea that it was a got-up affair. But we have not to deal with history but legal allusions.

In the Quarto the king only sentences Eleanor, but in the later play the story, as told by Hall and Hollinshed, is more closely followed, except that it is stated that all of the four prisoners taken with Eleanor were to be executed. This, as we know, was not the case; in the Second Part of "Henry VI." before sentencing Eleanor, the king, who, apparently, is supposed to be in a Hall of Justice, turns to the others and says—

> You four, from hence to prison back again;
> From thence unto the place of execution:
> The witch in Smithfield shall be burn'd to ashes,
> And you three shall be strangled on the gallows.
> [*He then sentences Eleanor.*]
> You, madam, for you are more nobly born.

following strictly the punishment as already stated, as given in Hollinshed.

This incident is of some interest as it is to be observed that the sentence of death follows the old form. You shall be taken back to the place from whence you came, and thence to the place of execution, &c. And these are the author of the play's words and not Hollinshed's.

It is also of interest, apart from any question as to who the author was, from the fact that at the time this trial and judgment is supposed to have taken place, there was no law, statute or otherwise, against witchcraft in England. Coke, in his 3 Institutes, in his famous article on this subject, tells us that before *The Conquest* the punishment was death and exile, but the first statute was long after the period of the play, viz., the 33 Hen. VII. c. 8, who first made it treason; this was altered by subsequent statutes, until, in Elizabeth's reign, it was only punishable by death, if death had been procured by the conjuring, or after conviction and a relapse, otherwise the punishment was the pillory and one year's imprisonment: and curiously enough, Coke, who does not appear to have studied Hall or Hollinshed, yet found traces of this matter, for he says:—

"I have seen a report of a case in an ancient register that in October, anno 20 Hen. VI., Margaret Gurdeman[1] of Eye, in Suffolk, was, for witchcraft and consultation with the devil, after sentence and a relapse, burnt by the King's writ *de heretico comburendo*."

He can only justify this on the ground not of positive law, but of scripture. It is to be noticed,

---

[1] Jourdain.

he says, she was burnt after conviction and a relapse, which is not mentioned by Hall or Hollinshed and no mention is made of Eleanor or the others. Now, this justification of acting outside or, rather, without the power of the law, is incidentally referred to in the play, for the king does not, although he calls it the sentence of the law, attempt to support his judgment by reference to the common or statute law, but says[1]—

> Stand forth, Dame Eleanor Cobham, Gloster's wife:
> In sight of God, and us, your guilt is great;
> Receive the sentence of the law, for sins
> *Such as by God's book are adjudged to death.*—
> You four, &c.

There is no such reference in the Quarto; it is there put—

Stand forth, Dame Eleanor Cobham, Duchess of Gloster, and hear the sentence pronounced against thee for these treasons that thou hast committed against us, our State and peers.

Penance was not a punishment for treason, but for an ecclesiastical offence. In this case, Coke evidently thought that the so-called witch was burnt without authority, or he would not have apologized for it. And the main fact is, that the same idea must have occurred to the author between the making of the quarto and the folio plays, for he introduces the Bible as the justification of the sentence as Coke does. I think, therefore, there is sufficient to prove that there is to be found in the first part of the contention as well as in the Second Part of "Henry VI.," the same evidence of legal knowledge and a fondness for using legal ideas and phrases which is so marked a peculiarity of some of the plays.

---

[1] Act II. Scene 3.

Hamlet.

"Hamlet" is one of the legal Plays. I will only cite one example from it, the case of Dame Hales, reported in Plowden. It was decided before Shakespeare was born, and was, I believe, not printed until after his death, and was not therefore a matter of current interest which would come under his notice. It has often been explained, but to make my study complete, I will refer to it shortly. The case really raised the issue whether a person com... the crime of suicide when he is alive or when he is dead. It was a good case for the lawyers, for so much was to be said on both sides. The husband of Dame Hales, Sir John, had drowned himself, and a jury had found a verdict of *felo de se*. He was a joint tenant with his wife of some land. If his death had occurred naturally she would have taken the whole by survivorship; but as a suicide his property was forfeited to the Crown. This would have made the wife joint tenant with the Crown, but by another rule of law, in such a case it was not considered consistent with the dignity of the Crown that it should be a joint tenant with the subject, and, as the weakest must go to the wall, the Crown would take the whole. The question, then, was whether the crime was committed in Sir John's lifetime. The sin undoubtedly was, but was Sir John guilty of the crime of suicide when he sank in the water. One side said "no," for he might have been recovered; the other "yes," because, as soon as death occurs, it relates back to the act that occasioned it. A man shoots another: if he dies at once, the murder is complete; but if he lives some days, his subsequent death makes that act murder which, until death, was not so. Even then it would be difficult to state *when* the crime occurred. The person who shot might not have been near his victim when the latter died. A good deal of discussion might take place, if it had to be decided on what day and where the murder took place. A similar difficulty, it appears, arose when the judges had to decide before the trial of the Regicides, in whose reign was Charles the First's head cut off. And as they could not decide this knotty problem, it was resolved at a council of the judges that the reign in which otherwise it would have been alleged the crime took place was not to be mentioned in the indictment.

Now this case of Sir John Hales was argued at great length. The counsel for Lady Hales alleged that it was not enough to consider an act, to resolve to put it into execution, and take all the steps necessary to do so: the act must be complete before the crime could be said to exist. Now the author of "Hamlet" was not going to weary the audience by a technical argument, but he played with the case and its nice distinctions and turns it inside out, views it in its comical aspect, and puts the jumble he makes of it in the mouth of a *Danish* grave-digger, who stops his work to explain in his way the puzzledom of English law to his companion, who, open mouth and astonished, wants to know if that be the law:

> Ay, marry, it is: crowner's-quest law.

King Lear.

"King Lear" is the last of the legal plays to which I shall at present refer; not that the list is exhausted, but my object is to prove my case, not to weary the reader. In the play of "King Lear," this peculiarity occurs: there are legal allusions which are to be found in the quarto and not in the folio, though apparently they have been introduced into modern editions. And in this play we find, as in the others, the same legal information introduced in and out of season; and the poor old king who lived in what may be fairly, I think, called pre-historic times, as far as English history is concerned, is made to know all about the difference between the common law and equity; and notwithstanding this, the fact that Lear did live in these remote times was clearly present to the author's mind or minds, can be shown, for where the king's fool gives his humorous prophecy in the third Act—

> When priests are more in word than matter;
> When brewers mar their malt with water,

he says, with a deliciously confused acceptance of "*nunc pro tunc*,"—

> "This prophecy Merlin shall
> Make; for I live before his time."

Yet the legal author cannot be kept quiet; his law, like Charles' head, is bound to come in; and the king in his madness twice thinks himself in a court of justice. In the first, he refers to the distinction between law and equity, a distinction which, as lawyers say, did not obtain in our courts till centuries after.

This scene is in the quarto, not in the folio, 1623.

Lear, when asked to rest, speaking of his ungrateful daughters, says [1]—

I'll see their trial first. Bring in the evidence. Thou

---

[1] Quarto, 1608.

robed man of justice, take thy place. And thou, his yoke fellow of equity, bench by his side; you are of the commission. Sit you two.

He afterwards says—

Arraign her first, 'tis Goneril, &c.

This refers to the practice of putting up one of several prisoners first before the jury. With regard to the persons, who are addressed, there are three present besides Lear and his fool, one to represent law, one equity, and one in the commission. This latter expression is doubtful. It may mean a justice of the peace, who is in the commission as such, and as we saw in "Measure for Measure" often sits on the bench in criminal trials, or it may refer to the practice of putting persons other than judges in the commission of assize. To those who are curious on the latter practice, it may be said that Henry the Second, and after him his successors, sent down the justices in eyre (*itinere*) to travel through the country and administer justice, and it appeared to be at the option of the Crown who were sent. But by an Act of Edward the Third one of the judges of the Common Pleas or King's Bench or a King's Serjeant had to sit, presumably to preside. But other people might sit with him if named in the commission. By an Act of the present reign, Queen's Counsel may also preside. It is, or was, customary, till lately, to put many names on the commission, archbishops, equity judges, &c., who, I daresay, never knew that they were there. It may therefore be, that Lear, in a true spirit of prophecy, refers either to the commission of the peace, or that of the assize. It is not very material which.

It is not my intention to do more than show the

nature of the knowledge displayed in the plays. But the reader who cares to inquire further will find that many of the other plays display such knowledge as Bacon or any other professional lawyer might possess. I may mention more particularly two plays, "Richard the Second," and "Henry VIII." In the one we have the ceremony and manners of the tournament, a knowledge of which, Bacon, who wrote, as we know, speeches for Leicester and others at the tilt-yard, might well have had. In "Henry VIII." we shall see particular attention is paid to, and a knowledge is shown of, the ceremony attaching to the position and dignity of the Lord Chancellor. The audience are shown the interior of the King's Council Chamber and there is generally a knowledge shown of the Ecclesiastical Law, both of that of Rome as well as of this country. But as I shall have to refer to those plays more at length hereafter, for the present I shall only direct the reader's attention to them.

The result of the examination of the legal Plays is, I think, to show that in Shakespeare's works we have not only the mere legal acquirements as collected by Lord Campbell, though they cover, as we know, a very wide range of law; but we have pictures drawn of the different members of the legal profession. We have, as a photographer would say, in "Measure for Measure" the English judge taken in four positions: the stern hanging judge, the kindly humane Escalus, inclined to trifle a bit on the bench yet doing justice after all. We have Escalus, prejudiced and misled, doing injustice on the bench, and we have him shamed and repentant. We have the argumentative barrister in the Temple, a sketch of life in Parliament, and a knowledge of its procedure, and lastly, we shall see in the play of "Henry VIII." a good deal about the Chancellor, Archbishop, the Lords of the Council, &c.

This is what we find in the legal Plays. Let us see what there is in the non-legal Plays.

CHAPTER III.

NON-LEGAL PLAYS: TITUS ANDRONICUS—MACBETH—OTHELLO, ETC.

IN the previous chapter many examples have been brought forward which show the legal information to be found in some of Shakespeare's plays. It is now proposed to examine the other plays in order that we may realise the absence of all that knowledge which one would expect to find in a professional lawyer. And, in considering these plays, it will be well to remember Lord Campbell's words, already, I believe, referred to.

"While novelists and dramatists are constantly making mistakes as to the law of marriage, of wills, and of inheritance, to Shakespeare's law, lavishly as he propounds it, there can be neither demurrer, nor bill of exceptions, nor writ of error."[1]

Titus Andronicus.

The play which is not often read is a very repulsive one, for which reason it is, I believe, that some of Shakespeare's admirers have tried to show it is not his. It is founded on a ballad which, like many other old ballads, has atrocity piled upon atrocity with an

---

[1] Page 108.

almost childish simplicity. To those who have not the poem at hand, an example will show what I mean. Titus describes his daughter's dishonour by the Empress's sons, who cut her tongue out, &c.—

> Then both her hands they basely cut off, quite,
> Whereby their wickedness she could not write,
> Nor with her needle on her sampler sew
> The bloody workers of her direful woe.

His revenge on the sons, &c. is thus told—

> I cut their throats, my daughter held the pan
> Betwixt her stumps, wherein the blood it ran;
> And then I ground their bones to powder small,
> And made a paste for pies straight therewithall.
>
> Then with their flesh I made two mighty pies,
> And at a banquet served in stately wise
> Before the Empress set this loathsome meat.
> So of her sons' own flesh she well did eat.
>
> Myself bereaved my daughter then of life,
> The Empress then I slew with bloody knife,
> And stabb'd the Emperor immediately,
> And then myself, even so did Titus die.

The earlier part reminds us of Fe-fi-fo-fum, who ground his guest's bones to make his bread; and the final catastrophe is told in almost as few words as that of the lover of the Ratcatcher's daughter, "who cut his throat with a pane of glass and stabbed his donkey arter."

The play follows the Poem and gives all these horrors with fidelity; but before the audience are introduced to them, there is a contest between the two sons of the late Emperor for the imperial throne. Titus has not yet returned with his victorious army; before his arrival the eldest son puts forward his claim in the following lines, which are the ones that first attracted my attention :—

> Noble patricians, patrons of my right,
> Defend the justice of my cause with arms;
> And countrymen, my loving followers,
> *Plead my successive title with your swords*;
> I am his first-born. . . .

It is very easy to understand the idea the author wishes to convey, but this idea seems to me to be clothed in the last words a lawyer would use. It was the duty of a patron to defend his client in the forum, but not with arms, but it is the fourth line that seems to me to be so wanting in the proper use of legal terms. Lord Campbell says,[1] "Having concluded my examination of Shakespeare's juridical phrases and forensic allusions, on the retrospect I am amazed not only by their number *but by the accuracy and propriety with which they are uniformly introduced.*" I do not think he could say that of the line,—

"Plead my successive title with your swords."

It is incongruous to speak of pleading with swords. Grotius speaks of the antagonism between the law and arms; how, in time of peace the former, and in war the latter, prevail? *Cedant arma togæ*, is the maxim for the first; *Inter arma sileant leges* for the second.

"Successive title" even shows more strongly want of legal training. Malone, I see, interprets it as meaning "my title to the succession"; no doubt this is its meaning, but successive title means one title succeeding another as successive waves, &c., and

---

[1] Page 107.

might perhaps be used where independent titles follow one another, a somewhat difficult thing to conceive as a title is continuous. If we say the Queen derives her title from Alfred, we speak as if the various links in the succession make up one title. But we might say at one time the successive titles of the Roman emperors were created by the clamour of the soldiers, &c., because here we mean there was no succession of interest, but as it were a fresh creation, every time a popular soldier was raised to the purple. But the expression also seems to me to be *improper* and inaccurate, even if we give the meaning to the words that Malone does. The word *title* imports a right to succeed, and, therefore, successive title, if it were accurate, which it is not, would be improper as being redundant.

I have dwelt somewhat at length upon this line, as it was the one that first led me to the belief that Shakespeare himself never mastered the intricacies of our law, and that consequently he must have been helped in those plays which show the accurate and proper use of legal ideas and expressions, which Lord Campbell refers to.

There was, as I have said, a desire to relieve Shakespeare's memory of the stigma of having written such a play as "Titus Andronicus." Be that as it may be, and it is not advisable to enter into any disputed questions that can be avoided, whatever reason there is for thinking that it was not the work of Shakespeare, there is still greater reason for thinking it could not be the work of any lawyer, especially of one who has shown such accurate knowledge as we find in Shakespeare's other plays. The whole play is not only offensively written, but it outrages every feeling and idea that a lawyer would possess. It tramples upon all his notions of right and wrong, justice and injustice; it seems not to have an idea that no society could exist without some approach to law and a legal procedure; in fact, it seems to do everything that a lawyer would not do, and leave undone everything that he would. It does not read like a serious play, but a sort of travestie that seems more like the work of one who had studied "Jack the Giant Killer" rather than the law books of the time, such as they were, or had gained his knowledge in the courts. As the whole question, to my mind, turns upon whether this view be correct or not, I propose, at some risk of wearying the reader, to take for consideration the treatment of the two sons of Titus as we find it recorded in the play, and then each one must judge for himself whether the story as there told is such a one as a lawyer would tell.

Titus has three sons left out of a very large family. Aaron, the villain of the Piece, has murdered the Emperor's brother, and thrown his body into a pit; he then persuades two of the sons to look into the pit, where, he says, there is a panther; one son tumbles in and the other follows trying to help his brother out. Aaron fetches the Emperor. The fact that they are in the pit with the dead body, with the help of a forged letter, is supposed to fix the guilt upon the sons, and the Emperor condemns them to death without further trial. They are subsequently brought in bound, on their way to execution, with Titus, according to the stage direction, "going before pleading." Of course, the officers of justice have no authority to pardon, and Titus is left grovelling on the ground bemoaning their and his hard fate instead of going to the Emperor who, as the Sovereign, alone had the power to interfere. If we compare this play with "Measure for Measure," we see the difference between a lawyer's treatment of the trial and condemnation of a prisoner and the way the appeal for mercy should be made to the Sovereign, with that given in this play. In "Measure for Measure" Claudio is properly condemned. I think the pre-contract with Juliet would, if it had been brought forward, have been a good defence; but it is not raised, and Claudio's sentence is properly discussed, and he is condemned to die as the law requires. His sister, when she wishes to implore mercy for him, goes straight to the sovereign for the time being, when she falters, her friend Lucio encourages her, and she is so far successful that Angelo tells her to come again, &c. All this seems a correct picture of what would be done in such a case. It is, however, useless to labour the comparison between the two plays. Any one has only to see how differently the arrest and trial of a prisoner is treated in "Measure for Measure" or in "Henry the Fifth," where the three conspirators are arrested for treason in due form, and then compare these plays with the stuff given in "Titus Andronicus," to at once see that the former plays show a knowledge of law and legal procedure, whilst the latter is the work of one who is remarkably ignorant of both. In "Henry the Fifth" we have an illustration of how the matter should be treated by any one who has any pretensions to being a lawyer. There, it may be remembered, Scroop, Cambridge, and Gray confess their treasons, and though Henry at great length addresses them on the enormity of their crimes, he does not sentence them himself, but says—

> Their faults are open,
> Arrest them to *the answer of the law;*—
> And God acquit them of their practices!

They are accordingly arrested for high treason in proper form.

Again the king says—

> Touching our person, seek we no revenge?
> But we our kingdom's safety must so tender,
> Whose ruin you three sought, that to her laws
> We do deliver you.

Though seeing that they have confessed he no doubt adds, knowing it to be a proper conclusion,—

> Get you, therefore, hence,
> Poor miserable wretches, to your death, &c.

The prisoners were, in fact, properly tried, for Hollinshed refers to their indictments. The fact that Shakespeare was the author of "Titus Andronicus" has, however, been so much doubted, that it is not perhaps advisable to waste further time upon it, especially as the same ignorance of law almost upon the same points is to be seen in "Macbeth." But it may be remarked that if "Titus Andronicus" is Shakespeare's work, I think it effectually disposes of the suggestion that Shakespeare learned his law when a boy at Stratford, because this must be his earliest play, and it is the one that most conspicuously displays his ignorance of law and want of legal training.

Macbeth.

"Macbeth" is placed by Lord Campbell amongst what I have called the legal plays on account of two expressions, or rather two words, which it is true are legal words, though they have, like many other such words, come into general use. The only two legal words that Lord Campbell refers to, are "bond" and "lease." Now Shakespeare, it is true, does use the words, but improperly and inaccurately in both cases.

The first he uses when he learns from the witch's second apparition that—

>> None of women born
> Shall harm Macbeth.

He replies—

> Then live, Macduff, what need I fear of thee,
> But yet I'll make assurance double sure,
> *And take a bond of fate:* thou shalt not live.

It is impossible to see, even by way of metaphor, how killing Macduff is taking a bond of fate. A bond is, as I have said, a deed whereby the giver is bound to pay a penalty unless something happens. In what way can Fate be said to be so bound, if Macduff were to die. It is mere sound, not sense, and the word is wrongly used, though both in the "Merchant of Venice" and in the Sonnets, as we have seen, the use and nature of a bond is correctly described. What was meant, I think, is, " I *will bind fate,*" or that *"fate shall be bound"* by his killing the person who was to kill him.

If a person is enslaved he is said to become a bondsman, or, if in prison, he may be put in bonds. But no lawyer would call this taking a bond from him.

NON-LEGAL PLAYS.

Lord Campbell seems to have noticed that the word "bond" has not been used with the propriety he so much admires in Shakespeare's works, though he relies upon it as evidence of Shakespeare's legal knowledge, for he says (citing the passage)—

"He, *rather* in a lawyer-like manner, resolves to provide an indemnity if the worst should come to the worst—without much considering what should be the penalty of the bond, or how he was to enforce the remedy if the condition should be broken."

A little reflection will show that Macbeth had no idea of making fate liable to a penalty upon the failure of any obligation, but, as suggested, simply to forestall it, and so overcome or bind it; and this does not seem an accurate or proper use of the word or one that "might be supposed to come from a professional lawyer."

So with the word "lease." Macbeth, when he learns, that he will not be vanquished till Byrnam Wood comes to Dunsinane, says, with glee—

> Our high-placed Macbeth
> Shall live the lease of nature, pay his breath
> To time and mortal custom.

What mortal custom means it is difficult to say, unless, perhaps, customary or common mortality. But it should be the lease *from* nature. A lessor A. leases Blackacre to a lessee B. B., therefore, has a lease of Blackacre *from* A. In the old Latin form A.'s lease would be *of* the thing leased in the genitive form,—*by* the lessor in the ablative. One can understand a farmer, perhaps, saying he wanted a lease "of his landlord," but, in saying so to any lawyer, he would be guilty of a gross absurdity, and, probably, he would only use the word "of" as meaning "off" or "from." A man's life may be put, poetically, as a lease from nature; but a lease of nature is nonsense. It is, however, not on such small points as these that I rely for my proof that "Macbeth" was not written by a lawyer. Though the examples given by Lord Campbell are, I consider, to refer to his own words, introduced neither with accuracy nor propriety.

The particular part of "Macbeth" which seems to me to most clearly prove the legal ignorance of the author is the story of Cawdor, as it is told in the play, which is founded on a short passage in Hollinshed's history, which tells us Macbeth and Banquo were sent against the rebels of the Western Isles, whom they defeated; but no sooner had Macbeth restored law and order, than Sweno, the King of Norway, landed in Fife. Ultimately, he was defeated, and a second landing took place, against which Macbeth and Banquo were sent and the invaders dispersed. It was on the return from this last victory Macbeth was saluted by the three witches as Thane of Glamis (which was his title, his father Sinell having lately died), Thane of Cawdor and King of Scotland, the latter being prophecies. For it was not till afterwards, as Hollinshed says, that the Thane of Cawdor "was *condemned* at Fores of treason against the king committed," and " his lands, livings and offices were given of the king's liberality to Macbeth;" the king Duncan was slain in battle, and buried at Elgin about the year 1046. The murder of Duncan, as described by Shakespeare, is taken from Hollinshed's description of the murder of king Duffe by his vassal Donnald, at the instigation of his wife, about the end of the tenth century.

It is to be observed that Cawdor, we are told, was condemned for treason at Fores, presumably in the ordinary course of law, but we are not told what those treasons were. Shakespeare has supposed them to be in some way assisting the Norwegian king, but in what way, whether in person or by sending assistance, neither he nor any of his characters seem to know. But, worst of all; he supposes that the king has the power to send a person to execution without any form of trial, or of his having an opportunity of defending himself. There is a very common form of error, *i.e.*, that of exaggerating the power of the Crown, an error, as we shall see, James himself fell into. Now, the story of Cawdor, as told in Macbeth, is very confused. After a preliminary scene which introduces the witches, in the second scene we are supposed to be at Duncan's court, where the king is informed by a wounded soldier that Macbeth has defeated the rebels of the Western Isles and was about to resist an attack of the King of Norway. He is unable to continue, and Rosse and Angus then enter bringing the news of Macbeth's victory. And Rosse thus describes Cawdor's treason—

> Norway himself, with terrible numbers,
> Assisted by that most disloyal traitor,
> The Thane of Cawdor, began a dismal conflict.

Apparently, this means that Cawdor was with the Norwegians on the field of battle: if so, after the battle he must have been either killed, Macbeth's prisoner, or a fugitive. Shakespeare, however, does not appear to have realised this, for he makes the king say, as if Cawdor was at the court—

> No more that Thane of Cawdor shall deceive
> Our bosom interest:—Go pronounce his present death,
> And with his former title greet Macbeth.

Rosse. I'll see it done.

The story grows still more confused as it goes on. Macbeth and Banquo, in the next scene, meet the witches, who salute him as Glamis, Cawdor and king, as already stated. Upon this, Macbeth says, in reference to Cawdor—

> But how of Cawdor? The Thane of Cawdor lives,
> A prosperous gentleman.

As if Macbeth had never heard of his being a disloyal traitor under arms against his sovereign, which fact Macbeth had himself sent Rosse and Angus to tell the king. Otherwise, Macbeth might reasonably have supposed that the result of his message would have been that Cawdor had ceased to be a prosperous gentleman, and probably had been put to death. The confusion, however, is increased when Rosse and Angus, in the same scene, meet Macbeth, and Rosse tells him that the king—

> Bade me, from him, call thee Thane of Cawdor, &c.

Macbeth again expresses his surprise—

> The Thane of Cawdor lives.
> Why do you dress me in borrow'd robes?

Whereupon Angus, who was joint messenger to the king from Macbeth and was present when Rosse made his statement which led to Cawdor's death, addresses Macbeth as if ignorant of the story, and at the same time informs him and Rosse that he does not know what was the exact crime that Cawdor had been guilty of, but he had a vague impression that he had been guilty of certain capital treasons *confessed and proved* (thereby proclaiming his ignorance of the well-known rule of law that when crimes were confessed they did not need to be proved).

In answer to Macbeth's remark that Cawdor was yet living, Angus replies—

> Who was the thane lives yet;
> But under heavy judgment bears that life
> Which he deserves to lose.
> Whether he was combined with those of Norway,
> Or did line the rebel with hidden help
> And vantage, or that with both he labour'd
> In his country's wreck, *I know not;*
> But treasons capital, confessed and proved,
> Have overthrown him.

I cannot think a lawyer, who is so accurate as the author is in other plays, could so far forget the necessity of there being *some* evidence to support a conviction, as to make one of the messengers, who had been specially sent by Macbeth to inform the king, amongst other things, of Cawdor's treason, state to Macbeth and his brother messenger, both of whom apparently now know nothing, that he was equally ignorant of what crime Cawdor had been guilty. And this want of legal accuracy is still further shown in the fourth scene, where the king says—

> Is execution done on Cawdor?
> Or not those in commission yet return'd?

This is an inaccurate and improper expression. I have pointed out in "King Lear" the proper use of the word "commission," meaning persons who were appointed to *try* prisoners, but the execution was left to the sheriff. Now, Cawdor had not been tried, and no commission would have been sent to execute him.

This condemnation of Cawdor to death without trial is the most convincing proof to my mind, that Shakespeare had no legal assistance in writing this play. As I have already stated, it is a very common form of error to exaggerate the power of the Crown—*omne ignotum pro magnifico*. And we have this travestied in "Alice in Wonderland,"[1] where "the queen never left off quarrelling with the other players and shouting, 'Off with his head,' or 'Off with her head'"; and I believe in "Richard the Third," as it was played, lines were introduced where Richard on being informed that Buckingham is taken, says—

>   Off with his head!
> So much for my cousin of Buckingham.

This is not to be found in the play.

I think it is evident that Shakespeare had the idea that the king had this power of life and death without the necessity of first trying a prisoner. For he makes Macbeth, in his interview with the murderers, expressly assert that this is so.

>   And though I could
> With bare-fac'd power sweep him from my sight,
> And bid my will avouch it; yet I must not.
> For certain friends that are both his and mine, &c.

Here Macbeth does not speak of assassination; he is choosing that mode of getting rid of Banquo when he is instigating the murderers to waylay and kill him as an alternative to doing what he says he might have done openly in the exercise of his kingly power. Now, however much the ignorant may magnify the power of the Crown, it is evident that no society could exist if its members only held their lives and property

---

[1] Page 136.

at the will of the sovereign. Something it is true like it existed for a short time when the Roman emperors used to send messages to those they wanted away (that it was for the good of the state that they removed themselves from this world). The times were very troubled then, and the persons seemed to have taken the hint; but in England it was well recognized that the king could only send a person for trial. This is very well put in the " Duchess of Malfi." Webster, the author, had been a parish clerk, and seems to have had some legal knowledge. It may be remembered that the Duke has had his sister killed, she having, in his opinion, dishonoured herself. Afterwards he attacks the instrument of his revenge.

> *Ferd.* By what authority didst thou execute this bloody sentence?
> *Bos.* By yours.
> *Ferd.* Mine? Was I the judge?
> Did any ceremonial form of law
> *Doom* her to nothing? Did a complete jury
> Deliver her conviction up in the Court?
> Where shalt thou find this judgment registered,
> Unless in hell? So, like a bloody fool,
> Thou forfeitest thy life, and thou shalt die for't.

If " Macbeth " was written after James' accession to the throne, which there is every reason to believe was the case—most authorities give the year 1605 as its date—there was a very particular reason why a common law lawyer, one who had some respect for the sanctity of the English law, should not have enunciated such opinions at this period, because James, on the 21st May, 1603, at Newark during his journey to London after Elizabeth's death, had sent a cutpurse to be executed without trial. The incident is thus described in Nicholl's "Progresses of James I,":—

"In this towne and in the Court was taken a cutpurse doing the deed; and being a base pilfering theefe, yet was a gentleman-like in the outside. This fellow had a good store of coyne found about him, and upon examination confessed that he had from Barwick to that place plaied the cutpurse in the Court. His fellow was ill mist, for no doubt he had a walking mate; they drew together like coach-horses, and it is a pity they did not hang together; for his Majesty hearing of this winning gallant directed presently a warrant to the recorder of New-warke to have him hanged, which was accordingly executed."

It appears, however, that this act was greatly censured by various historians, Rapin's remarks being[1]:

"He must, at the time I am now speaking of, have conceived a larger notion than had been hitherto formed of the power of an English king; since, when he came to Newark, he ordered a cutpurse to be hanged by his sole warrant and without trial. It cannot be denied that this was beyond the lawful power of a king of England, and directly contrary to the privileges of the English nation. Probably care was taken to warn him of the ill effects such illegal acts might produce among the people, since he refrained from them afterwards."

This proceeding was clearly illegal by the English law as provided for by the well-known 29th Chapter of Magna Charta. *Nullus liber homo* was to be taken, &c., or in any way destroyed; nor was the king to pass upon him, nor condemn him, but by lawful judgment of his peers, *nisi per legale judicium parium suorum*, or by the law of the land, *vel per legem terræ*, that is, by a jury of the man's peers, nor without being brought in to answer by due process of the

---

[1] See note, vol. 2, p. 159.

common law.[1] And so jealous was the law of the liberty of the subject, that even a villein or serf had the protection of this provision. Coke tells us that he was entitled to be treated as a *liber homo*, as he was a free man to all the world except only as regards his master. And as the masculine includes the feminine, women are equally entitled; but Coke tells us that certain of the aristocracy—duchesses—had the Act specially made to include them, perhaps thinking that as *Homo* only included woman, a lady of title might be left out in the cold; unfortunately they only named some of the aristocratic titles, and as special mention of some is supposed to exclude those not so mentioned, apparently countesses, &c., were not entitled to the protection of the clause. But Coke thinks they would, as a matter of fact, come under the general word *homo*.

It is said that the king was warned, that he had exceeded the law. Probably Bacon was one of those who did so. He was not likely to miss an occasion of giving the king advice if he had the opportunity; at all events, the matter created some scandal. Jesse describes the act as—a sort of Orientalism, which was afterwards canvassed in such a manner as to prevent the probability of its recurrence. If this be so, I think neither as a lawyer, nor as a courtier, nor in his usual position of running with the hare and hunting with the hounds, would Bacon have ventured to have revived the scandal by allowing his character to say, as Macbeth does, that he had a right to send a man to execution without trial.

This being the view of the law as I think it would

---

[1] Coke's Institutes, p. 51.

then be understood by an English lawyer, let us turn to the way Duncan sentences Cawdor to death :—

> No more that Thane of Cawdor shall deceive
> Our bosom interest:—Go pronounce his present
> death, &c. . . . .

Rosse. I'll see it done.

There is great reason for believing that in the description of Cawdor's death a picture was drawn of Essex's last moments.

> Nothing in his life became him
> Like the leaving it.

Let us carry this idea a little further and substitute Elizabeth for Duncan, Raleigh for Macbeth. Let Essex, in his jealousy against Raleigh, have invited over the French, as, I believe, he once thought of doing. Let Raleigh be sent by the Queen to resist the invaders and let us suppose him to defeat them, finding Essex with them, or believing he can prove Essex had helped them, and he sends two of his officers to inform the Queen of his victory and Essex's treason, and the Queen thereupon says "no more Essex shall deceive me," and directs, not a member of her court or an officer of justice, but one of the messengers, to pronounce Essex's death, and the officer in a casual manner, as if he was ordering her carriage, says, "I'll see it done." The idea is, of course, absurd. He might arrest Essex, but he could not hand him over to proper custody without a warrant, nor would he be executed before trial. It may, perhaps, be urged that Shakespeare departed from his rule, and no longer gave us English law, as he has done on all other occasions in whatever age or place his play may be laid, as I and others have already pointed out. But that in this case he is referring to the unknown law of Scotland.

It may, of course, be said that this was the law or supposed law of Scotland. But it appears that this was not so, and, according to Jesse, the illustrious Buchanan endeavoured by every means in his power to instil very different ideas in the mind of his sovereign-pupil, and, indeed, published his work "*De jure regni apud Scotos*" with this object.

Hollinshed, copying Boethius, says Cawdor was condemned, which means, I think, by a proper tribunal; but even if there had been no information on the subject, an English lawyer would, I conceive, draw the unknown from the known, his learning and instinct would teach him. Whatever the society was, an important noble could not be sent to the scaffold without trial and without evidence upon mere statements of those who afterwards admit they know nothing about it. To make it appear probable to his audience, as well as to himself, he would make the process at least reasonable. Even the griffin at Temple Bar, though it may have an extra turn to its corkscrew tail, has its limbs fashioned with some regard to the bones and muscles of real animals, and I think the lawyer who so carefully painted the English judge presiding over a court of justice in Vienna, and so solemnly and with dignity made Henry the Fifth deal with his traitors, would not have hurried poor Cawdor off the scene as he has been in the play of "Macbeth."

When we compare the philosophical calm of Hamlet who reasons everything out, and the wild language of Macbeth, I think we have some measure of the work done by Shakespeare writing alone, and the nature of the assistance he obtained from his legal friend.

Twelfth Night.

In comedy we have "Measure for Measure" full of law and "Twelfth Night" without it, as this play contains, I think, only two legal references and both wrong.

One where Sir Toby and Fabian are persuading Sir Andrew Aguecheek not to give up his pursuit of Olivia, Sir Ague says,—

S'light! will you make an ass o' me?
Fab. I will prove it legitimate, sir, upon the oaths of judgment and reason.
Sir Tob. And they have been grand jury-men, since before Noah was a sailor.

Of course, this is wrong, witnesses prove matters upon oath. Jurymen find verdicts or bills. The doubt I have in my mind is whether this mistake is intentional as in "Measure for Measure" where Elbow considers an action for battery the proper remedy for slander. The joke does not appear self-evident enough to have been put in on purpose, apparently there has been confusion between the duties of a witness and those of a grand juryman. That Shakespeare or his friend knew what a juryman was, is to be seen in "Henry IV.," when Falstaff not only assaults and robs the travellers but insults them.

On, bacons, on! What, ye knaves? young men must live. You are grand-jurors, are ye? We'll jure ye, i' faith.[1]

The other law reference also mis-states the law, though, as in the former case, the mistake may have

---

[1] Act II. Scene 3.

been intentionally introduced to show Aguecheek's ignorance. The law then, as in the present time, was that he who commences a fight by assaulting another first, cannot maintain an action (unless excessive force is used, though this was not laid down till the reign of Anne). Now, Sir Aguecheek being urged to assault Viola, apparently a boy, comes upon Sebastian who gives him his blows back with interest, whereupon Aguecheek, who has had enough, says :—

I'll go another way to work with him; I'll have an action of battery against him if there be any law in Illyria: though I struck him first, yet it's no matter for that.

Here Aguecheek mistakes the law which is that a person who assaults another first, cannot bring an action for the beating he gets from his provocation. This was the law in Shakespeare's time though, as I have said, in Anne's reign, the judges allowed an action to be brought where excessive violence was used. Thus, if a woman pushed a man, he was not entitled to knock her down with a cudgel. But I do not think these two allusions, both of which are doubtfully, if not wrongfully, used, can put the play amongst the legal class. If not, I think it would be sufficient for Shakespeare's reputation if he had written this play alone, being, as it is, one of the most delightful of comedies.

It is curious to my mind to consider how the interest of the piece is made to depend on the three boys who were required for the parts of Olivia, Viola, her brother Sebastian, not to mention Maria. It shows how well the stage must have been furnished with clever boys, that such a play could be written or played.

The Tempest.

This play is generally supposed to be the last Shakespeare wrote: in it I find no legal allusions, but some expressions which I consider a lawyer would not use, particularly the misuse of the word executor, which I shall refer to hereafter.

If this be so, we have Shakespeare's earliest play, "Titus Andronicus," if it be his, and his last play showing no legal knowledge, so that he could not have acquired his law and then forgotten it, or have started ignorant of it and afterwards acquired it. But I shall have hereafter to speak of the time when the majority of these non-legal plays were written as coinciding, according to the best evidence we have of the dates when they were written, with Bacon's improved fortunes which commenced with the accession of James the First in 1603.

Othello.

This play occupies a very curious position in relation to the legal test which I have applied to other plays. In some, as we have seen, the law is clear and unmistakeably the correct English law of Shakespeare's period, and in others there is no trace of law to be found; and in others we find a want of appreciation of those principles and ideas which we should expect a lawyer to possess.

In this play we find a somewhat lavish use of legal expressions and allusions, which are uniformly (though not wrong in themselves) expressed in a wrong way. There seems throughout the play an attempt to use legal phrases by one not trained in their use. In nearly every instance I think it will be seen that where legal expressions are used they are generally inappropriate, and expressed in a manner which we should not expect a lawyer to use.

It is as if one was examining a number of documents, in some of which we find idiomatic French phrases properly introduced; in others these are absent; in a third class we have the writer expressing opinions which we should not expect from a French scholar; and in the last we have a copious display of bad French. Thus, in "Measure for Measure" we find an accurate knowledge of law; in "Julius Cæsar" no reference to law; in "Macbeth" ideas inconsistent with a legal education; and in "Othello" we find an attempt to speak as a lawyer by one who does not know how to do so.

This may appear strong language to use of what is perhaps, one of Shakespeare's finest plays; but I think that, for some reason or other, the author has in this play introduced legal expressions without a very clear idea of what they mean and how they should be used. Instead of being accurate or appropriate, as Lord Campbell says Shakespeare's law universally is, in "Othello" it will be seen to be inaccurate and inappropriate. If a workman is well skilled in the use of his tools, his work will show evidence of his manual dexterity. We do not expect him to turn out something which may serve the purpose, though it is made in a rude and bungling way, as the work of an untrained person would be.

It may be said that, as long as the author makes his meaning clear, it is mere criticism to look too closely to the language he uses, and that a great deal is allowed to poetical licence. But this is not the object of this inquiry. We are considering whether the expressions used are those which a learned lawyer like Bacon *would use;* and as to this each reader must judge for himself, after having his attention directed to the particular expressions.

I do not propose to do more than point out what I consider the most striking examples of the author's "prentice hand." In fact the difficulty would be to find anything in "Othello," notwithstanding the lavish display of good law in other plays, as Lord Campbell says, which would not justify the belief that the author is pretending to knowledge which he does not possess. I think this will be seen from the following examples.

At the commencement of the play Iago tells Roderigo that, "though three great ones of the city in personal suit asked Othello to choose Iago as his lieutenant, Othello had 'non-suited his mediators.'" Now a non-suit, strictly speaking, is where a plaintiff withdraws his case from the jury; it is, according to the dictionaries, a renunciation of a suit by the plaintiff upon the discovery of some defect which prevented the jury giving a verdict in his favour; as where the evidence is insufficient. As this is for the judge to determine, popularly he is said to non-suit the plaintiff; but in reality it is the act of the plaintiff himself, who elects to be non-suited, thereby escaping an adverse verdict, so that upon paying costs he can recommence, which he could not do if the verdict were against him. The question is whether any lawyer would apply the expression as Iago does. Bacon, for instance, often employed Essex to use his influence with Elizabeth to obtain him some appointment, but in vain; Bacon was no favourite with that robust-minded lady. One would hardly expect Bacon, when writing to a friend of his disappointment, saying that Essex had been non-suited again by the queen. It is easy enough to understand what is meant, and there might be no objection to a poet using the expression, though that I hesitate to admit, its use seems so artificial and inappropriate.

Brabantio's charges against Othello.—As soon as Brabantio is satisfied that Desdemona has gone off with Othello, after one of those Shakesperian double speeches, made partly to himself and partly to others, he asks Roderigo—

> Are there not charms,
> By which the property of youth and maidhood
> May be abused?

And thus prepares the audience for the charge of witchcraft, &c., which he brings hereafter. There has been a previous scene between Othello and Iago, when the latter, speaking of Brabantio, says—

> He will divorce you;
> Or put upon you what restraint and grievance
> The law (with all his might, to enforce it on,)
> Will give him cable.

When Brabantio meets Othello, he says—

> O thou foul thief, where hast thou stow'd my daughter?
> Damn'd as thou art, thou hast enchanted her:
> * * * *
> I'll have it *disputed on;*
> 'Tis probable, and *palpable* to thinking.
> I therefore *apprehend* and do *attach* thee,
> For an *abuser of the world*, a *practiser*
> Of arts *inhibited* and out of *warrant:*—
> Lay hold upon him, if he do resist,
> *Subdue* him at his peril.

All these expressions sound to me like bad French

would to a Frenchman. He may understand what is meant, but the unaccustomed words jar upon his ear. Brabantio might easily have used the English law as so many other characters of Shakespeare have done, and alleged that Othello had been guilty of the crime of abduction. The 3 Hen. VII. c. 2 made it felony to take away for the sake of lucre any heiress without her consent even to marry her. Brabantio was evidently rich, he had only to say that Othello took Desdemona away from his custody for her wealth, and that her apparent consent, being obtained by witchcraft, was no consent at all, and the charge would have been properly framed. But Brabantio is as ignorant of this law as he is of the peculiar custom of Shakespeare's characters of knowing English law, and prefers to rely upon the charge of witchcraft.

Let us take the expressions used in their order. In the first place Iago tells Othello that Brabantio will divorce him. If Desdemona's consent had been obtained by witchcraft, as I have stated, this might be held no consent, and the divorce might have been obtained; but Iago knows nothing of this alleged witchcraft, and, therefore, had no grounds for his suggestion. On the other hand, Brabantio, who brought forward the charge, does not, as he might have done, ask for a divorce. It may be urged that Iago was a soldier and not a lawyer, with any other author this might be a reason, but Shakespeare's practice was to make all his characters know our law. If Venus knew all about a common money bond, why should not Iago know about our marriage laws? and with regard to his alternative suggestion of putting "restraint and grievance" upon the bridegroom, that seems to be taken from the practice of the Chancellor when one of his wards had been married without his consent, of clapping the man into prison until he had purged his contempt and made suitable settlements; but this was only applicable to an heiress who was a ward of chancery, and the author has forgotten to make Desdemona one. I suppose this must be the explanation of what is meant by "restraint and grievance," otherwise, there is no better-known rule of English as well perhaps of all other civilized law than that a daughter becoming a wife is freed from a father's control. But as we have seen Brabantio does not propose to invoke the aid of Chancery, nor rely upon Desdemona being his heiress, but intends to prefer a charge of the use of spells, &c. But he does not do this in anything like a legal way, he begins to argue that it must be so, and says, "I'll have it *disputed* on," meaning, I suppose, he is going to bring the matter before a court of law, for he says "I therefore apprehend and do attach thee." One cannot fancy any lawyer using the phrase "I'll have it disputed on," and "attach" as used here is inaccurate. Attachment is distinguished from arrest; the law dictionaries say, that a person attaches another who has received a warrant to keep the person in his *own* custody until he brings him before the Court. But arrest means to take a person into custody for the purpose of handing him over to others; this is what Brabantio proposes to do, for he says he is to go to prison. *Inhibit* is wrong. The word is known to Ecclesiastical and Scotch law, but the common law equivalent is prohibited; "out of warrant" is nonsense, and subdue is hardly the word which would be used to a resisting prisoner. A lawyer, I think would have said—

> If he do resist,
> He does so at his peril.

But the best way is to compare these lines with those where the offence against Gloster's wife, Dame Eleanor, is stated by Buckingham, "Henry VI." Pt. II.—

> A sort of naughty persons, lewdly bent,—
> Under the countenance and confederacy
> Of Lady Eleanor, the protector's wife,
> The ringleader and head of all this rout,—
> Have practised dangerously against your state,
> Dealing with witches, and with conjurers:
> Whom we have apprehended in the fact;
> Raising up wicked spirits from under ground,
> Demanding of King Henry's life and death,
> And other of your highness' privy council.

I have already discussed this charge of witchcraft and shown, though in Elizabeth's time it might be properly made, it was not so in the time of Henry VI. But I cite it here to show the difference between its accurate and legal language and these inaccurate and confused phrases of Brabantio's. To join a conspiracy and to practise against the state contain definite ideas which a lawyer could understand, but it is difficult to attach any legal meaning to "abuser of the world, a practiser of arts inhibited," &c.

The same want of accuracy and definition pervades the play in all legal matters. Othello asks where he is to go to answer Brabantio's charge. Brabantio replies—

> To prison: till fit time
> Of law, and course of direct session,
> Call thee to answer.

I can only guess that the author had only a confused idea of the distinction between a trial in due course of law as opposed to one by a special commission, and has, therefore, jumbled them together, and means to say " to prison, where you shall be tried in due course by the ordinary sessions," otherwise these words are without meaning.

Compare this with the arrest in " Henry V." of the conspirators.

> Their faults are open,
> Arrest them to the answer of the law ;—
> And God acquit them of their practices!

I do not wish to labour the subject, so I will refer shortly to a few more instances that prove the author's want of legal training.

Take, for example, the Duke's speech to Brabantio—

> Who ere he be, that, in this foul proceeding,
> Hath thus beguiled your daughter of herself,
> And you of her, *the bloody book of law*
> You shall yourself read in the bitter letter,
> *After your own sense.*

What should we think of a judge who tells the prosecutor that he shall interpret the law against the prisoner after his own sense? On the other hand, the Duke speaks as a judge should when Brabantio says—

> I therefore vouch again,
> That with some mixtures powerful o'er the blood,
> Or with some dram conjur'd to this effect,
> He wrought upon her.
>
> *Duke.* To *vouch* this, is no proof;
> Without more certain and more overt test,
> That these thin habits, and poor likelihoods
> Of modern seeming, do prefer against him.

But though the sentiment is judicial, the language is not what a lawyer would use. Vouch is in law generally confined to a step in a common recovery, when the crier of the Court is vouched by the defendant, yet it is used here instead of some such word as assert or allege. Test is a poor substitute for the proper word evidence. I do not understand what is meant by thin habits. A lawyer might express it thus: Mere assertion is no proof without some better evidence than surmises and poor suspicion.

Desdemona says to the Duke—

> Let me find a *charter* in your voice,
> To assist my simpleness.

Othello says—

> Vouch with me, Heaven.

It should be, I think, "Vouch *for* me"; &c.

Desdemona says to Cassio—

> I give thee *warrant* of thy place,

which only Othello could give; and she says—

> For thy solicitor shall rather die,
> Than give thy cause away.

A lawyer would say in those days attorney. A solicitor was one who practised in the Equity Courts, and had to look after Chancery suits, not common law causes.

One of the most remarkable expressions is in a speech of Iago to Othello—

> Who has that breast so pure,
> Wherein uncleanly apprehensions
> Keep leets, and law-days, and in sessions sit
> With meditations lawful?

At first I did not understand the words as used here—leets and lawdays. I thought it must have meant lent and law terms. I, however, looked the matter up, and in Jacobs and other somewhat modern law dictionaries I found lawdays were said to be the days on which inferior courts, such as the Courts-Leet, &c., were held, and that leet was the same as lawdays.

" Keep leets, and law-days," therefore seemed to be a correct expression. The word keep is properly applied to the observance of certain periods or days, as keeping lent, keeping holy the sabbath day, &c. But further investigation showed me how necessary it is to be very careful to get at the root of things. I found those law dictionaries which I had consulted were misleading, if not absolutely wrong, being themselves perhaps misled by this very line from Shakespeare. I found that *lawdays* did not, as the word seemed to mean, stand for the days on which the Court-Leet was held, but meant the Court itself. And I could find no evidence that the word ever had the meaning modern dictionaries give it. I found that Spelman had the true meaning of the word. And whatever may have been its original meaning, by one of the well-known changes in the use of words, it must have very early come to mean not the days of the court but the Court itself, and in that sense only is leet or Court-Leet the same as lawdays.

It may not be uninteresting to the reader to have the evidence that this is so. The Court-Leet was a Saxon meeting, generally in the open air, of all the residents between the ages of twelve and sixty, except peers, clerks, women, and aliens, whether master or servant. These, Coke tells us, owed personal suit and attendance to this court, where they would be sworn to their fealty and allegiance.[1] At this court the view of frank-pledge was held (*visus franci pledgii*), that is, the examination or survey of the nine sureties for good behaviour every man not specially privileged was required to have. In the early writers on law,

---

[1] 2 Inst. 120, 121.

Bracton and others, the word leet is not to be found; the Latin title, *visus franci pledgii*, is used instead. But subsequently to these writers, and even before them in charters, Acts of Parliament, and reported cases, the proper word used was "lawdays," which is given in either a French or barbarous Latin form when the Court-Leet is referred to.

Thus, in a charter of the 39 Hen. III., we have—

"Et quod eorum terræ imperpetuum quietæ sint de sectis comitatum et hundredorum nostrorum de visu franci pledgii et *lawdayorum*,"[1] &c.

In a charter of Glastonbury Abbey we have—

"Debeant facere sectam ad hundredum prædictum ad duos *Lagedaies* per annum; unum ad festum beati Martini et alium ad le Hokedaie."[1]

The first of these frees the particular lands from the control of the divisions of counties, of that of the hundreds, and of the frank-pledge and lawdays.

The latter, apparently (for I am not quite sure of the meaning of *facere sectam*, *secta* in old law Latin being in the nature of a witness), requires the abbot and monks to attend with witnesses at the named hundred, at two Courts-Leet during the year, one at the Feast of St. Martin, the other on Hook Tuesday, which, Cowell says, is the second Tuesday after Easter week.

Now Bracton tells us that the *visus franci pledgii*, that is, the Court-Leet or lawday might be granted away by the Crown as its other possessions could be. —"Sed ut per donum libertatis summondenses fiunt et attachamenta et visus franci plegii et omnia quæ pertinent at coronam,"[2] &c.

---

[1] Cowell's Law Dictionary, Art. Lawdays
[2] Bracton, f. 36 (b).

NON-LEGAL PLAYS.

It is amusing to see how lawyers eked out their Latin with latinised English words.

We see in later days the word still used as meaning the Court-Leet itself. In the Act of 1 Ed. IV. c. 2, the expression occurs more than once.

"A lour tourn" (the sheriff's court) "ou lawdaies," and finally we have two cases reported, one in Benloe and one in Dyer, which I give in their barbarous Norman-French, with a translation, for the benefit of those who have not studied that delightful language. It will be observed that the marginal note, which explains the report, uses leet, and the body of the report, lawday.

"*Grant de leet.*—Trois co-parcen d'un manor sont et le Roi grant a eux un *lawday* et ils font feffment del manor non obstant ils averont *ladway.*"[1] There are three co-parceners, and the king grants them a lawday (or Court-Leet), and they make a feoffment of the manor notwithstanding they shall have the lawday, *i.e.,* it did not pass with the manor. This case was decided in the 25 Hen. VIII., and a case is reported to the same effect in the same year in Benloe, 11.

"*Leet ou lawday extinguishment.*—Nota per l'opinion des justices del Common Bank que si iii coparcens, sont seisies d'un manor en fee a qui un leete ou lawday est appert et le roi purchase ii parts de meme le manor oue les appertenants, que uncore cest leete per tel purchase n'est extinct mes cest leete remaine uncore appert à le tierce parte de meme le manor."

This is translated by the editor of Dyer. Three

---

[1] Dyer, 30 (b).

coparceners seised of a manor whereto a leet belongs and the king purchases two parts, yet the leet by such purchase is not extinguished, but remains appurtenant to the third part of such manor.

I have taken some pains to go into this matter. Lord Campbell, in his introduction and in his notes to "Othello," twice cites it as evidence of Shakespeare's legal knowledge. But I think the author of "Othello," where he speaks of keeping leete and lawdays, does not seem to have realised that the lawday meant the Court itself, and not the day on which it was held. He might have made a mistake about lawday, but he speaks of leete as he does of the former. Now a lawyer would not say that a person who attends a court keeps it. The judge held a court, others attend it; the person who keeps the court is a servant who looks after it.

I think a lawyer of the time of Shakespeare would not have been ignorant of the correct meaning of the words as the author seems to have been. The meaning of the sentence, I take it to be, that no one's mind is so pure that unclean thoughts do not come to it as well as lawful ones, as good and bad men attend the Court-Leet and sit in sessions there. But, as I have said, I think improper use has been made of the word "lawdays," and even the expression, "sitting in sessions," I do not think a lawyer would use when speaking of the Court-Leet, where the residents probably stood. To a lawyer the expression would mean rather the Court of General or Quarter Sessions, or Parliament, than a Court-Leet.

Desdemona, when speaking of Othello, says:—

> Beshrew me much, Emilia,
> I was (unhandsome *warrior* as I am)

> *Arraigning* his unkindness *with* my soul ;
> But now I find I had *suborned* the *witness*,
> And he's *indicted* falsely.

Now here we have a number of technical words used, so that we can gather the author's meaning, though they are all used so as to make a jumble of an imaginary criminal proceeding. The ordinary barrister who has had plenty of time to spare, which he has passed with more or less profit to himself in the Crown Court, has too clear a picture of what takes place to have made the mistakes we have here. He has too often seen a number of prisoners arraigned together, which Coke tells us is done by bringing the prisoners to the bar to hold up their hands to their names, that the Court may be certain they are respectively the proper persons and that they may plead, after which, if they plead not guilty, they are given in charge to the jury. He is also well acquainted with the part the judge plays on the bench, and the witness in the witness-box. I do not think he would, in the first place, call the person who is instituting these proceedings a *warrior*, he has a more familiar expression with which to convey his meaning, prosecutor, or in this case prosecutrix. Again, when he has got Othello's unkindness in the dock, a shadowy personage, but sufficiently tangible from a poetical point of view, he would not put Desdemona's soul alongside so that the two might be arraigned together. He would put her or it on the bench and say,—

> Arraigning his unkindness *before* my soul.

Then who is the witness who has been suborned, is Desdemona's soul to play that part too ? If the witness is suborned, then the verdict might be wrong, but the indictment would not be false, and a lawyer would not change the personality of the prisoner from Othello's unkindness to Othello himself. The whole speech seems to be written with a confused idea of what really takes place in a criminal court, which a barrister of a very few years' experience knows only too well.

One more example, and I think I have pointed out sufficient for my purpose,—Iago misuses the word dowry. Speaking to Cassio who wishes to get Desdemona's assistance to be reinstated by Othello, he says:—

> Now if this suit lay in Bianca's dowre.

Meaning, I suppose, in her gift. The Quarto of 1622 says "power," which makes better sense, but is not so powerful as dowry if it were permissible to use it in the sense of "gift." But to a lawyer dowry means the wife's share to her deceased husband's property.

There can only be, I think, two explanations of these mistakes, one is that they are due to carelessness or poetical writing, the other is ignorance; in either case they do not rank with the correct law that is so often found in Shakespeare's plays, and to me seems to be the work of a different mind. If Bacon assisted Shakespeare, as I think it is possible he did, in "Measure for Measure" and the other legal plays, I do not think either he or any other lawyer of any real experience prompted or assisted Shakespeare in "Othello."

Misuse of Words.

Besides the plays of "Titus Andronicus," "Macbeth," and "Othello" which, from the reasons I have given, appear to me to show by the way in which they are written, that their author had no legal training, there are, scattered throughout the plays and other works, examples where words and phrases are used as no lawyer would use them. I think the misuse of a simple word would in many cases be sufficient to show that the person using it was not a member of a particular profession. Perhaps I may be permitted to give an example from my own experience. When in the army, I, at one time, had charge of the Verne, a large work on the Island of Portland. It was said to have been originated by the Prince Consort who conceived the idea of taking out a great part of the material required for the breakwater from an excavation which should be the ditch of a large fortress. The consequence is that this ditch is very wide and deep. I was one day showing a party of friends round the works and from the top of the parapet we looked into the ditch. An old clergyman surprised me by saying, "I suppose this *Fosse* is the largest in the world." I said, using the proper word, I thought the ditch might be; but he stuck to his own word fosse. It is many years ago, and I have no doubt he has long since joined the majority, but like many other matters, small as they seem, his mistake is useful; it illustrates Shakespeare's legal mistakes. In fortification, most of our terms are derived from the Italian through the French; thus parapet is against the breast, *para petto*, but for some reason English engineers have chosen the Saxon word ditch, and though *fosse* is not actually wrong, no English military engineer would use it. If ever used it has become obsolete. This, to my mind, illustrates the use by the dramatists and poets of the Elizabethan era of the words "executor," and "doom," and others, which I propose to show have been used not illegally, but as no lawyer would, I think, use them.

The following is a wrong use of a word which I find, as far as I have searched, only in "Macbeth."

Name.—It is recognised by lawyers that the king is the fountain of honour, and may *create* such titles as he pleases. He can, it is said do this by summoning a person by a title to the House of Lords. But the act is always spoken of as a creation. He is said to create or make him. Hollinshed tells us Duncan *made* his eldest son Malcom, Prince of Cumberland, which was the title given to the appointed successor to the Crown, and that after Macbeth's death earls were first *made* in Scotland. Now Shakespeare goes out of his way to use the word "name," thus,—

Dunc. Our eldest son whom we *name* hereafter the Prince
          of Cumberland.

Again—

Mal.   My thanes and kinsmen,
Henceforth be earls, the first that ever Scotland
In such an honour *named*.

This is not a lawyer's speech. The king makes: the country cannot *name*. A good deal may be said for poetical licence, but it is to be noticed that in other plays the proper word "create" is used where a peer is made without any loss of poetry, as in "John," Act II. Scene 2—

                        We'll heal up all,
For we'll *create* young Arthur duke of Bretagne
And earl of Richmond.

Again in "Henry VI." Part I. Act III. Scene 4—

> For these good deserts,
> We here *create* you earl of Shrewsbury;
> And in our coronation take your place.

Here the proper word is used. To the ordinary spectator it makes, I think, no difference whether the word "create," "make," or "name," is used; but I think a lawyer would not, without any reason, go out of his way to use a word he was not accustomed to, whereas Shakespeare persists in using the word "named." Thus, where Rosse is discussing with Macduff Duncan's death, he says—

> 'Tis most like,
> The sovereignty will fall upon Macbeth.
> *Macduff.* He is already *named;* and gone to Scone
> To be *invested.*

The word should, I think, have been "chosen" or "elected." Macduff does not, I think, mean he "has been spoken of," but actually created or made king; and it may also be remarked that kings are not said to be invested. That is usually applied to the case where some superior bestows an office or dignity upon another. The proper word is used by Malcom in the two last lines of the play:—

> So thanks to all at once, and to each one,
> Whom we invite to see us *crowned* at Scone.

Doom.—This is one of the words that is used in the plays in a way that it seems to me showed even in Elizabeth's time that the person using it was not a lawyer. The word is an old Saxon word connected, so Richardson's Dictionary says, with deem and damn. The latter, curiously enough, apart from that peculiar use that makes it familiar in some men's mouths as household words, seems to be confined to the theatre, where, I believe, it is still permissible to talk of damning a play without offending the proprieties. Deem is still used in the sense of "considering," as "I deemed it not safe," and is preserved in its original legal sense in Deemster, the office of justice in the Isle of Man, with which Mr. Hall Caine's novel has made us familiar. These words all originally had the meaning of exercising the power of the judge; and in Blunt's Law Dictionary of 1691, the nearest I can get to the time in question, doom or dome (Saxon Dom) is a judgment, sentence, ordinance, or decree. And under the word oath it said, "Anciently, at the end of a legal oath was added, 'So help me God at his holy *Dome*, *i.e.*, judgment.'"

But long before Shakespeare's time the law had changed its Saxon dress for a Latin one; the legal terms that were fitted to the *Leges Edwardi Confessoris* had for the most part dropped out of use in our courts. The lawyer spoke of judgment, sentence, decree, &c., but not of "doom" as a legal word. The very explanation given by Blount in 1691 shows that the ordinary lawyer required to be told that dome meant judgment. Now, in the plays, we find the word used in its original sense of a judgment in some places, whilst almost side by side the ordinary legal words of judgment, &c., are also used. It is not worth while wearying the reader with too many quotations; those who wish to investigate the matter for themselves have only to turn to Mrs. Clarke's Concordance, and there will be found a number of instances in which "*doom*," is used for "*judgment.*" The modern idea is rather that of fate, as "one doomed to be unhappy," "the doom of the great city." But in the plays it is used as the decision of a tribunal or princely power. Thus in "Two Gentlemen of Verona," where Valentine gives his account to the outlaws why he had left Milan, *i.e.*, that he had killed a man.[1]

Out. But were you banish'd for so small a fault?
Val. I was, and held me glad of *such a doom*.

The doom was not always against the person. There might be a doom of mercy as of punishment, of life as of death.

Thus, of Jack Cade's followers, Clifford says[2]—

Humbly thus, with halters on their necks,
Expect your highness' *doom* of life or death;

and in the third part of "Henry VI."[3], where Clifford dies, Edward says—

See who it is; and, now the battle's ended,
If friend, or foe, let him be gently used.
Rich. Revoke that *doom* of mercy, for 'tis Clifford.

It has already been suggested by some that Greene may have been the author of the third part, an opinion in which I concur; and I read the plays we have of his, including the doubtful one of "George-à-Greene," and I found that Greene used the word in this sense.[4]

The judge of truth, the patron of the just,
Who soon will lay presumption in the dust,
And give the humble poor their heart's desire,
And *doom* the worldlings to eternal fire.

Prince Edward, stop not at the fatal *doom*,
But stab it home.[5]

Fond Ate! *doomer* of bad boding fates.

---

[1] Act IV. Scene 1.
[2] Henry VI. Part II. Act IV. Scene 9.
[3] Act II. Scene 6.
[4] Looking Glass for London and England.
[5] Friar Bacon.

He also uses the word "deem" in the sense of considering.[1]

> Whereon *deems* Lord Douglas all the while.

This, Mr. Dyer in a note suggests, should be "dreams," but deems is correct.

In "George-à-Greene," the Scotch king says—

> I protest by the Highest Holy God,
> That doometh just revenge for things amiss.

Webster also uses the word in the "Duchess of Malfi" several times, but he may have followed our author.

I think, therefore, we may fairly conclude that play-writers preserved the old meaning of the word, as on the stage the ancient meaning of the words "to damn" has been kept.

It may be said that if this be so, why does this use of doom show that the author was not a lawyer? It seems to me for this reason, a lawyer uses special words for special purposes, and he would refrain from using others that were not appropriated to the idea he wished to convey. In the same way, I think a clergyman would refrain from speaking of a damned play. And when we find the word judgment used in other places instead of doom, it seems unreasonable to suppose a lawyer would use one time the word to which he was accustomed, at another a word that was obsolete, as far as his profession was concerned. Thus, in the trial scene in the "Merchant of Venice" judgment is several times used, as—

> "A second Daniel come to judgment!"

But doom is not once used in the play.

---

[1] James IV. Act II. Scene 2.

Enfranchise.—This is another word, which originally meant to give the franchise or freedom of a city or town to one who had it not. And afterwards it meant to free a slave and thus make him a citizen. In modern times it has been used for turning copyholds into freeholds, the Act speaking of "the enfranchisement of copyholds." In the present dictionary of Mr. Murray it is pointed out that Shakespeare frequently uses the word as meaning to set free. He, of course, ranks as a classical writer of English, and, therefore, what he has written is of authority. But I think no one would expect a well-trained lawyer to say to his servant, "take my horse to the field and there enfranchise him," or "the prisoner is pardoned, enfranchise him," or to a lady who is under lock and key "to-night I will come and enfranchise you." Yet we find the word used in these senses in the following examples :—

Thus, in "Venus and Adonis," we have Adonis' horse thus described—

> How like a jade he stood, tied to the tree,
> Servilely master'd with a leathern rein !
> But when he saw his love, his youth's fair fee,
> He held such petty bondage in disdain.
>   Throwing the base thong from his bending crest,
>   *Enfranchising* his mouth, his back, his breast.

In "Two Gentlemen of Verona,"[1] Valentine speaks of his friend to Silvia :—

> This is the gentleman, I told your ladyship,
> Had come along with me, but that his mistress
> Did hold his eyes lock'd in her crystal *toils*.
>
> *Sil.* Belike, that now she hath *enfranchis'd* them
> Upon some other *pawn* for fealty.
>
> *Val.* Nay, sure, I think she holds them prisoners still.

---

[1] Act II. Scene 4.

In the same play, when Silvia is locked up in a tower, the Duke by a trick gets a letter Valentine has written to her, wherein he reads:—

"Silvia, this night I will *enfranchise* thee."
Duke. 'Tis so, and here's the ladder for the purpose;

and Banquo speaks of keeping his conscience clear, as having his "bosom franchised."

Of course it may be said that this is poetical licence, and no doubt that is so. No one complains of the word being used as it is. The question is whether that legal mind which is so full of its own learning, that it scatters it over the pages of the plays in and out of season, as we have seen, would use the word out of its strict legal sense.

Executor.—This word to a lawyer has only one meaning, *i.e.*, the person entrusted with the duty of carrying out the provisions of a will. It is so explained in all law dictionaries. In Richardson's dictionary we have also the words execut*er* and execut*ress*. But executor and executrix have only one meaning to a lawyer. In Murray's new dictionary an executor is described as one who executes, and a quotation is given of an executor of charity. But the word for centuries before Shakespeare's time had been a specialized word for lawyers, and I doubt if any lawyer would have used it as it is used in "The Tempest."[1]

Fer.   I must remove
Some thousands of these Logs, and pile them up,
Upon a sore *injunction*: my sweet Mistress
Weeps, when she sees me work; and says, such baseness
Had never like *executor*.

---

[1] Act III. Scene 1.

This word is pronounced here as the lawyers say it—exec-utor, and not as one would think the word would be spoken, if meaning one who simply executes. Now, the lawyers have so carefully appropriated the word executors to those who execute a will, that when they speak of one who most of all really executes—the headsman, he is called not exe-cutor, but exe-cutioner; yet our author, like my old friend the clergyman, sticks to his own word.

I find that executor is also used for executioner in "Henry V.," where there is a rather fanciful analogy drawn between a state and a hive of bees. Where the author supposes there is a division of labour, certain bees being told off to bring in the honey, others to fetch the wax, whilst some guard the hive, others build the cells, &c. I do not know whether this is so, or whether the working bees do not all perform these different duties in turn, but however this may be, speaking of the slaughter of the drones, the author says:—

> The sad-ey'd justice, with his surly hum,
> Delivering o'er to *executors pale*
> The lazy yawning drone.

It seems to me that the verse requires the word executor to be pronounced not as it usually is by lawyers, but exe-cùtor, not exèc-u-tor, and there is no necessity for the misuse of the word, for the proper word executioner might have been used instead of executors pale, and the line I think would have read as well—
> Delivering o'er to executioners.

Here, as in many other places, the author seems to have gone out of his way to use the wrong word, though when the author sought the assistance of his legal friend we find the word used properly.

Thus in "Richard II." Act III. Scene 2—

> Let's talk of graves, of worms, and epitaphs;
> Make dust our paper, and with rainy eyes
> Write sorrow on the bosom of the earth.
> Let's choose *executors*, and talk of wills.

I have not attempted to exhaust the subject. If I have found sufficient to establish, to the satisfaction of the reader, that there is evidence to prove that the author of the non-legal plays had no legal training, then I have gone as far as I consider necessary. I have not relied on my own judgment alone, but have submitted the facts to those whose opinion I value, and their opinion is that there is evidence to show that the author uses expressions no lawyer would; and as there is also evidence of legal knowledge in the legal plays, the conclusion seems inevitable that the poet-author had a legal friend who helped him.

The majority of those plays which contain no law—*i.e.*, the non-legal plays—are, as far as I have examined, plays that are supposed to have been written after Elizabeth's death. She would not advance Bacon. She was a good judge of character; and we have her own opinion of him, which Essex gives, as coming from her, in a letter he wrote to Bacon (*docketed le* 18me *de May*, 1594). He reports the result of an interview with the Queen, when he had urged Bacon's "extraordinary sufficiency," proved "by the opinion of all men." To the first she answered:—

"That the greatness of your friends, as of my Lord Treasurer and myself, did make men give a more favourable testimony than else they would do, thinking thereby they pleased us. And that she did acknowledge you had a great wit and an excellent gift of speech, and much other good learning. *But in law she rather thought you could make show to the uttermost of your knowledge than that you were deep.*"

Besides this, she had Essex's death to forgive, in which Bacon played too important a part. But when James ascended the throne in May, 1603, Bacon found an opportunity of pushing himself into favour, which he was not slow to avail himself of. And, I think, now that his ambition had a chance of growing, he would have neither the inclination nor the time for play writing. I must, however, leave to others who desire to pursue the matter further the task of seeing whether there is any legal play written after 1603.

I should be very much surprised if any play, written after the latter date, may be fairly termed a legal play in the sense with which I have used the expression, always excepting "Henry VIII.," which, for reasons I shall show hereafter, stands by itself. If this be so, it may, of course, be only a coincidence: in any case, any conclusion to be drawn from it must depend upon our possessing accurate knowledge when the different plays were written, which knowledge we do not possess. Although, therefore, it may be of use as confirmation of any proof we may possess that Bacon did help Shakespeare, it does not, by itself, amount to proof.

I propose now, therefore, to consider what evidence there is that Shakespeare wrote the plays, and that *Bacon helped him.*

CHAPTER IV.

SHAKESPEARE—THE AUTHOR.

IF the distinction drawn between the two classes of plays, the legal and non-legal, is accepted as being proved, then it must also be admitted that the principal author or poet must have received assistance from some legal friend in writing the legal plays. Here this inquiry might well be closed, for most persons would agree that if this be so, Shakespeare was the poet, and probably, Bacon assisted him.

In the course, however, of collecting the necessary materials for this study, a great deal of evidence has been gathered bearing on these last two facts, which may prove of interest, and it is, therefore, proposed to give the same as shortly as possible.

It appears that the argument of the Baconians may be stated as follows :—

1. The impossibility of a person educated as Shakespeare was, being able to write plays.
2. The similarity which is to be found in many respects between the ideas, language, &c., which are found in Shakespeare's alleged plays and those in Bacon's works.

The second may be dealt with first. Whatever similarity there may be would arise as well if Bacon were only the legal friend, as if he were the sole author; and though there might be found points of resemblance between Bacon's writings and the non-legal plays, with which it has been sought to show Bacon could have had no connection, yet the close intimacy which must have existed between the two, if Bacon assisted Shakespeare in the legal plays, may well account for some of Bacon's ideas finding their way into those plays in which he had no part.

With regard to the first objection, it no doubt has great weight if we take the commonly-accepted view of Shakespeare's early career; but one of the objects of this inquiry, it will be seen, is to show that the idea of Shakespeare's inability to be a great poet is based upon a groundless assumption, which there is no reason for believing to be true.

The position taken up by some, is, that Shakespeare was no writer, but only a successful actor and shareholder in Burbage's theatres, that he never wrote nor was capable of writing any of the works attributed to him, but allowed his name to be used as the *nom de plume* for some person in the background, who really wrote the plays; and they say that there is no evidence he ever personally claimed to be the author of these plays. They further say his name was put to some of the Quartos, without his authority; and the Folio of 1623 was published after he had been dead seven years, and though there is contemporary evidence of his being an actor and even author of certain poems, which they say are far inferior to the plays, he is hardly ever spoken of as a dramatist, but even if he were, it was only because the person doing so had not discovered that he was not the real author.

This view is to many men strengthened by the mystery of Shakespeare's life. In dealing with the history of bygone times, there are certain events with which we come face to face as if we had been present: we get hold of some contemporaneous account and know as much and perhaps more about the facts than those who were living at the time. There are others which we can only see through the brains of those who too often surround them with the halo of romance. We have no doubt that Cicero wrote his speeches, or Cæsar his Commentaries, or that Bacon, Ben Jonson, Beaumont and Fletcher, authors about Shakespeare's time, wrote what the world imputes to them. But with Shakespeare all is confusion, and from an entirely different reason from that which might lead us to doubt the authorship say of the Homeric poems, namely the lapse of time and the difficulty of handing down history unaltered. Homer may be a name; Shakespeare was a person who lived, whose life may be traced, without much detail it is true, from his birth-place to his grave. The plays exist as they were given to the world, we have the actual books; there is no confusion about what they were, for as they were so they are. There is no doubt of the actual existence of the man and of the works. But directly we attempt to connect the two the difficulty commences. As a rule writers are egotistical and self-asserting. Shakespeare as an author is always in the background. He is like *Madame Benoiton*, who is never at home, never appears on the stage. Except in the sonnets he never seems to speak in the first person. We never seem face to face with the man as he was. Married, making a large income, buying land, ambitious of local success, trying to get a grant of arms for his father, living and dying in his native place, all this we can gather from others, but he tells us nothing of himself. We see a man and an author in the Folio of 1623, but we are looking across a grave that has been filled for seven years, and see only a shade, who is not more silent about himself, being dead, than he appears to have been in his fifty-three years of life.

To some it seems impossible that if he were the voluminous writer he must have been if he were the author, the fact is not brought home to us by evidence which could not be disputed. But such people seem to think that if he were only a name to hide the identity of some other writer, that which appears mysterious becomes natural. In such a case the man would be in the back-ground, his individuality suppressed, and when he retired to the country home busy with his own affairs, he would be careless of what was being done in London with his so-called plays. He would possess no books with marginal notes in his hand-writing. No manuscripts would exist of the old plays he altered and adapted; he would leave when he died no pile of papers; no desk at which he worked; no library which he consulted; no correspondence with his publishers; in fact, no circumstances would be found confirming him in an authorship which did not belong to him. It has been suggested that the Fire of London may have destroyed all the papers that would have proved who and what he was. But there has been no such fire at Stratford, where he died; having lived there for several years before; and as his house has been pulled down, there has been no for-gotten cupboard with its door papered over which contains his papers. All these facts, no doubt, have, in a great measure, given the mystery to his life—a mystery which has perplexed so many and has led more than one person to fabricate the evidence which he has failed to find. But after all, this is merely negative; it may justify suspicion but proves nothing; and I think the difficulties suggested will disappear when we deal with the facts of his life, so far as they are known, and leave the region of conjecture for that of evidence, particularly that of Shakespeare's contemporaries.

Shakespeare's Early Life.

Generally where there is an inquiry into the past, the belief and opinion of those who were cotemporary with the matters under consideration are accepted as evidence of repute, which, no doubt, is liable to be rebutted by other evidence, as the discovery of secret documents, which are permitted to come to light when the necessity for their concealment has passed away. But in the absence of such new matter being found, it does seem that due weight must be given to the views expressed by those who apparently knew more of the subject than we do. The answer of the Baconians is, that the true facts were carefully concealed from Shakespeare's cotemporaries, who were consequently deceived, and attributed to him powers which he did not possess, and that therefore their evidence was of no more value than that of any one else who was deceived by a trick, as the audience is by a conjurer. And the principal reason which seems to have led persons not without intelligence to this belief—for there are a large number of persons who have a lurking idea that there is something in the Baconian theory—is the generally-accepted view of Shakespeare's training and early life, which renders it almost impossible that he could be the author.

The story that has generally been received of Shakespeare's youth is that he was born at Stratford, where he remained and grew up in a small country town, living his life away from cultivated society—a mere rustic yokel, who married and had children. Then took to a little poaching, became a fugitive from justice, found his way to the metropolis, where he sank to the low livelihood of holding horses for those who came to the theatre. Thence made a start as an employer of other boys to hold horses for him, found his way in some humble capacity into the theatre, and suddenly became the greatest dramatist the world has ever known, his lines, though often exuberant, showing a great command of the English language, and a power of description never equalled. This sudden metamorphosis of the butterfly from such a chrysalis is unknown in human nature; we have no example, as far as I know, of persons becoming great artists late in life, their childhood having been passed amidst uncongenial surroundings. The first question we have therefore to consider is, what truth there is in this story. Now, when we come to the consideration of the actual documents which have come down to us, as given by Halliwell, we shall see there is no evidence in support of these views of his early life; and when we find that though Jonson was never allowed to forget that when a boy he was put by his step-father to the work of a bricklayer, in all the reflections he and others cast upon Shakespeare, there is not to be found a single allusion to these deer-stealing, or horse-holding stories, I think we are, at least, at liberty to search for ourselves, and try, as far as possible, to distinguish between actual facts and modern fiction.

Shakespeare's early Surroundings.

The first step is to have some idea of Shakespeare's early life. We have little direct evidence on the subject, but we know his father was, when Shakespeare was a boy, fairly well-to-do, and became bailiff or mayor of Stratford; during his year of office, we find, I think, the first connecting link between his son and the stage, for there is evidence that twice a company of actors visited the town, and apparently this had not occurred before. There is also evidence to show that many of those who were actors with Shakespeare belonged to the neighbourhood. Now we know more about the father, John Shakespeare, than we do about the son, William. We have certain original documents collected by Halliwell, to which I shall refer, which prove that the father was either a bad man of business, or an unscrupulous one. I do not think he was the latter, because there is reason to believe that to the last he retained the sympathy and affection of his son, whose object in life, apparently, was not to have himself handed down to posterity as the greatest dramatic author the world has known, but to put his father back to his original social position. I think I shall be able to show that this was so, and that the son was much ridiculed for so doing. It is said our great novelist, Dickens, in drawing the character of Micawber, had in view his own father, and he has painted the miseries of his early days owing to the poverty of his family. Shakespeare has left us no such picture, but he probably felt the *res angustæ domi*, and the endeavour of his life was to put his father in that position he thought he ought to occupy. And it may be the same causes that spurred Dickens onwards in his own successful career may have had their influence upon William Shakespeare.

John Shakespeare, in 1578, mortgaged his wife's property to one Edmund Lambert for 40*l*. This sum had to be repaid at Michaelmas, 1580. At this time, Halliwell says, he was in prison for debt. Be that as it may, the money was not repaid, and, from what after appears, the mortgagee levied a fine of the property so as to make his title good, and prevent John Shakespeare from afterwards redeeming it. Nevertheless, we find, after Edmund Lambert's death, in 1589, John brought an action against the son, John Lambert, for a further sum of 20*l*., which he alleged that John Lambert had promised to pay him on consideration that Shakespeare and his wife Mary with their son William would assure the premises to John Lambert with their appurtenances, and would deliver all writings and evidence concerning the said premises to him, and then followed an allegation that they were willing to do so, but that John Lambert would not pay the 20*l*. This claim Lambert meets with a denial that he made any such promise. Nothing appeared to have taken place further, and we shall see John Shakespeare afterwards setting up another and entirely different claim.

It is evident either that Lambert made no such promise, or John Shakespeare had not acted in a business-like way in having the bargain properly witnessed. In 1598, when his son William was at least a rich and successful actor and part-owner of one, if not two theatres, John Shakespeare made an attempt to recover the property itself, on the ground that he had tendered the money when it was due, viz., Michaelmas, 1580, to Edmund Lambert, who refused to receive it. The petition refers to the position of the Shakespeares; it alleges that—

"John Lambert is of great wealth and ability, and well friended and allied amongst gentlemen," but that "Your orateurs (petitioners) are of small wealth and very few friends in the (said) county."

The defendant denied that the money was paid or tendered as alleged, and said that not being so paid, his father had levied a fine upon the premises, and so had become absolute owner.

"That the value of the property was then generally raised, for which reason only the complainants troubled and molested the defendant by unjust suits at law, &c."[1]

Nothing further seems to have been done in this suit, but, like the former action, it was allowed to drop. As nothing was done, the only observation that occurs is either that John Shakespeare must have been reckless in his attempts to recover the property after eighteen years had elapsed from the time when the money was due in 1580; or the other alternative is that John Shakespeare did tender the money—though if he were in prison for debt this is hard to believe—but did not take the proper steps to be able to prove it.

Traditions.

The facts, so far as we can gather them, are in the case of William Shakespeare very few; we have, in fact, to start and work back from his tombstone to get even an idea of the date of his birth. He died, we are told by that authority, on the 23rd April, 1616, aged

---

[1] Halliwell, p. 589.

fifty-three years. Supposing the age to be correct, and it is very often difficult to ascertain how old a person is when he dies, this would take his birth back to 1563. There is a reason why this age of fifty-three may not be reliable, viz., it does not give the months and days of his age, but only the round number of years; whereas, if the date of his birth were known these would have been given, unless he died on the same day of the month on which he was born, when the fact would probably have been stated. Curiously enough he was baptized on this day, and it is, therefore, often supposed he was born on the 23rd April, 1563, the 23rd April, 1564, being the date of his baptism, the 23rd April, 1616, being the date of his death; the date on which he was married is not known, but the bond given in anticipation of it is dated November, 1582, and he had children born subsequently, the last of them, twins, being born 2nd February, 1585.

Now it is usually supposed by modern writers that it *is unlikely* that Shakespeare left his rustic home till after the birth of these twins, that is to say, when he was about twenty-two years of age, when his ideas and habits would be formed, and his dialect fixed. I cannot see upon what grounds Malone and others have made this assumption. As he was married at Stratford and his children were born there, it is, of course, to be presumed that he had his home there; but, so far as we know, this he always had, though he might be frequently away in London acting and writing, until he retired and settled down at Stratford. If he did this after the children were born, why should he not have done so before? He was undoubtedly attached to his father, and if he had gone as a boy to London and worked at his career, as I think there is far more reason for believing than that he wasted his youth at Stratford; he would, as he did in after years, return from time to time to Stratford, and then as he came back in all his pomp and pride as a London gallant, or as he calls it, a "Strutting Jack," he may have captivated the affections of the fair Anne Hathaway, whom he afterwards married.

It is very material to show that there is no necessity for believing that Shakespeare stayed at Stratford till he was grown up; but that the necessity is rather for the opposite belief, as this would account for that absence of provincialisms which are found in his earliest writings (except where they are introduced on purpose) and would afford him an opportunity for leading a life surrounded not only by men of learning but by women of rank and fashion who were both likely to foster and develop his talents. But before we discuss this, let us see what grounds Malone and others have for believing Shakespeare stayed at Stratford till he was between twenty-two and twenty-three years of age, instead of leaving much earlier, other than his assumption that it was unlikely. Now if we turn to his writings and to the traditions that have come down to us regarding his early career, untrustworthy as the latter are, we shall, I think, find nothing to support Malone's view, but such evidence as it is, is the other way. The traditional history so far as it was reduced to writing has been collected by Halliwell in his life of Shakespeare where the original records will be found copied.

The first of these is from the note-book of a former vicar of Stratford written 1662. This extract is, perhaps, more likely to be accurate than the others; it mentions that he frequented the plays all *his younger time*, which by no means limits his acquaintance to theatres until after his marriage, and the birth of his younger children in 1585. This extract also mentions that Shakespeare in his retirement supplied the stage with two plays a year, and finally tells us the cause of his death, all of which facts, if they be facts, we learn for the first and only time.

The next extract is from Aubrey's Lives of Eminent Men[1] and is as follows as given by Halliwell, dated 1680, sixty-four years after the poet's death.

"Mr. William Shakespeare was born at Stratford-upon-Avon in the county of Warwick; his father was a butcher, and I have been told by some of the neighbours, that when he was a boy he exercised his father's trade, but when he killed a calf he would do it in high style and make a speech. . . . This William being inclined naturally to poetry and acting came to London, *I guess about eighteen*, and was an actor at one of the playhouses, and did act extremely well.

". . . He began *early* to make essays at dramatic poetry, which at that time was very low, and his plays took well. . . . He was wont to go to his native county once a year. . . . Though, as Ben Jonson says of him that he had but little Latin and less Greek, he understood Latin pretty well, for he had been in his younger years a *schoolmaster* in the county."

The value of a statement, which makes Shakespeare a butcher (with the nonsense of his killing his calves in a high style with a speech), and also a schoolmaster in the county before the age of eighteen, when he is supposed to have gone on the stage, cannot be of

---

[1] Page 695.

much value, especially as Shakespeare's father was not a butcher, according to modern authorities; but what weight it has is in favour of Shakespeare having left Stratford before and not after his marriage, for he would have been eighteen years old before the 23rd April, 1582, and he was not married until after the 28th November in that year. This evidence may be of little value for the purpose of proving affirmatively that he went to London before he married, but it shows that there is no authority in these traditions for the opposite statement, and this we shall see is the case in the other traditions.

The next extract is not in the order as given by Halliwell, but is from a manuscript written by a person named Durdall about 1693.[1]

Speaking of Shakespeare's tomb, he gives the epitaph, which concludes—

>Obiit. A. Dni. 1616.
>Ætat. 53. Die. 23 Ap.

He then continues—

"The clerk that showed me this church is above eighty years old. He says that Shakespeare was formerly in this town bound apprentice to a butcher, but that he ran from his master to London, and there was received into the playhouse as a servitor, and by this means had an opportunity to be what he afterwards proved."

The last extract is partly in date before the one just given, but partly after; and as it is this latter part which is only material, I have given it last. It purports to be an extract from certain notes preserved at Corpus Christi College, Oxford, the original

---

[1] Page 697.

being made by the Rev. William Fulman before 1688, seventy-two years after Shakespeare's death, in which he says,[1]—

"William Shakespeare was born at Stratford-on-Avon, in Warwickshire, about 1563-4. From an actor of plays he became a composer. He died April 23, 1616," &c.

To these notes another reverend gentleman, not having before him the fear of sin, commits a literary forgery by interpolating, according to Halliwell, before 1708 (ninety-two years after death), the tradition about his stealing venison and rabbits, which we hear of for the first time, and was utterly unknown to Shakespeare's cotemporaries.

Nothing is said that Shakespeare's Hegira took place after his marriage. Malone, who is the only person who seems to have brought original research to the inquiry into what evidence we have of Shakespeare's early life, has disposed of these traditions, but in vain. He has shown that Shakespeare could not have stolen Sir W. Lucy's deer in his park, for the best of all reasons—the gentleman had no deer and no park. That is to say, unless in a properly constituted place, deer were *feræ naturæ, i.e*, wild animals, in whom no one had property; and Sir W. Lucy's property had lost its privilege before he came into it. He also shows how the idea was first put into writing by the reverend gentleman, who did not fear to commit literary forgery, as I have already pointed out, and that Rowe was the first person to put this story into print—a story utterly unknown to Shakespeare's cotemporaries. He also shows how the story of Shakespeare's holding horses outside the theatre arose, and

---

[1] Page 696.

was the creation of later days, a century or so after Shakespeare's death. But all without effect. We find Knight, Collier, and even Halliwell all referring to these idle tales, as if Malone had never written a line—another example of how difficult it is to disabuse people of anything they wish to believe in. However worthless these traditions may be, they have the negative value that they do not state Shakespeare continued at Stratford up to the date of 1585, the birth of his children, but suggest that he left as a mere lad.

Shakespeare has travelled over so wide an area, and has touched upon almost every subject; but other persons have made extracts from his works to support their particular views, so that I am not unreasonable in citing the following lines to show that he was well aware of the evil effects upon a young man passing his youth at home, and I think these lines confirm the view I take that Shakespeare got to work early and did not waste his youth, but went on the stage as a boy.

> This morning, like the spirit of a youth
> That means to be of note, begins betimes.[1]

Guiderius.   We, poor unfledged,
Have never wing'd from view o' the nest; nor know not
What air's from home. Haply, this life is best,
If quiet life be best; sweeter to you,
That have a sharper known; well corresponding
With your stiff age: but, unto us, it is,
A cell of ignorance; travelling abed;
A prison for a debtor, that not dares
To stride a limit.

---

[1] Antony and Cleopatra, Act IV. Scene 4.

Arviragus. What should we speak of,
When we are old as you? . . . .
. . . . We have seen nothing:
We are beastly.[1]

So, in the "Two Gentlemen of Verona" (Act I. Scene 1), Valentine says:—

> Home-keeping youth have ever homely wits;
> Wer't not, affection chains thy tender days
> To the sweet glances of thy honour'd love,
> I rather would entreat thy company,
> To see the wonders of the world abroad,
> Than living dully sluggardiz'd at home,
> Wear out thy youth with shapeless idleness.

So, in the same play, Panthino speaking to Antonio about his brother[2]—

> *Pant.* 'Twas of his nephew, Proteus, your son.
> *Ant.* Why, what of him?
> *Pant.* He wonder'd that your lordship
> Would suffer him to spend his youth at home;
> While other men, of slender reputation,
> Put forth their sons to seek preferment out:
> Some, to the wars, to try their fortune there;
> Some, to discover islands far away;
> Some, to the studious universities.
> For any, or for all these exercises,
> He said, that Proteus, your son, was meet:
> And did request me, to importune you,
> To let him spend his time no more at home,
> Which would be great impeachment to his age,
> In having known no travel in his youth.
> *Ant.* Nor need'st thou much importune me to that
> Whereon this month I have been hammering.
> I have consider'd well his loss of time;

---

[1] Cymbeline, Act III. Scene 3.
[2] Act I. Scene 3.

> And how he cannot be a perfect man,
> Not being tried and tutored in the world:
> Experience is by industry achieved,
> And perfected by the swift course of time.

If, therefore, a youth who stays at home is of a homely wit, knows nothing, has nothing to talk of, cannot be a perfect man, nor mean to be of note, I think we have a fair inference that, as Shakespeare was not a homely wit, knew almost everything, and had a great deal, if not to talk, to write about; and as our author was a "perfect man," and one who meant to be of note: if all this is true, then the syllogism is true that he did not pass his youth at home; and that his father, a man of slender reputation, "put forth his son to seek preferment out."

I think, therefore, we may fairly come to these conclusions. It is very improbable that a person of Shakespeare's abilities would have wasted his life at home a burden upon his father, who was undoubtedly getting poorer and poorer. It seems almost impossible, if he had so wasted his youth, that he could have got rid of his provincialism, and removed all trace of rustic ignorance, and become the poet of all time. That there is nothing in the traditions which have come down to us, nor in his writings which supposes that he stayed idly at Stratford until his children were all born; that what evidence there is, is the other way; and that all we have to support this view is a hasty expression of Malone's, which every later writer seems to have adopted. The suggestion that he went in early life on the stage seems the more reasonable one.

There was no doubt a very early connection between

the actors of Shakespeare's time and the Shakespeare family. A considerable number of them came from the neighbourhood of Stratford. We find several names amongst them who are believed to be Stratford men, or, if not so, to have come from the vicinity. And we have already seen that when John Shakespeare was mayor two companies came to Stratford for the first time. I see no improbability, therefore, in the idea that Shakespeare, possessing, as he undoubtedly did, gifts that fitted him for the stage, when he desired to get his living found no difficulty in getting on to the London boards. At this time there were two companies in London, one belonging to Henslowe, who has left us his diary, whose principal actor was his son-in-law Alleyne, who made a large fortune with which he founded and endowed Dulwich College. The other was Burbage's of which Shakespeare became a member and, ultimately, a partner.

It is by no means impossible, therefore, that Shakespeare went forth as a mere lad to improve his fortunes, that he found an easy introduction to Burbage's company, and when there either himself played women's parts, or was an associate with lads of his own age who did; that he may soon have been in receipt of a good income, and have mixed in good society. His talents would have given him introductions everywhere.

All this is very speculative, not amounting to evidence, but of that we have none. We can only speculate, and my object is to show that the possibilities, if not the actualities, of his early life are very different from those hitherto taken for granted.

But it may be said, what does it matter when

Shakespeare went to London? In reality it is very important. In one case we have him bred up in a rustic life, surrounded by poverty, with the cares of a family on him and scanty means for its provision—none of the graces and comfort of prosperity. In the other, we have him in early youth rapidly growing rich, for the actors, as is well known, were highly paid, surrounded by all the amenities of fashionable existence, introduced into the best society, a friend, perhaps, of young men of good position, perhaps taken in hand by some high-born and well-bred ladies who taught him those high notions of the other sex which he afterwards embodied in his heroines. All is mystery about him. But this, I think, we may say: there is nothing improbable in the suggestion that he early lost his rustic manners and provincialisms of thought and speech in the cultured life of the metropolis.

If this be so, and we have not evidence to say one way or the other positively, it removes the principal objection that has been raised, viz., his want of opportunity for improvement and education. I propose now to examine into the evidence that shows as a matter of fact that he was a dramatic writer.

CHAPTER V.

EVIDENCE THAT SHAKESPEARE WAS A WRITER OF PLAYS.

THERE are at least three writers who, having private means of knowing the fact, have acknowledged Shakespeare as a dramatic writer. In the case of two, it is impossible to understand how they could have been deceived by any secret arrangement, if such existed, between Bacon and Shakespeare, as the one wrote before either of them, as far as we know, had written or published any play, the other, with full knowledge of who the real author of the plays was. In addition, there is another piece of evidence, viz., the publication of the two poems by Shakespeare himself. I propose to deal with these in their order in time. They are, therefore—

1. The reference to Shakespeare by Robert Greene.
2. The publication of the poems.
3. The evidence of Meres.
4. The statements by Ben Jonson.

First, as to Robert Greene.

In order that this evidence may be properly appreciated, let us for a while allow our imagination to go back three hundred years. Let us suppose that it is not the end of the nineteenth century, but that of the sixteenth, when London was very different from what it is now. But then, as now, a Queen was on the throne, and as now, so then, the period was one of great literary activity. It is a curious thing, by the way, that under our three queens we find the same high position taken by literature—the Elizabethan poets, Addison and his followers, the penny papers, and the voluminous journals, novels, &c., characterize the reigns of our three female sovereigns. But to return to our supposition. It is the *fin du siècle*, the last ten years of the century, and they are slipping by as the years are slipping away from us now; and during these years matters are occurring which, I think, if rightly looked at, must establish to all but the prejudiced the right of Shakespeare at least to the title of poet.

At this period, 1590, he was about twenty-seven years of age. His youth had passed and, as far as we know, he had published nothing. The date of "Titus Andronicus" is uncertain, but, with the exception of that blood-curdling drama, there was nothing that there is the slightest reason to suppose had been produced so early as 1590. The first mention of him as a writer is, in fact, not made till 1592. Before then we get no evidence that such a person as William Shakespeare was in existence. If our records ended with 1590, the William Shakespeare who was baptized, married, &c. at Stratford might have died long before. But in 1592, we do find evidence that he was in existence, and was at least attempting to write poetry. The evidence is of the best kind, for it is evidence not given by a friend and admirer, but of one who was speaking bitterly of him, not seeking to hold him up to admiration, but pointing at him as a person to be feared, as one who was taking, or ready to take, the bread out of the mouths of starving poets. I refer to the evidence which has so often been stated, *i.e.*, that of the dying Robert Greene, who was one of the best, I consider, of the poets of this period. He was the only person, I think, of that period who had the power of composing a story. Nearly all the writers of plays of that time wrote upon old plots. Their subjects were taken from the classics, history, or older plays. It may be that the public preferred old favorites. But any reader of the old writers knows how one author copied from another. One may trace anecdotes from Gil Blas back to Boccacio, and still further on to Apuleius and his "Golden Ass," and his stories have their foundation in old Greek myths taken from Egypt, but who in time stole from that India, which seems to be the cradle of our fiction as well as of our philosophy. Nowadays, every young lady can create her plots fast enough. The framework of the story can be put together though it may not be skilfully worked out. In past times plot making seems to have been either an unknown art or one that had been forgotten. But Robert Greene could tell a new story, and tell it well too. We have one of his novels[1] on which Shakespeare founded his "Winter's Tale." Dyer, in his short account of Greene's life and works, says it is unknown where he got the story from, never apparently conceiving that he created it. Now, there is strong reason for believing that Shakespeare and Greene were at one time on terms of intimacy. It is very likely that it was so, if the view here taken of Shakespeare's early career was correct, that he was an industrious lad wishing to make money and to raise his family. Greene was one who had misspent his life, but was of great talents, and he was one who

---

[1] Pandosto, 1588.

might well offer an attraction to Shakespeare as likely to assist him in his studies. On studying Greene's history and writings, perhaps others may take the same view, perhaps not. It is only indirectly connected with the present inquiry; but it is of interest if we can see how Shakespeare may have learned to write plays.

Mr. Dyce, in his account of Greene's life and writings, says he was supposed to have been a clergyman of the Church of England, and quotes a statement supposed, curiously, to have been made on the authority of Shakespeare himself. He says,[1]—

"A copy of *The Pinner of Wakefield* exists, on the title-page of which are the following notes in handwriting of about the time (1597) when the play was printed.
"Written by . . . . a minister, who acted the piners pt in it himselfe. Teste Wm. Shakespeare.
"Ed. Juby saith it was made by Ro. Greene."

For this reason Mr. Dyce includes this play amongst Greene's works. Greene appears to have led a very dissipated life, to have lost his preferment, if he had one, to have lived apart from his wife, and rapidly to have sunk lower and lower. He was born about 1550, so that he was about forty-two when he died; he was a man of considerable education, for he took his degree both at Oxford and Cambridge, and in some of his works he describes himself as "*Utriusque Academiæ in Artibus Magister.*" And he appears to have studied physic, and, from his writings, he must have made himself master of some of the rudiments of law, as he uses many legal expressions correctly, though

---

[1] Greene and Peele, by Dyer, 1861, p. 4.

EVIDENCE THAT SHAKESPEARE WROTE PLAYS. 159

they are only such as he might have learned at the University. In no place does he show that sympathy with the life and ideas of a lawyer which are to be found in some of Shakespeare's plays—and in his alone. After a life of debauch he was taken ill and was sheltered and kept alive by the charity of some humble people; ill and deserted by his former friends, particularly the actors, who left him in his poverty, his mind became filled with self-reproach, and no doubt he tried to sell some of his writings. He, however, died (3rd September, 1592), leaving a bond for ten pounds for those who sheltered him, with a letter to his deserted wife, praying her to see it paid. It is generally supposed he died from starvation, but this does not appear to be the case; he died in poverty but not in actual want.[1]

After his death another author, named Chettle, was employed by some of those who had Greene's manuscripts to prepare them for publication. And as he tells us—

"About three months since died Mr. Robert Greene, leaving many papers in sundry booke-sellers' hands, among others his '*Groatsworth of Wit*,' *in which a letter written to divers play makers is offensively by one or two of them taken*," &c.

Of this "Groatsworth of Wit" Chettle goes on to say—

"I had only in the copy this share; it was ill written, as sometimes Greene's hand was none of the best, licensed it must be e'er it could be printed, which could never be if it might not be read. To be brief, I writ it over, and as near as I could followed the copy, only in that letter I put something

---

[1] Halliwell, p. 449.

out, but in the whole book not a word in, for I protest it was all Greene's, not mine nor Master Nashe's, as some unjustly have affirmed it."

This "Groatsworth of Wit" is remarkable as containing the first reference, though an indirect one, to Shakespeare as a dramatic writer; but the reference is the more valuable as it is made in a hostile spirit, and was made before either Shakespeare or Bacon, if he were the author, had published either of the Poems, Sonnets, or Plays, so that he could not have been misled by Bacon's writing in Shakespeare's name. It is addressed by the writer:—

"To those gentlemen, his quondam acquaintances, that spent their wits in making plaies, R. G. wisheth a better exercise and wisdom to prevent his extremities."

The letter then proceeds to address three persons in succession, generally supposed to be Marlowe, Lodge, and Peele. It is not necessary to quote his addresses to each of them, which are given in Halliwell[1] and many other writers, though it may not be out of place to remark that the words savoured of impertinence, as we may see when he addresses all three and warns them from the players, and in so doing refers to Shakespeare as a would-be author.

"Base-minded men all three of you, if, by my misery ye be not warned, for unto none of you (like me), sought those burrs[2] to cleave; those puppits I mean that speak from our mouths, those antics garnished in our colours. Is it not strange that I to whom they have all been beholding, is it not like that you to whom they have all been beholding, shall (were ye in that case that I am now) be both at once

---

[1] Page 445.   [2] The actors.

EVIDENCE THAT SHAKESPEARE WROTE PLAYS. 161

of them forsaken. Yes, trust them not; for there *is an upstart crow, beautified with our feathers, that, with his tyger's heart wrapped in a player's hide, supposes he is as well able to bombast out a blank verse as the best of you, and being an absolute Johannes factotum,* is in his own conceit the only *shake scene* in a county. Oh, that I might entreat your rare wits to be employed in more profitable courses! And let those apes imitate your past excellence and never more acquaint them with your admired invention.[1] I know the best husband of you will never prove an usurer, and the kindest of them all will never prove a kind nurse; yet whilst you may seek you better masters, for it is pity men of such rare wit should be subject to the pleasure of such persons."

Now this seems to me very easy to understand. There is a well-known picture of a poverty-stricken author appearing at the banquet of the actors who were flushed with wine and good living. And there is no doubt at this period the literary work of the author was poorly paid in comparison with the large earnings of the actors. We have extracts from Henslowe's diary of the small sums paid to the authors, and we know from the papers of 1635, discovered by Halliwell and set out in his book,[2] that the players' share was £180 of money of that period, being ten or twelve times the value of this sum at the present time. It also appears that out of the actors' share had to be defrayed "all wages to hired men, apparel, *poets*, lights, and other charges of the house whatsoever." It is easy, therefore, to understand Greene's bitterness when he reflected on all the money he had assisted the actors to make, and how little of it came into his own hands. This irritation

---

[1] New works.   [2] Page 476.

would, I think, have been greatly increased if he had lived long enough to see Shakespeare doing double work, taking not only the bread out of the poets' mouths, but their ideas, and more particularly a good deal from Greene himself.

In "Orlando Furioso" Sacripant, Orlando's rival, hangs his slanders about Angelica on the trees; these Orlando reads, and for the time goes mad. In "As You Like It" we have a similar incident, but rather as comedy than tragedy.

There is in the same play the scene, with which it opens, with the suitors, which reminds one of a similar scene in the "Merchant of Venice."

In Greene's "James the Fourth," we have Oberon, who disturbs a Scot named Bertram, who has taken up his residence in a tomb. This Bertram has two sons, and he causes a play to be acted before Oberon, in which the two sons appear in their own persons, yet as characters in the play. In "A Midsummer Night's Dream," we have in the play Oberon, but also Titania and Puck added. In Greene's play we have the incident of a queen flying in the disguise of a man, being the object of love by another woman, and of the jealousy of her husband. But the subject is very differently treated from the way it is in "As You Like It." But the principal assistance Shakespeare derived from Greene was from the prose novel "Pandosto," the story and incidents of which are believed to be the invention of Greene. On it was founded the "Winter's Tale," almost incident for incident, except the slandered wife actually dies, after the oracle is read and her character cleared, upon hearing of the sudden death of her son. So much has the novel been copied, that whereas in the novel the lost daughter and her lover on their voyage came to the coast of Bohemia, in the "Winter's Tale" Bohemia is spoken of as being on the sea. I think if Greene could have foreseen Shakespeare's future still more would he have spoken of him as an upstart crow beautified with our feathers. The reference can only be to William Shakespeare. Now, we are not trying whether all his ideas were original, or whether he did not as all else have done, borrow from other authors; but the question is whether he wrote plays.

All those who have written on Shakespeare, at least since Malone's time, have made a very curious mistake about this incident of Greene's "Groatsworth of Wit." It may be remembered it was published by Chettle after Greene's death, and Chettle, in his preface to "Kind Hearts Dream," explains the part he took in writing it out legibly,[1] and that it being a "letter written to divers play makers, is offensively taken by two or three of them." Speaking of these who thus took offence, who are clearly the *play-writers* to whom the letter was addressed, Chettle goes on to say—

"With neither of them that take offence was I acquainted, and with one of them I care not if I never be; the other, whom I did not so much spare, as since I wish I had, for that as I have moderated the heat of living writers, and might have used my own discretion (especially in such a case), the author being dead; that I did not, I am as sorry as if the original had been my fault, because myself have seen his demeanour no less civil than he (*sic*) excellent in the quality he professes; besides, divers of others have reported his uprightness of dealing, which argues his honesty, and his facetious grace in writing that approves his art."

---

[1] Halliwell, p. 448.

Here Chettle's meaning is quite clear. The letter of Greene was addressed to three play-writers, said to be Marlowe, Lodge and Peele. Two of these complain. One of those complaining he does not know nor care to know; the other he is sorry for, as he is of very excellent demeanour, &c. These two, I consider, must be Lodge and Peele, for of the first, Marlowe, he speaks separately. He continues:

"For the *first*, whose learning I reverence, and at the perusing of Greene's book, struck out what there in conscience I thought he in some displeasure writ, or had it been true, yet to publish it was intolerable, him I would wish to use me no worse than I deserve."

This is also clear. Marlowe was the Nestor of the rising literary world—the giant whom they all respected. Chettle simply submits himself to his judgment, but deals with the other as pointed out. Yet Malone twisted this apology of Chettle's to "one of the two play-makers to whom the letter was written, and who had taken offence," as an apology to Shakespeare. It is difficult to see how the language could be so understood, even by one of his most ardent admirers. The letter was not addressed to Shakespeare; he was not one of the play-writers; he was a pretender in Greene's eyes, and as far as one can see he was severely left alone by Chettle. Of course it is immaterial whether Chettle apologized to him, or to Peele or Lodge. But it is material to see whether a whole succession of writers, Malone, Stevens, Dyce, Collyer, Halliwell, Knight, and a host of minor authors, are so blinded by their admiration for Shakespeare, that they cannot read a simple document correctly, or are simple followers of Malone, that they have adopted his mistake and made no inquiry for themselves.

One hesitates to express an opinion in the face of so much, apparently, consensus of opinion, but I have read the document very carefully, and can see no construction to put upon it except the one given. If this be so, whatever evidence we may find in Greene's attack that Shakespeare was in 1592 pretending to bombast blank verse, we have no right to turn Chettle's apology to Lodge or Peele into a testimonial, as Knight or so many others put it: "that Chettle recognized Shakespeare's uprightness of dealing, which argues his honesty, and his facetious grace in writing that approves his art." Expressions that would hardly have been used about one who, as far as we know, had never published anything, whatever he may have done privately.

Be this as it may, we have, if Greene's upstart crow and shake scene refers to Shakespeare, the actor-writer, contemporaneous evidence as early as September, 1592, that he, Shakespeare, supposed himself able to bombast a blank verse as well as the best of the writers.

It is no doubt impossible to decide positively upon what, after all, is a matter of opinion. But, as I have said, there is some ground for believing that Shakespeare and Greene must have one time stood in the relation of master and pupil to one another. It has been pointed out that Shakespeare uses some words, as *doom*, as Greene does, in the sense of judgment, and that many of Shakespeare's plays and scenes are taken from Greene's works.

Whatever may have been their relations, we have, as I have said, this undoubted fact, that before Shakespeare either published anything himself, or any one else published anything in his name, Greene had written of him as one who fancied he could bombast blank verse. And in saying this, he could not possibly have been misled by any arrangement between Bacon and Shakespeare that the former should write plays which the latter should adopt, for at the time Greene wrote, as far as we know neither Bacon nor Shakespeare had written anything. The whole tone of Greene's observations is not that of a person speaking of one who was already before the world as an author; but he is, as it were, announcing some one who was not yet known, as racing men put it "speaking of a dark horse," one who might come forward and be a competitor in the badly-paid work of play-writing. And in this way it seems that Greene's evidence is most valuable, as proving that long before any arrangement could have taken place between Shakespeare and Bacon, Shakespeare had begun to write blank verse.

The next piece of evidence which, I think, constitutes part of the proof that Shakespeare was the poet-author of the plays, is the publication of the two poems of "Venus" and "Lucrece." It has been already shown that in these two poems, as well as in the sonnets and those plays which I have termed legal, there is that introduction of law in and out of place, which is so marked a characteristic of these writings. Besides this mixture of poetry and law, there are many resemblances in ideas and expressions to be found in the Poems, Sonnets, and Plays which I will not stay to describe at length.

We have, therefore, enough to show that the poet-author of the poems wrote the plays and sonnets, and that Shakespeare was the author of the poems, which, up to the present, no one has ever disputed, as they have generally been considered of inferior merit to the plays. The argument, in fact, generally has been, that the poems are so inferior to the plays that Shakespeare could not have written both. But if the evidence adduced is sufficient to establish that poems and plays are by one author, then those who assert that Bacon was the author of the plays must go so far as to say that he also wrote the poems. But the poems stand on a very different footing to the plays; the latter, as far as we know, were never published by Shakespeare as his own or claimed to be so by him. But of the poems, the first, "Venus and Adonis," was not only published by Shakespeare as his own in his lifetime, but was printed by Richard Field, a fellow-townsman of his. Halliwell tells us that Shakespeare's father made an inventory of Field's father's goods in 1592. And one author, Mr. William Blades, has written a book[1] showing the intimate technical knowledge of printing that is to be found in the plays, and, in fact, he suggests that Shakespeare may have worked in Field's shop.

Richard Field, Mr. Blades tells us, was not only "Shakespeare's own townsman," but being about the same age and social rank the boys probably grew up together as play-fellows. We are also told that—

"Early in 1577 young Field came up to London, and at Michaelmas was apprenticed for seven years to George Bishop, printer and publisher; and in 1588 he married the daughter of Thomas Vautrollier."

---

[1] Trubner, 1872.

Field's father-in-law was a Frenchman, who had settled in London as a printer and publisher. He died the same year that Field married his daughter, and Field succeeded to his premises and business. Mr. Blades somewhat humorously supports his view by showing that the illustrations given of Shakespeare's use of technical printing terms are very curious. Such as when a book is finished, there are often found vacant leaves of the last sheet where it is usual to put the typographer's *imprint*. Mr. Blades quotes[1] :—

The vacant leaves, thy mind's imprint will bear.—
Sonnet, lxxvii.

Shakespeare also knew the use of "Quoins," of "Locking-up," the "Register," &c.—

By the four opposing coigns
Which the world together joins,[2] &c.

We have therefore these facts: "Venus and Adonis" published in Shakespeare's lifetime as his own work, and printed by his friend and fellow townsman Richard Field in 1593. It is dedicated to Henry Wriothesley, Earl of Southampton, and William Shakespeare's name is attached to the dedication, wherein he terms it "the first-heir of my invention." This poem was followed by that of "Lucrece," which is also dedicated to Lord Southampton. This nobleman was at the time a member of Gray's Inn, and there is a probability that Bacon was a party to these poems being addressed to so distinguished a member of Bacon's own inn.

It is also generally considered from the absence of errors, &c., that Shakespeare himself passed the poems through the press. In fact, that Shakespeare

---

[1] Page 48. [2] "Pericles," Act III. Scene I.

EVIDENCE THAT SHAKESPEARE WROTE PLAYS. 169

wrote and published these poems is proved by as good evidence as any work of that date can be proved to be written by its author. If so, the chain of reasoning seems complete. If there be unity of authorship between the poems, sonnets, and plays, and Shakespeare wrote the first, he must have written the other two.

It may be noticed that the references made by Shakespeare's cotemporaries are, with the one exception, I believe, of Francis Meres, made to these poems and not to the plays. Halliwell has collected these references, to which the reader can refer.

The Testimony of Francis Meres.—

In September, 1598, Meres published a comparative discourse of our English poets (painters and musicians), with the Greek, Latin, and Italian poets (painters and musicians). In it he mentions Shakespeare's name several times, first as the honey-tongued Shakespeare:

"*Witness* his 'Venus and Adonis,' his 'Lucrece,' his sugared sonnets among his private friends."

These sonnets were not published in 1598, in fact not before 1609, and it is to be noticed that Meres speaks of them as if they were only privately circulated amongst Shakespeare's friends, and thus professes to have a knowledge of Shakespeare not only in his public but private life. He further says, as Plautus and Lucrecia are accounted the best for comedy and tragedy among the ancients, so Shakespeare among the English is the most excellent in both kinds for the stage.

"For comedy witness his 'Two Gentlemen of Verona,' his

'Comedy of Errors,' his 'Love's Labour Lost,' his 'Love's Labour Won,' his 'Midsummer Night's Dream,' and his 'Merchant of Venice.' For tragedy his 'Richard II.,' 'Richard III.,' 'Henry IV.,' 'King John,' 'Titus Andronicus,' and his 'Romeo and Juliet.'

"As Epius Stilo said that the muses would speak with Plautus' tongue, if they would speak Latin; so I say that the muses would speak with Shakespeare's fine filed phrase if they would speak English."

He afterwards says there are eight descriptions of poetry: (1) Heroic, (2) Lyric, (3) Tragic, (4) Comic, (5) Satiric, (6) Iambic, (7) Elegiac, and (8) Pastoral, and mentions Shakespeare's name amongst others under 2, 3, 4, and 7. Now, it may be said that we have no knowledge of the means of information possessed by Meres, he may have been deceived like others if there had been a Bacon-Shakespeare conspiracy. No doubt to a certain extent this is so, but it is to be noticed that in the case of the Sonnets I have pointed out that he speaks as one having a personal knowledge of Shakespeare and his private friends, and therefore was not so likely to be deceived as another might be. We have, therefore, the evidence of Greene, that Shakespeare was a writer of blank verse, though unknown as such to the world; of Meres, that Shakespeare was the writer *par excellence* of all descriptions of dramatic verse, and, as we shall see, we have that of Ben Jonson who says Shakespeare was a very voluminous writer, one who wrote "with that facility, that sometimes it was necessary he should be stopped."

CHAPTER VI.

BEN JONSON'S STATEMENT ABOUT SHAKESPEARE'S PLAY-WRITING.

IN considering the evidence of Jonson, who so often expressed his opinion about Shakespeare and his plays, it must be remembered that he was a great friend and admirer of Bacon; he wrote masques for him. Bacon was so friendly with Jonson, that when the latter was starting to walk to Scotland he met the former, who said that he did not like to see poetry going on other feet than dactyls and spondees. This we have from Jonson's own account to Drummond. And when Bacon fell Jonson visited him, and it is believed helped him in his literary work. The Baconian idea is that at this time the folio of 1623 was being brought out. It is impossible to believe that, if the plays were Bacon's, he could have done this without letting Jonson into his secret. Jonson wrote the verses to the portrait, the lines to Shakespeare, and not only this, but he is supposed to have written the addresses of the players; and we know that certain verses were written by Digges which Jonson kept out, because he adopted some of the ideas but did not use the lines, which, however, have come down to us and will be given hereafter. If this be so, then it follows that Jonson as soon as he knew Bacon was the real author, must have known Shakespeare was not, and would therefore have no reason to criticise Shakespeare's writings, which he was always doing long after Bacon and Shakespeare were both dead; nor would he have had any reason to leave papers for posterity continuing this criticism. It might be said that he did so for the purpose of throwing the world off the scent. But if this were his object, one would think he would have been very careful when writing about Bacon not to say anything which would lead posterity to attribute the authorship to Bacon; if he wished to conceal the secret he would not have alluded to Bacon filling up all numbers, nor used the same expressions about Bacon as he has about Shakespeare. It is these expressions of Jonson's which are so often relied upon as evidence of Bacon being the author. But if Shakespeare was the voluminous and sometimes careless writer and Bacon only assisted him, then Jonson's conduct is easily understood, he praised and alluded to his friend and patron Bacon, he criticised and quarelled with his rival Shakespeare. As an actor, Shakespeare was not in Jonson's way; if he had been no more, Jonson, so far from quarrelling with him, would have looked to him for employment. But as an author, Shakespeare was an opponent to be fought. It is not necessary to go into the quarrel between the two, except so far as it relates to Shakespeare's position as a writer of plays. And we shall see that Jonson objects to Shakespeare putting battles on the stage, to his choice of plots, to his dialogue, and careless writing; and not content with this, attacks him personally. And Shakespeare answers him on more than one occasion : all of which seems to be inconsistent with the fact that Bacon was the real author; if that had been so, it seems a fair observation that Jonson would not have attacked Shakespeare for Bacon's works, nor would he, looking at the admiration he had for Bacon, have attacked the works themselves; nor would—and this seems important—Bacon have replied in *his* plays to these attacks upon Shakespeare.

It seems, therefore, that the strongest and best evidence that Shakespeare was a writer of plays is to be found in the statements made by Ben Jonson. The evidence is so strong that it is difficult to understand how anyone could maintain that Bacon was the real author of the plays, and Shakespeare only allowed his name to be used. It seems that such a theory could only be put forward by those who were unacquainted with that which Jonson had written about his great rival. About the end of the sixteenth century Jonson, it appears, first began to try and earn his living by the precarious profession of a playwriter. He had had a somewhat unhappy and chequered career. His mother was a widow who had married for a second time a master builder, who, perhaps, for the better educating the boy in his trade, compelled young Jonson to work as a bricklayer. And not many years ago, some old houses were pulled down in Chancery Lane on which, tradition said, young Jonson had actually worked. However this may be, there is no doubt that he actually did use the trowel, a circumstance which was never forgotten. It has already been referred to that, when people were not pleased with his poetry, on more than one occasion he was told with a sneer that he had better go back to his old trade of bricklaying. He appears, however, like Dickens, to have escaped from his uncongenial employment, and under the protection of the great Camden, who was the head master of Westminster School, he acquired a good education. He afterwards served some time as a soldier, and finally returned to England and wrote plays. At this time, as far as we know, Shakespeare had the command of the stage. Marlowe and Greene were both dead, and, though there were others, Shakespeare, at all events of all those who have come down to us, was the chief. There were many causes which may have led Jonson to attack his successful rival. He was himself a man of considerable education; master of classics, one who had been present in actual battle, and he appears to have somewhat sneered at Shakespeare's attempt to put on his scene with the aid of a few serving-men the pomp and circumstance of actual war. In these days on our large stages we sometimes have actual troops with real guns and horses, and a very fair representation of what one might see in actual warfare; but Shakespeare had none of these accessories, and though Richard III. might call "A horse, a horse," it is very doubtful if one could possibly have been got on the stage in answer to his call. All this seems to have irritated Jonson. Shakespeare, on the other hand, considered that he had a right to leave a good deal to the imagination of his audience, as we find in the opening chorus of "Henry V." This play must have been written some time in the middle of 1599, as it refers in the chorus to the fifth act to Essex being in Ireland. This gives us, therefore, the date when Shakespeare, no doubt in answer to

Jonson's objection, stated what he considered an author had a right to expect from his audience.

After wishing he could play his piece with real personages and a kingdom for the stage, he asks pardon for his audacity in making his stage a battle-field, but justifies it, that as figures may represent millions, so with the "force of imagination" (which he, with his usual reckless writing, calls "imaginary forces") imperfections can be pieced out with thought, and one man supposed to be a thousand—

> Think, when we talk of horses, that you see them
> Printing their proud hoofs in the receiving earth;
> For 'tis your thoughts that now must deck our kings,
> Carry them here and there, jumping o'er times,
> Turning the accomplishment of many years into an hour-glass.

It must not be considered that in recalling what Jonson has said about Shakespeare is for the purpose of criticising the latter. Posterity has, for a long time, settled the respective merits of the two authors. But we have to consider what evidence there is that Jonson, who as I have shown was in a position to know what part Bacon took, treated Shakespeare as being a writer.

It appears that Jonson left behind him certain short essays, which he called "Discoveries made upon Men and Matter." These were published after his death, in the folio of 1641, but are supposed to have been mostly written after 1630. He refers therein to both Shakespeare and Bacon. Though the paragraph in which he refers to Shakespeare is well known, as it is a direct and final testimony that Shakespeare himself was a writer, it is given here. The folio of 1623 could not have been published without Jonson knowing how far Bacon was mixed up with the authorship of the plays, and it is, therefore, very material if we find Jonson, after Shakespeare and Bacon are both dead, still repeating his complaint of the reckless way in which Shakespeare wrote. For unless Jonson was wilfully lying to posterity in order to conceal the fact that Bacon was the real author, his "Discovery," which relates to Shakespeare, seems to be conclusive. And, as I have said, we cannot suppose Jonson would have gone out of his way to state what he knew to be false to hide Bacon, for it is what Jonson has himself written about Bacon which has led persons to attribute the plays to him and not to Shakespeare. However, it is upon a due study of all the evidence that we must form our conclusions, and, at present, we have to deal with the "Discovery," referring to Shakespeare, which is as follows :—

" *De Shakespeare Nostrat Augustus in Hat.* I remember the players have often mentioned it as an honour to Shakespeare that in his writing (whatsoever he penned) he never blotted out a line. My answer hath been *would he had blotted a thousand*, which they thought a malevolent speech. I had not told posterity this, but for their ignorance. *Who choose that circumstance to commend their friend by* wherein *he is most faulted* and to justify my own candour, for I loved the man and do honour to his memory on this side idolatry as much as any. He was (indeed) honest, and of an open and free nature ; had *an excellent phantasie, brave notions and gentle expressions, wherein he flowed with that facility that sometimes it was necessary he should be stopped. Sufflaminandus erat,* as Augustus said of Haterius. His wit was in his own power : would the rule of it had been so, too! Many times he fell into those things " (? which) " could not escape laughter. As when he said in the person of Cæsar one speaking to him, 'Cæsar, thou dost me wrong,' he replied 'Cæsar never did wrong but with just cause,' and such like, which were ridiculous. But he redeemed his vices with his virtues. There was ever more in him to be praised than pardoned."

We have also two remarks made by Jonson when he was staying in Scotland with William Drumond of Hawthornden. It appeared that Jonson's sayings were noted by his host, and these notes have been preserved.

We find under the heading—
 "*His censure of the English Poets was this*":—
That Shakespeare wanted arte.

Again, under
 "*Particulars of the actions of other Poets and Apothegms,*"—
Shakespeare in a play brought in a number of men, saying they had suffered shipwreck in Bohemia, where there is no sea near by some 100 miles.

However much we, who are accustomed to consider Shakespeare as an object for our unqualified admiration, may admire Jonson's audacity in damning him with faint praise and sneering at his errors, yet Jonson speaks far more kindly of him here than he generally does. Of course he, like all men, was many minded, thinking one thing at one time, at another, another. And Jonson, when he wrote his "Discoveries," may have persuaded himself that he dearly loved the man, and honoured his memory "on this side idolatry [he is careful to add] as much as any." But when Shakespeare was alive there did not seem to be much love on either side; but at present we have to deal with the statements which Jonson has left behind him. And in these we have the evidence of a rival, one of a very jealous nature, who must have known if it were the fact that Shakespeare's work was all done for him by Bacon, who has left for the information of posterity, "that Shakespeare not only wrote many a thousand lines," but in his opinion wrote them very badly, and that he sometimes wrote nonsense into his plays, and sometimes showed his ignorance, as in the examples given.

We do not care for Jonson's opinion whether Shakespeare was a good or bad poet; but the evidence is of great value when one rival admits that the other was a fertile writer of verses and plays, and this is strengthened if he couples with the statement that, in his opinion, the verses and plays were sometimes very bad. It shows, at least, that he does not err on the side of undue partiality.

Jonson had other objections to Shakespeare. He objected to him that he copied or stole his plots from other authors, and that his dialogue was too often picked up from actual conversations with the lower classes of society. Jonson was not himself above mimicking what he heard others say, as we find in "Bartholomew Fair," and other plays. But he chose to consider in Shakespeare's case that it was beneath the dignity of the drama to give the conversations of the lower orders, which Shakespeare was so fond of doing in his "Dogberrys," "clowns," &c.

"*Shakespeare's Plagiarism.*"—There is no doubt that Shakespeare not only took his plots from others, but also many of his scenes and situations; whatever he wanted he no doubt took, but he improved all that he did take. Thus, for example, the celebrated scene in the churchyard, where Hamlet takes up Yorick's skull and moralises; this seems to me to be copied from a scene in Dekker's "Honest W——," where a forlorn lover similarly moralises over a skull, with very similar language, only in "Hamlet" we have the incident made natural by the skull being thrown up by a grave-digger at his work; Dekker's scene is affected and improbable, for it takes place in a room where the disconsolate individual has retired with the lady's portrait and a skull. The treatment of the idea in "Hamlet" is such an improvement on Dekker's that Dekker's must have been the original one. It seems that, as far as the public are concerned, it is immaterial where a poet gets his plot, &c., from; it is what effect he produces. We may find a comparison in painting; there may be a photograph which is correct, but idealises nothing; a sketch which is effective; a study which may be laboured and commonplace; and a finished picture, the value of the last depending on the skill of the artist. It contains besides nature something of the artist's individuality, which gives it great or little value, as the case may be. Now Jonson objected to all this. He objected to old plays being worked upon, or to an author making studies from low life, forgetting that there is nothing which can really be said to be original, least of all in thought, which at its best only differs from mere copying, so far as it is supported and strengthened by independent research.

This question has been considered at some length, because it is very material to realise exactly what Jonson thought of Shakespeare. Let us take Jonson's own words, so far as they refer to these plays. Amongst Jonson's minor pieces we find the following:—

"*Our Poet Ape.*"

"Poor poet ape! that would be thought our chief,
  Whose works are e'en the frippery of wit;
From brokage, is become so bold a thief
  As we, the robbed, leave rage and pity it.

> At first he made low shifts, would pick and glean,
>   Buy the reversion of old plays; now grown
> T' a little wealth, and credit in the scene,
>   He takes up all, makes each man's wit his own;
> And told of this, he slights it. Tut! such crimes
>   The sluggish, gaping auditor devours;
> He matters not, whose 'twas first, and after time
>   May judge it to be his as well as ours.
> Fool! as if half eyes will not know a fleece
> From locks of wool, or shreds from the whole piece."

These verses are generally considered as referring to Shakespeare, though Gifford, Jonson's editor, tries to throw doubt on this being so by a sneer; but it seems to me the allusions are too clear. When we remember that Shakespeare's crime, in the eyes of Greene and others, was that he adorned himself with other people's feathers, and when we trace, as we do, that he very often took old plays and re-wrote them, there is very little doubt but that at this time, at all events, Jonson referred to Shakespeare. He speaks of one who has grown to a little wealth and credit in the scene. It must not be forgotten we are not considering, as I have said more than once, whether Jonson's attack was justifiable, but whether he did not believe, at this time at all events, that Shakespeare was the author of "The Plays." The matter, however, does not rest here, for, in "Cynthia's Revels," in the Introduction, Jonson expresses himself more strongly. He makes one of his boys say,[1] speaking on behalf of the audience:—

"They could wish your poets would leave to be promoters of other men's jests, and to waylay all the stale apothegms or old books they can hear of, in print or otherwise, to farce

---

[1] Page 146.

their scenes withal. That they would not so penuriously glean wit from every laundress or hackney man, or derive their best grace with servile imitations from common stages or *observation of the company they converse with*, as if their invention lived wholly upon another man's trencher."

Again—

"That feeding their friends with nothing of their own but what they have twice or thrice cooked, they should not wantonly give out how soon they had dressed it," &c.

The last passage refers to a statement made that Jonson worked so slowly that he only produced a play a year. This Jonson seemed to have particularly resented, for he refers to it in the prologue to "The Fox":—

And when his plays come forth, think they can flout them,
   With saying he was a year about them,
To this there needs no lie; but this his creature,
   Which was two months since no feature,
And though he dares give them five lives to mend it,
   'Tis known five weeks fully penned it
From his own hand, without a coadjutor,
   Novice, journeyman, or tutor.

I do not wish to overburden the reader with references. I shall, therefore, only show that Jonson persevered in this view to the last. On the 19th January, 1629, long after Shakespeare's death, Jonson produced the "New Inn" with its absurd plot and weak imitation of Shakespeare. The play was "completely damned." The absurdity of the situations and a great deal of the dialogue prevented its being heard to the conclusion. There are, undoubtedly, some fine lines in it, but the whole plot was ridiculous. If this was the result of Jonson's originality, it is easy to understand how Shakespeare's works were thought otherwise. Jonson wrote an ode to himself, apparently to console himself for the adverse criticism; which harps on the same old complaint.

>   Come, leave the loathed stage
>   And the more loathsome age,
> Where pride and impudence, in faction fit,
>   Usurp the chair of wit,
> Indicting and arraigning every day
>   Something they call a play.
> * * * * * *
> If they love lees, and leave the lusty wine,
> Envy them not their palates with the swine.
>
>   No doubt some mouldy tale
>   Like Pericles, and stale
> As the Shireve's crust and nasty as his fish,
>   Scraps out of every dish,
> Thrown forth and raked into the common tub,
>   May keep up the play club;
>   These sweepings do as well
>   As the best ordered meal.
> For who the relish of these guests will fit,
> Needs set them but the almsbasket of wit.

This was Jonson's view of Shakespeare's works, but he went further and attacked Shakespeare not as an author only, but personally, making fun of his desire to be thought a gentleman, and even of his father, who, it may be remembered, made, no doubt at his son's instigation, at least two attempts to obtain a grant of arms.

John Shakespeare's Coat of Arms.—Now, this attempt of William Shakespeare to improve his father's social position turned out unfortunately. It so happened that between the two first drafts, which, as we shall see, were in 1596 and 1597, Camden, who had been Jonson's friend and schoolmaster at Westminster, was made Clarencieux King of Arms. We generally find out, even in these days, that the world is very small: it must have been smaller in 1599. Jonson probably learned from Camden of Shakespeare's application; at all events, I think there is reason to believe that in the first three or four of Jonson's plays, he ridiculed not only Shakespeare but his father. It may not, however, be out of place to recount shortly what is known of these so-called grants of arms, so far as they can be ascertained from the records of the Heralds' College. And for this purpose, I propose to quote from Mr. Hunter's work on Shakespeare, as he seems to be the best authority on the subject.

Amongst the other documents that refer to Shakespeare and his family, Mr. Halliwell has given us the two drafts, one of a grant proposed to be given in 1596 and the other in the year 1599. Mr. Hunter, in his new illustrations of Shakespeare,[1] says, p. 19, from 1596 to 1599, there were communications between Shakespeare's "family and the College of Arms touching a grant of coat armour." The application, it appears, was made on behalf of the father, and Mr. Hunter supposes a grant was actually made, though no formal copy exists, and only *three* drafts are to be found, or, rather, as Mr. Hunter calls them, "studies for the grant, confusedly written, being full of corrections and interlineal matter."

It appears that the second of these three is practically the same as the first, being of the same date, &c. which may account for Halliwell taking them as being

---

[1] Nichols & Sons, 1845.

two only. The subject of these proposed grants is very fully examined by Mr. Hunter, who, from his position as a Fellow of the Society of Antiquaries and an assistant-keeper of the public records, knew as well as any one how to collect and deal with the evidence. I propose, therefore, only to refer to those facts which are material to the present inquiry. The grants are supposed to be justified by the fact that John Shakespeare's ancestors and parents had been rewarded by Henry VII. for their services to him, with a grant of land, &c., and had since lived in good reputation and credit. But Mr. Hunter says this rested on a vague tradition, and that the most material fact to which Mr. Hunter calls our attention is that in 1599, when the celebrated Camden was Clarencieux, he was joined with Dethick, Garter King of Arms, in the proposed grant (see Halliwell, p. 458). Complaints were made by one Brook, a member of the College, against Camden and Dethick,[1] "that they had not exercised a sound discretion in the grant which they had made." It appears that Mr. Hunter could not find any copy of Brook's complaint, but that several copies are in existence of the answer given by Camden and Dethick, showing that the complaint was serious enough to be fully answered. This defence seems to have been directed to two points, *i.e.*, that the coat was too like that of the old Baron Mauley, and the person was not of sufficient quality to have a grant made. The answer to the latter was that John Shakespeare had been a magistrate (as mayor), his estate was worth £500, and he had married a daughter of Arden, "a gentleman of worship." There seems

---

[1] Hunter, p. 26.

to be sufficient evidence to show that at this period, so far from John Shakespeare possessing an estate worth £500—equal, Mr. Hunter says, to £4,000 of our money—he was in pecuniary difficulties. Mr. Hunter mildly puts it that "John Shakespeare had carried to the utmost extent consistent with truth his claim to hereditary gentility." But whether that be so or not, I think it was the position of his son as an actor which was the real objection to the grant of arms to his father, which objection was pressed, not by Brook only, but by Jonson, with all the ridicule he could bring to bear.

Now, when we come to consider the plays of Jonson and Shakespeare, so far as they relate to this matter of a grant of arms, we shall find Jonson making a number of allusions to the matter and ridiculing the presumption of those seeking to be made gentlemen, particularly when they were actors; and Shakespeare seems to have been a little sore upon the subject, and to have shown his mortification that his family were not considered of sufficient gentility to bear arms.

If this be so, then I think Bacon, had he been the author, would have taken no interest in the matter, or, if he did, would, one would think, have supported Jonson's view that it was presumption for an actor, who was either a vagabond by law or a nobleman's servant, to try and get a grant of arms. So that though not of great weight, yet I think the conflict between Jonson and Shakespeare on this subject is of some value, as evidence that Shakespeare was the author of the plays.

To take first the evidence that we find in Shakespeare's plays. There we find traces of some bitterness in the author because only *gentlemen* were allowed to bear arms. Thus, the grave-digger in "Hamlet" says :—

1 *Clo.* Come, my spade. There is no ancient gentlemen but gardeners, ditchers, and grave-makers; they hold up Adam's profession.
2 *Clo.* Was he a gentleman?
1 *Clo.* He was the first that ever bore arms.
2 *Clo.* Why, he had none.
1 *Clo.* What, ar't a heathen? How dost thou understand the scripture? The scripture says Adam digged: Could he dig without arms?

The last two speeches are not to be found in the Quarto of 1604, and the subject is not mentioned in that of 1603, though the jest about who builds stronger than either the mason, the shipwright, or the carpenter, is to be found in both.

In the "Taming of the Shrew," Katharine strikes Petruchio, he says :[1]—

I swear I'll cuff you, if you strike again.

She replies—

So may you lose your arms :
If you strike me, you are no gentleman ;
And if no gentleman, why, then no arms.
Pet. A herald, Kate? Oh, put me in thy books.
Kath. What is your crest? a coxcomb? &c.

This reference in the second Quarto may have been put in by Shakespeare to show that he could afford to make a jest of the matter; but I think Jonson's allusions must have been made to annoy him, or why should Jonson have inserted them in all of his first three plays?

Now, in his first play, "Every Man in his Humour,"

---

[1] Act II. Scene 1.

supposed to be first acted about 1596 (the first application of Shakespeare's father was in 1596, the second in 1599), we have Jonson making the following allusion: There is a character, one Master Matthews, whose verses, however, are said to be stolen, and whose pockets are turned out at the end of the play and found to be full of stolen stuff, which is burned to purify the air. Justice Clement says:—

Is all the rest of this batch? Bring me a torch; lay it together and give fire. Cleanse the air [*sets the papers on fire*]; there was enough to have infected the whole city, if it had not been taken in time. See how our poet's glory shines brighter and brighter! still it increases. Oh, now it is at its highest, and now it declines as fast! *Sic transit gloria mundi.*

Knownall. There's an emblem for you, son, and your studies.

Shakespeare's works show traces that the author made use of the Italian writers on "Emblems," and I think, from the opinion Jonson always had of Shakespeare, that Matthews was intended for him. When he is introduced on the stage, he meets Cob, the water-carrier, who boasts of his lineage as being descended from the first red herring that was broiled in Adam and Eve's kitchen, whence he fetched his pedigree from the Herald's Book, Cob being, as I understand, another name for a herring. That Matthews is meant to represent Shakespeare seems pretty clear; he composes verses which are a parody after the manner of Shakespeare's sonnets.

> To thee, the purest object of my sense,
>   The most refined essence Heaven covers,
> Send I these lines, wherein I do commence
>   The happy state of turtle billing lovers,
> If they prove rough, unpolished, harsh, and rude,
> Haste made the waste, thus mildly I conclude.

This, Matthews calls a toy of his; later on he is introduced to us as reading some of his verses to Mistress Bridget, which are described as being nothing but stolen remnants. And the lady is told she cannot in conscience give him less than a shilling, for the book he had his muse out of must have cost him sixpence[1] at least. If Jonson intended Matthews for Shakespeare, his summing up by Cob[2] must have been very galling to Shakespeare.

Cob. "You should have. Some now would take this Master Matthews to be a gentleman at the least. His father's an honest man, a worshipful fishmonger and *so forth*, and now he does creep and wriggle into acquaintance with all the brave gallants about the town, such as my guest is (Bobadil) . . . And they flout him invariably."

Now posterity has been good enough to bestow several trades on Shakespeare's father, such as making him a butcher, glover, wool merchant, &c.; but there is no reason to suppose he was a fishmonger. This, if Matthews was meant for Shakespeare, could only have been said to annoy him, the so forth being particularly contemptuous. But Shakespeare appears to have to put a bold front on the matter, as in "Hamlet" we find the well-known lines:[3]—

Pol. Do you know me, my lord?
Ham. Excellent well: you are a *fishmonger*.
Pol. Not I, my lord.
Ham. Then I would you were so honest a man;
    For to be honest, as this age goes, is to be one man picked out of ten thousand.

Polonius afterwards said:—
    He called me a fishmonger.

---

[1] A tester.
[2] Act I. Scene 2.
[3] In the Quartos of 1603 and 1604.

These are the only times the word is found in Shakespeare.

In the second of Jonson's plays, "Every Man out of his Humour," 1599—60, we find reference made to the purchase of a grant of arms; Sogliardo, wishing to become a gentleman, is advised by Carlo[1] to get arms, which he does.

In the third of Jonson's plays, "The Poetaster," there is the same allusion. Shakespeare's name consisting of the verb, *shake*, and a substantive, *speare*, it was easy to make a joke on it by changing the substantive; thus he is alluded to by Greene as "Shake-*scene*,"[2] and by Jonson in the dedication to the Folio, 1623, as "Shake-*stage*." This is carried out in "The Poetaster," speaking to one Crispinus Chloe says,—

Chloe. Are you a gentleman born?

Cris. That I am, lady. You shall see mine arms, if it please you.

Chloe. No, your legs do sufficiently show you are a gentleman born, sir; for a man borne upon little legs is always a gentleman born.[3]

Cris. Yet I pray you, vouchsafe the sight of my arms, mistress; for I bear them about me to have them seen. My name is *Crispinus* or *Cri spinas* indeed, which is well expressed in my arms—a face *crying* in chief, and beneath it a bloody toe between three thorns *pungent*.

Chloe. Then you are welcome, sir; now you are a gentleman born, &c.

It is clear that Jonson in these allusions intended to

---

[1] Page 100.
[2] *Ante.*
[3] This appears to have been an old joke.

refer to some actor, for in "The Poetaster," Lupus says,—

Indeed, master Ovid, these players are an idle generation.

Tucca adds :[1]—

They are grown licentious, the rogues, libertines, flat libertines. They forget they are in the statute (*which made them rogues and vagabonds, unless enrolled as some nobleman's servants*), the rascals, they are *blazoned* there, there they are *tricked*, *they* and their *pedigrees*, they need no *other heralds*, I wiss.

"Blazoning" meaning setting forth a coat of arms in its proper colours; "tricking" to draw it with a pen only. Now we have no evidence that any other actor, besides Shakespeare, was ambitious of getting a grant of arms, so that it can hardly be said that these allusions to arms are accidental. I do not find them in other plays, and, as far as I have read, Jonson does not make any reference to the subject, except in these three plays, so that it is a fair conclusion that they were made there for the purpose of throwing ridicule on Shakespeare and his pretensions to gentility; for at the time these three plays were written, Jonson was, I believe, not friends with Shakespeare.

It must not be supposed that Shakespeare submitted meekly to these attacks of Jonson. We know from a play, "The Return from Parnassus" (which was registered the 16 October, 1605, but printed in 1606), that Shakespeare could hit back in his turn. The lines have often been quoted. In the 4th Act, Scene 5, Burbage and Kempe, the two well-known actors, come to Cambridge looking for possible actors whom Burbage

---

[1] Act I. Scene 1.

hopes to get cheap; but Kempe says the slaves are somewhat proud and complains of their stage business, to which Burbage replies—

"A little teaching will mend these faults, and it may be beside they will be able to pen a part."

But Kempe objects—

"Few of the university pen plays well; they smell too much of that writer Ovid and that writer's Metamorphosis, and talk too much of Proserpina and Jupiter. Why, here's our fellow Shakespeare puts them all down, aye and Ben Jonson, too. Oh! that Ben Jonson is a pestilent fellow, he brought up Horace giving the poets a pill[1]; but our fellow Shakespeare hath given him a purge that made him bewray his credit."

It has been generally supposed that this purge, which Shakespeare administered to Jonson, has not come down to us. It may be so, but I have already pointed out that the allusion to a fishmonger being an honest man, may have been Shakespeare's answer to Jonson's impertinence. It may not be admitted, however, that this is so; if not, we have in "Macbeth" an allusion to one of Jonson's characters which I do not think can be disputed.

In Jonson's second play "Every Man out of his Humour," each character has his particular failing, which Jonson calls his humour, which is cured at the end of the piece, and so each man is out of his humour. One of these characters, a farmer, has hoarded up corn in hopes that there will be a bad harvest, so that he may get a good price for what he has put away. The harvest is likely to be a good one, so he hangs himself. He is, however, cut down in time, and repents with the others.

---

[1] The Poetaster, published 1601.

In "Macbeth," we find, after the murder, when there comes that terrible knocking at the gate which must have struck such terror to Macbeth and his wife, the sleepy porter soliloquizes so as to let the knocking go on—

Porter. Here's a knocking, indeed; if a man were porter of hell-gate, he should have old turning the key. (*Knock.*) Knock, knock, knock. Who's there i' the name of Belzebub? Here's a farmer that hanged himself on the expectation of plenty. Come in time, have napkins enough about you: here you'll sweat for it, &c.[1]

If this refers to Sogliardo, the name of Jonson's farmer in "Every Man out of his Humour," as it seems pretty clear it does, it shows that "Macbeth" must have been written some time after the publication of Jonson's play which was 1603.

In "Hamlet," we have another hit at Jonson in the well-known lines about the "ayre" of children, which refers to the Blackfriars Theatre, then leased to Evans. I shall have occasion to refer to this at more length hereafter. For the present, it is sufficient to say that this theatre, being built by Burbage, helped by Shakespeare and others, was not allowed to be opened as a theatre, and was taken by Evans to bring up boys as choristers. But, gradually, these boys took to acting plays, and Jonson took his plays there, and no doubt, for a time, these boy-actors became the fashion. We find allusions made to this by Hamlet, who points out that these boys will probably become actors, and that they are injuring their future professions when they attack grown-up actors.

---

[1] Act II. Scene 3.

Ham. What, are they children? who maintains 'em? how are they escorted? Will they pursue the quality no longer than they can sing? will they not say afterwards, if they should grow themselves to common players (as it is like most, if their means are not better) *their writers do them wrong to make them exclaim against their own succession.*

Rosen. 'Faith, there ha's been much to do on both sides; and the nation holds it no sin, to tarre them to controversie. There was, for a while, no money bid for argument, unless the poet and the player went to cuffs in the question.

Ham. Is't possible?

Guild. Oh, there has been much throwing about of brains.

This, no doubt refers to the plays of Jonson and perhaps others, which were acted at Evans' theatre by the children of the Queen's Chappel, and it may be this is the "purge" alluded to in "The Return from Parnassus;" for it must be remembered Ben Jonson had a great deal to do with the publication of the Folio in 1623, and he may have softened this passage down.

We have, therefore, not only Jonson's attacks upon Shakespeare, but the latter's defending himself and his brother actors. Of course, Bacon might have taken up the cudgels on Shakespeare's behalf, but, looking at the friendship that existed between Jonson and Bacon, it is difficult to conceive the former keeping up his complaint against Shakespeare for hasty and bad writing, long after he must have known the fact, if it were so, that it was not Shakespeare's works he was abusing, but that of his friend and patron.

CHAPTER VII.

BACON AND SHAKESPEARE.

THE question now for consideration is, what evidence have we of who it was that assisted Shakespeare. It is not likely we shall find any direct proof. If such assistance was given it was kept a secret, jealously guarded from the world. But still, a careful investigation of the circumstances, so far as we know them, may help us to determine the identity of this unknown legal friend with some degree of certainty.

Although the precise knowledge and training displayed in the legal plays are very remarkable, there is no reason why they should be Bacon's more than any other trained lawyer's. In the present day, many members of the Bar could supply a dramatic author with this information. The law, the sketches of the courts, &c. taken from life, may be very accurate, but there are many persons who could draw upon their everyday experience and reading to supply all the law we find in Shakespeare's writings. In Shakespeare's time, though, the number of men at the Bar were much fewer than at present. But I think Shakespeare would have had no difficulty in getting assistance from several sources. There is therefore no *primâ facie* reason why we should suppose the information was supplied by Bacon. In fact, there are some reasons why one should attribute the legal assistance, say, to Coke, rather than Bacon. Many circumstances might be suggested as pointing to the former. In the first place we have no reason to believe that Bacon was particularly well read in the technicalities of our law; he never seems to have seriously followed his profession. He was, no doubt, able to get together sufficient to write his speeches out, but when suddenly called upon he had not that fund of legal knowledge that only deep and extensive reading can give. Mr. Spedding states that, when he went in state to take his seat for the first time as Lord Chancellor, he invited his friends to witness his dignity. He had carefully prepared his speech, and all went very well until some real business took place for which he was not prepared, and he lamentably broke down. And we have Elizabeth's opinion of him, that he was no great lawyer, though he was able to make a display of what law he possessed.

Again, in the second part of "Henry VI.," we have the trial of the so-called witch. Now Coke speaks of this trial as something he had discovered, as I have already stated. So the study of Escalus as an English judge upon the bench dealing with criminal matters is a description of an office which Coke had filled and Bacon had not. So the description of the Temple Gardens; and the manners and customs of the Templars already referred to, might with more propriety be attributed to Coke, who was a Templar, rather than to Bacon, who was a member of Gray's Inn; though, as I shall have to point out, in Bacon's time there was a strong alliance between Gray's Inn and the Inner Temple. I think, therefore, that we must not presume because we find traces of legal learning in the plays that Bacon was the only man who could have furnished it. I think, though I may be able to adduce historical evidence that Bacon was Shakespeare's friend and assistant, the mere legal knowledge by no means proves it.

But if Shakespeare was assisted, some one must have done so. And there has been for many reasons a suspicion that Bacon was the person; we have to see whether there is any foundation for this view which seems to be founded upon the many parallel passages to be found in Bacon's writings and Shakespeare's works. Mr. Donnelly in his first volume has taken great pains to collect these various passages, which do go a great way to establish that Bacon had some part in Shakespeare's works, the coincidences are so numerous. He classifies them as follows:—

(a) *Identical expressions.*

Bacon says:

Custom! an ape of nature.

And Shakespeare:

Oh, sleep, thou ape of death; &c.

Bacon: (b) *Identical metaphors.*

In the third place I set down reputation because of the peremptory tides and currents it hath, *which, if they be not taken in due time, are seldom recovered.*

Shakespeare:

There is a tide in the affairs of men, which, taken at the flood . . . &c. *And we must take the current when it serves, or lose our venture.*

(c) *Identical opinions.*

Bacon speaks of:

States corrupted through wealth,
Or too great length of peace.

And Shakespeare of:

The cankers of a calm world and a long peace.

Bacon: (d) *Identical quotations.*

The wisdom of crocodiles that shed tears when they would devour.

Shakespeare: As the mournful crocodile
With sorrow snares relenting passengers.

(e) *Identical studies.*

Both study gardens, flowers and plants; both give the same explanation of a knot being found in a tree, by the sap being gathered at the spot, and thus branches are caused there.

Bacon:

The cause whereof is that the sap ascendeth unequally, and doth, as it were, *tire* and stop by the way. And it seemeth they have some closeness and hardness on their stalk, which hindereth the sap from going up, until it hath gathered into a knot and so is more urged to put forth.

Shakespeare: Checks and disasters
Grow in the veins of actions highest reared,
As *knots* by the conflux of meeting sap
Infects the sound pine and diverts his grain,
Tortive and errant from his course of growth.

Both apparently had studied physic, and were not unacquainted with the names of Galen and Paracelsus.

(f) *Identical errors.*

Both misquote Aristotle; both believe in spirits pervading nature, even when inanimate; both believe in spontaneous generation. But these seem to me to be errors common to all men of that period, at least, if not of all periods, witness table turning, &c., of our days.

Mr. Donnelly gives us further examples of identity in the use of unusual words, such as hurly burly, &c., of character and of style. But I must refer my readers to the first volume of Mr. Donnelly's work for further illustrations of these alleged similarities. On the other hand, it is alleged that we have only to refer to another author or set of authors to have a great number of examples given where Bacon's writing is supposed to be dissimilar to that of Shakespeare.

Some point out that Shakespeare's poetical description, say of a horse, is entirely different from the non-poetic treatment by Bacon of the same subject. Others refer to some very mediocre paraphrases of the Psalms, which Bacon has left, as showing that he had not the gift of poetry.

The presence of parallelisms and of discrepancies between the acknowledged works of Bacon and those of Shakespeare, though a good argument against those who insist that either Bacon or Shakespeare was the sole author of the plays, is evidence in favour of the view that they worked together.

With regard to Mr. Donnelly's second volume, in which he attempts to prove that there was a story running through the plays, concealed in his so-called cryptogram, which has provoked so much ridicule, one author having gone to the trouble to compose and publish a travestie of his explanation. I can say that I have honestly tried to understand the explanation, and I have come to the conclusion that instead of mastering his subject Mr. Donnelly has been mastered by it. Of course, it is very easy to go through any large page of printed matter and pick out a word required to make sense, and, having obtained such a word, to formulate some arithmetical reason for choosing it. By counting from the top or the bottom, adding or subtracting the number of the page, &c., you can arrive at any particular word you choose. But this is not the way the person who created the cryptogram would proceed. He would, it is assumed, have the power of so arranging his composition that, when in print, the particular word would occupy a definite place. If this was in his power (which seems impossible to believe) he would not require to change the position of the concealed word, so that on no two pages it occupied the same place as is the case with Mr. Donnelly's so-called cryptogram. If the first, twentieth, or say, the last word, on each page, when read together, made a consecutive story, we might believe that this was not accidental. But why should a person who can put the word where he likes, put it the nineteenth on one page, the thirty-seventh on another, and so on. It is easy to understand where the cryptogram is a delusion, a person picking out the nineteenth word on one page and the thirty-seventh on another and then trying to find reasons for his selection. But there seems to be no reason why the contriver of such a system should alter his formula for each word. The final cause of a cryptogram is, I suppose, that someone should discover its meaning, or why take the trouble to write it. And this is not to be done where the words are put anyhow and anywhere. Whatever opinion we may, however, have of this theory of a cryptogram, there can be but one opinion as to Mr. Donnelly's first volume showing considerable learning and care, and being a valuable help to the student of Shakespeare.

In addition to these parallel passages, we shall see, I think, that Bacon took steps to qualify himself to assist Shakespeare.

Promus.—Amongst the works left by Bacon was a MS. written, Mr. Spedding tells us, in Bacon's own hand entitled "Promus of Formularies and Elegancies." This collection, he also tells us, fills more than forty quarto pages, and is of the most miscellaneous character, and seems, by various marks on the MS., to have been afterwards digested into other collections which are lost.[1] I have not seen this MS. but I have the work published by Mrs. Potts, where she tries to prove that the selected sentences have, for the most part, been used in the Shakespeare's plays, &c. But the examples in the "Promus" do not seem connected with the extracts from the plays sufficiently to show that the one sprang from or was created by the other.

In the "Promus" we find noted a number of short sentences taken from many sources. The Bible is often laid under contribution for short texts, as John x., 32.

For which of the good works do ye stone me?

Mrs. Potts has found some sentences that seem to be connected with the "Promus," as in the above case she cites from "Winter's Tale," IV. 2.

I cannot tell, good sir, for which of his virtues it was, but he was certainly whipped out of court.

The difficulty is to feel certain that the one sentence sprang from the other. It may have been so, but it may not. A text, as we understand the word in modern days, is a sentence from the Bible which, as it were, takes root in a preacher's mind and springs up and opens out in the sermon, but it would be impossible to show the connection between the text and the ideas and sentences it leads the preacher's mind to. The text need not be a religious one, to take

---

[1] Query Shakespeare's plays.

a homely proverb "That a bird in the hand is worth two in the bush." One can conceive a person thinking on this as a text, saying, "A reality outweighs a chance, the first is to be depended on, the latter is not," "Therefore live on what you have and not on what you expect, for with great expectations you may starve," "And paupers ere now have been found to be heirs to large fortunes"; or he might dispute the proverb and say, "Without risk there is no gain," "No seed is sown or cargoes sent across the sea except for the greater wealth they may produce," "No one has a right to bury his talent in a napkin, but must part with it that it may return with interest," &c.

We may be able to trace the connection between the text and the sermon when we know it exists, but I think no one would be justified in working backwards, and saying, where we find an author writing "That with great expectations you may starve," his idea sprang from the proverb "a bird in the hand," as a matter of fact it did spring from it; but it seems as impossible to trace back such an expression to the text that gave it birth as it would be to trace back a stream to its underground sources. However this may be, Mrs. Potts has failed to convince the world that Bacon wrote the plays, because he formed the collection called the "Promus;" the references she gives do not seem to belong naturally to the sentences from which they are supposed to spring; the connection may have existed, but it is by no means self-evident now. This has led, I think, to the real fact, which is of interest with regard to the "Promus" being overlooked, and that is not that any substantial connection can be shown between the "Promus" and the plays to establish that they were the work of the same author; but that the "Promus" is undoubtedly a collection made by Bacon, and is such a one as he might have been expected to make if he were preparing to write or assist others in writing works like those we know as Shakespeare's; standing by itself, the "Promus," I think, proves nothing. But if we lay a foundation for believing Bacon had some hand in Shakespeare's works, then the "Promus" is just such a commonplace book as he might have made to assist him in his work.

There are other *scraps* of evidence which I may have to refer to; in some cases I have already done so, such as statements made by Bacon as to being a concealed poet, or of Jonson's statement that Bacon had filled all numbers, meaning, apparently, had written all kinds of verse, and Toby Matthew's letter in which he speaks of returning "Measure for Measure." "Measure for Measure" is the most legal of the legal plays in my opinion, and the one I have principally relied upon as showing the legal knowledge displayed in some of Shakespeare's plays. It seems to me the true position of this class of evidence —viz., the similarity of ideas and expressions Mr. Donnelly gives us; the "Promus"; and these scraps; to which I have referred—is this, they are matters which are capable of being explained in many ways; but one of these explanations undoubtedly is that Bacon either wrote or assisted the author of the plays. They are like the circumstances that often weigh with a jury when considering their verdict. A prisoner charged with murder may have been near the spot, he may have quarrelled with the murdered man, &c.; all this class of evidence is consistent with the prisoner's guilt, would freely give rise to suspicion, but is clearly capable of being explained away, as if at the actual time of the crime an alibi could be proved, &c.; and in any case few juries would convict on mere matters of suspicion, matters which it is easy to see are capable of an explanation inconsistent with guilt. But if there are good grounds for believing the prisoner was the man who committed the crime, then this evidence comes as strong confirmation. I think, therefore, we have to inquire whether there is any real evidence, that is, evidence which is capable of only one explanation which connects Bacon with Shakespeare, and this evidence, I think, exists, only for some reason it has hitherto escaped notice.

Before proceeding to state what this evidence is, I wish to clear the ground and deal with one or two objections which have been suggested as showing that Bacon could not have had anything to do with the plays.

One is that there is no evidence that Bacon or Shakespeare ever knew one another.

Another is that Bacon never acknowledged the authorship, or claimed to have any part in the plays.

With regard to the first, I shall, I think, be able to show that there is evidence that Bacon and Shakespeare were acquainted with one another. But even if this were not so, nothing is to be presumed from the fact that Bacon and Shakespeare do not mention one another. Shakespeare, as we know, has left no record of his private life. But his rival, Ben Jonson, has left us a considerable number of personal recollections. And from his writings we know that he and Bacon were well acquainted. In fact, Jonson is supposed to have helped him with his Latin translations at or about the time when the folio of 1623 was being prepared for the press. And there was such intimacy between them that, as I have mentioned, when Jonson met Bacon and told him he was going to walk to Scotland, Bacon said, "He loved not to see poesy go on other feet than poetical dactylus and spondæus." And in the "Discoveries," Jonson speaks of Bacon in these words:—

"My conceit of his person was never increased towards him by his place of honours, but I have and do reverence him for the greatness that was only proper to himself in that he seemed to me ever by his work one of the greatest of men and most worthy of admiration that had been in many ages. In his adversity, I ever prayed that God would give him strength, for greatness he could not want. Neither could I condole in a word or syllable for him, as knowing no accident could do harm to virtue, but rather help to make it manifest."

Besides this, we have evidence that Bacon on one occasion, at least, had a masque written by Jonson, which was produced at Gray's Inn, of which I may have occasion to speak hereafter.

Yet Bacon, as far as I have discovered, never mentions Jonson's name nor makes any allusion to him in either his works or correspondence, so that if posterity depended only on what Bacon has left behind, it would have no evidence that such a person as Jonson ever existed.

I do not therefore think that the conclusion is to be drawn from Bacon not mentioning Shakespeare, that they were not acquainted. If he did not mention Jonson, it was perhaps because he considered his connection with him did not add to his dignity or increase his chance of that promotion, which he so sedulously sought for all his life, and could not keep when he got it, and therefore he ignored him; and the same influence may have operated against his mentioning any intimacy with Shakespeare, if it existed. If, however, Shakespeare had left his papers carefully preserved as Jonson did (those at all events which were not destroyed by the fire at his house), we might have found references to the intimacy which, I think, I shall be able to show from other sources, did exist between him and Bacon.

With regard to the second objection, that Bacon never made any claim to being the author of the plays, I think those who try to draw any inference that Bacon had nothing to do with the plays, because he made no claim to them, do not sufficiently consider the history of the period. Bacon's mother, as Mr. Spedding tells us, belonged to the Puritan party, and was therefore opposed to the court and theatrical life of her times.

At the close of Elizabeth's reign and during that of her successor, there had been growing up a strong feeling in the minds of the Puritans against the Crown and against the theatre. Elizabeth was a woman and a wise one, and for a time the feeling was kept back, but James had no hold on the affections of the English people, and his son Charles had not the cunning of his father, and, as we know, his conduct led to civil war and his own death. It is not my province to consider who was right or who was wrong; I have only to call attention to the fact that this opposition during Shakespeare's time was growing. We find traces of it in our law books, where we find the power of the Crown was often questioned in a way, I think, Henry VIII. would never have permitted. It may be remembered that Charles himself, in one of his speeches to Parliament, comments upon this fact. Now one of the most important matters of dispute between the Court and Puritan parties was the existence of the stage, to which, for some reason or other, the puritanical party were strongly opposed. At this time the city authorities refused to allow a theatre to be erected within the city, and attempted, with more or less success, to close Burbage's Theatre in the Blackfriars, and Elizabeth's Parliament made travelling actors by statute rogues and vagabonds, unless they were the servants of some nobleman, and this was only permitted by the intercession of Leicester. Elizabeth, too wise to run counter to public opinion in matters such as this, only recognized players as such servants. But James by patent constituted them "the King's servants," and a second company became "the Queen's," and afterwards a third was known as "the Prince's." This recognition of the players by the sovereign no doubt was a mistake, and I have little doubt that in the struggles that were to come, the Puritans gained many an adherent who might have fought on the king's side, were it not for the prejudice they had against plays and actors. As in chess the game is often concentrated about one piece, and as in actual warfare the objective point of attack at first may be an outlying province or a distant fortified place, so I think the theatre was the seat of war in the commencement of the struggle between the Court and the Puritans. The ultimate contest was, as we know, between personal and parliamentary government, but the initial sore, the one that produced bad blood and prejudice, was, in the early years of the seventeenth century, the stage; and this bitterness was not lessened by the writings of the dramatic poets. We find Dekker having the bad taste to bring puritan women on to the stage and making them drunk, and Ben Jonson holding them up to ridicule in many of his plays, as the discomforture of Bussey by the puppets in Bartholomew fair. In fact I think we find the earliest references to the puritan party in the impertinences of the playwriters of Shakespeare's time. Now, when we come to his plays we find references to the Puritans, it is true, but none which seem to be written in a hostile spirit, with the exception of the porter's speech in "Henry VIII.," to be referred to hereafter. It is true that we find some sly hits at their foibles, but written in a friendly spirit.

As in "All's Well that Ends Well," Act I. Scene 3—

Though honesty be no Puritan, yet it will do no hurt; it will wear the surplice of humanity over the black gown of a big heart, &c.,

a very different style from the sneering abuse of Jonson; but he was allied to the Court party, was the first Poet Laureate and wrote the masques which Charles and the ladies of his Court acted, and by so doing created the scandal which found a voice in the malevolent tongue of Prynne. But Bacon was no particular favourite of Elizabeth's court, and his mother was a Puritan. If any one could run with the hare and hunt with the hounds he was that man, and I think, if he did assist Shakespeare, he would not care to raise up enemies gratuitously. His object was self —a luxurious life, personal distinction, and above all money—not scandal. I think the last thing he would wish would be to be known as a playwriter—an object of contempt and hatred to thousands. Policy, it seems to me, would have kept him silent, if he had anything to do with plays and actors, as being a connection not likely to add to but detract from his dignity.

Bacon's concealed authorship.—I think that there is one fact that should be noticed before I proceed to the historical evidence which, I think, shows a probability that Bacon may have helped Shakespeare, and that is Bacon's habit of writing secretly for other people, not only letters, but proclamations for his sovereign, observations on passing events, &c., all of which he has carefully left behind him. Mr. Spedding has given us an edition of his works properly so called; he has also given us seven volumes of what he terms "His occasional works, namely, letters, speeches, tracts, state papers, memorial devises, &c. And in these seven volumes we find a large number of writings far too numerous even to mention wherein he seems to have written out his ideas at great length upon passing events, which he very often intended other people to use as their own. There is no evidence that these were always used; some were, as when he wrote a letter for Essex to his brother Anthony to be shown to the queen. But many may have never left his desk; but whether they did or not is immaterial. That he was a most voluminous writer, and that he was always willing to compose matter for others to use seems undoubted. Thus, in the commencement of the second volume, Mr. Spedding, speaking of certain "Letters of Advice from the Earl of Essex to the Earl of Rutland," and a "Letter of Advice from the Earl of Essex to Sir Foulke Greville on his

Studies," says of the first letters, *i.e.*, those to Earl Rutland, that—

"These letters[1] (or at least two of them) were sent and received as from Essex himself, circulated in his name, and meant to be received as his composition—there is, I presume, no doubt. But we know as a fact that both before and after he did occasionally accept Bacon's help, and there was no occasion on which he was more likely to avail himself of it than this."

Again, he says—

"We have direct evidence that a few years after Essex would sometimes employ Bacon to draw up letters for him about his own most personal affairs, letters which he was himself to sign."

Of the second he says—

"It is a letter of advice addressed to Fulke Greville (date unfortunately not known) all about books and studies, such a letter as Bacon would undoubtedly have wished Essex to write, and the queen to know he had written."

Mr. Spedding has included these among Bacon's works as being "very Baconian in matter and manner," though, it is true, he leaves it to the reader to decide for himself whether they be Bacon's or not. But we have some of which he was undoubtedly the author, which he intended to be put forward by others. Thus, when James entered England, he drew up more than one proclamation[2] for the king, some of which were "prepared but not used,"[3] and one Mr. Spedding cannot find was ever used, though, apparently, one—*Proclamation for Jurors*—was adopted and printed.[4]

I do not propose to give further examples, they may be found scattered through the volumes of Occasional Works.

---

[1] Spedding, vol. 2, p. 5.
[2] *Ibid.* vol. 3, p. 67.
[3] *Ibid.* p. 385.
[4] *Ibid.* p. 389.

CHAPTER VIII.

BACON AND SHAKESPEARE—*continued*.

It has been often noticed that there is no evidence that Shakespeare and Bacon were ever acquainted with one another, and that neither mentions the other's name. But it has been already pointed out that Shakespeare has left no writings beyond his works, and that Bacon, who undoubtedly was on terms of intimacy with Ben Jonson, does not mention the latter any more than he does Shakespeare.

There is, however, one account which has come down to us, which does bring Bacon and Shakespeare together under circumstances which render it very probable that Bacon was actively assisting Shakespeare, if not in the authorship, at least in the production of one of his plays; and even if the person who did so assist Shakespeare is not absolutely shown to be Bacon, yet there is proof that Bacon must have known of Shakespeare's existence, for we find him substituting something of his own when Shakespeare's play proved a fiasco. I refer to the revels at Gray's Inn, usually known as the "Gesta Grayorum." These consisted of a series of entertainments lasting about three months from Christmas, 1594, to Lent in the following year.

In Nicol's "Progresses of Queen Elizabeth," we

have the account of these revels printed, as we shall see, from a pamphlet which, in its turn, was printed from a MS. discovered by accident. Unfortunately the original MS. is not known to exist and there are very few copies of the pamphlet—one is in the Gray's Inn Library; and Nicol's "Progresses" is itself not a very common book, so that there may be some reason why, in the numerous inquiries that have been made as to both Bacon and Shakespeare, the evidence of this account, so far as it shows them to be, if not friends and allies, at least present together, should have been overlooked. These revels are, it is true, occasionally mentioned as giving the date of the first production of the "Comedy of Errors," the first of Shakespeare's plays, it is believed, to be produced. But no notice seems to have been taken of the special part played by Bacon, not in the play itself, but in getting up and carrying through these revels.

In Elizabeth's time Gray's Inn was the leading Inn of Court; its numbers were nearly double that of the Inner Temple, and it numbered amongst its members the leading men of the day. The Burghleys or Cecils, the Bacons, Lord Southampton, to whom Shakespeare dedicated his two poems, and many other well-known names, to describe whom would be too long. And amongst other peculiar customs, was the friendship which existed between Gray's Inn and the Inner Temple, the coat of arms of the one being on the gate of the other. This being so, we may more fully understand the proceedings that took place in the years 1594-5, an account of which, apparently written at the time, was preserved, and was printed for W. Canning at his shop in the Temple cloisters in the year 1688. Who the author of this account was? how it came to be preserved? how it came into the hands of the publisher? we have no direct evidence, but I think there is enough to show that it was either written by Bacon himself—and thus is an illustration of his concealed authorship—or it was written by someone who had some reason for not mentioning Bacon by name. For while we shall be able to show that Bacon was taking a very, if not the most, active part in getting up the plays, devices, &c., his name alone seems to be conspicuous by its absence. Nearly every other name is carefully given, his equally carefully omitted.

The account on the face of it bears the impress of being written with authority, and we are fully justified in accepting it as evidence, though the original MS. appears to be lost.

The person who was selected to preside was one Mr. Henry Holmes or Helmes, who must have been a person of some enterprise as he was one of the youngest members of the Inn having only been called in the middle of the year 1594. Yet he kept the whole entertainment going for some three months. Amongst other things, he went to court and performed a masque before Elizabeth at Greenwich, who apparently was so pleased with it, that when the courtiers wished to dance after it was over she said, " What, shall we have bread and cheese after a banquet?" and she had the Gray's Inn men presented to her next day and gave them her hand to kiss,[1]—

"With most gracious words of commendation to them particularly, and in general of Gray's Inn as an house she

---

[1] Nicols, vol. 3, p. 319.

was much beholden unto, for that it did always study for some sports to present unto her. The same night there was fighting at Barriers: the Earl of Essex and others challengers, the Earl of Cumberland and his company defendants, into which number our Prince was taken and behaved himself so valiantly and skilfully therein, that he had the prize adjudged due unto him, which it pleased her Majesty to deliver him with her own hands, telling him, 'That it was not her gift, for if it had it should have been better; but she gave it him as that prize which was due to his desert and good behaviour in those exercises, and that hereafter he should be remembered with a better reward from herself.'"

The account, after giving the value of the prize as being 100 marks, concludes with so much that is Baconian in manner, that I give it here:—

Thus, on Shrove Tuesday, at the Court were our sports and revels ended, so that our Christmas would not leave us till such time as Lent was ready to entertain us, which hath always been accounted a time most apt and wholly dedicated to repentance. But now our Principality is determined, which although it shined very bright in ours and others' darkness, yet at the Royal Presence of her Majesty, it appeared as an obscured shadow; in this, not unlike unto the Morning star which looketh very cheerfully in the World so long as the Sun looketh not on it; or, as the Great Rivers that triumph in the Multitude of their Waters until they come unto the Sea. *Sic vinci, sic mori pulchrum.*

To return to the proceedings which appear to have consisted, as I have said, of the installation of Mr. Henry Helmes as the Prince. A very considerable retinue was assigned to him, amongst whom, however, we do not find Mr. Bacon mentioned, although, from the circumstances, on the authority of Mr. Spedding, his biographer, he must have taken an active part.

Mr. Spedding says, Vol. I. p. 325 :—

"But as Mr. Bacon's name does not appear upon the face of the narrative, and as his connection with it, though sufficiently obvious, has never, so far as I know, been pointed out or suspected, I assume that the little story I am going to tell, presenting as it does a very curious and picturesque illustration of the manners of the time and the licences of the people among whom all his early and middle life was spent, is not so familiar to the students of his works, but they will be glad to see it here."

Again, he says (p. 342)—

"That Bacon had a hand in the general design is merely a conjecture. We know that he had a taste in such things, and did sometimes take part in arranging them: and the probability seemed strong enough to justify a more detailed work than I could otherwise have thought fit. But that the 'Speeches of the Six Councillors' were written by him, and *by him alone,* no one who is at all familiar with his style, either of thought or expression, will for a moment doubt."

The "Speeches of the Six Councillors," to which reference will be made, is therefore directly attributed by Mr. Spedding to Bacon alone; but he says it is a matter of conjecture whether he had a hand in the general design. From this I feel inclined to differ. I think that when we come to examine the account already referred to, as published in 1688, and afterwards given in Nicol's " Progresses of Queen Elizabeth," there is a strong presumption that Bacon took the active and principal part in getting up the plays of the "Comedy of Errors" and "Masque," and the account itself was written by himself. I do not mean to say that there is that kind of evidence which would entitle a jury to convict a prisoner; but there is, I think, sufficient to convince an unbiassed mind that it is probable that Bacon arranged, and was reponsible for, the "Masque," though he may have been assisted by others. To show this is so, I propose to refer shortly to the account as given by Nicol's "Queen Elizabeth," Vol. III. p. 262.

The title of the masque is thus given :—

Gesta Grayorum;

OR

THE HISTORY OF THE HIGH AND MIGHTY PRINCE HENRY;

Prince of PURPOOLE, Arch-Duke of STAPULIA and BERNARDIA, Duke of HIGH and NETHER HOLBORN, Marquis of ST. GILES and TOTTENHAM, Count Palatine of BLOOMSBURY and CLERKENWELL, Great Lord of the Cantons of ISLINGTON, KENTISH TOWN, PADDINGTON and KNIGHTSBRIDGE, Knight of the Most Heroical Order of the HELMET,[1] and Sovereign of the same, who reigned, and died A.D. 1594. Together with a Masque as it was presented (by his Highness's command) for the Entertainment of QUEEN ELIZABETH, who, with the Nobles of both Courts, was present thereat.

There was a very large list of names of those forming the court of the pseudo prince, and, as I have said, Bacon's name was conspicuous by its absence. The proceedings seem to have been of a very elaborate character—too much so modern persons might think, for what was after all but mere fooling. The hall was fitted with staging, and a theatre erected on the 20th December, St. Thomas's Eve. The account tells us the Prince went to the great hall and took his seat upon a throne under a rich cloth of state, the councillors and great lords placed about and before him.

---

[1] It appears that Mr. Helmes' crest was three helmets.

At a lower table sat his counsel and lawyers. His ridiculous titles were proclaimed by the king of arms, and his champion, in complete armour on horseback, rode into the hall about the fire and made his challenge, offering to fight anyone who, as a false traitor, said his sovereign was not rightly Prince of Purpoole, &c.

It appeared that a letter had been addressed—

"To the Most Honourable and Prudent the Governors, Assistants, and Society of the Inner Temple"

asking that an ambassador might be sent to the State of Purpoole, &c.—

"Your most loving friend and ally,
"GRAY'S INN.

"Dated at our Court of Graya, &c. this 14th December, 1594."

To this there was a reply sent—

"To the Most Honourable State of Grayans"

accepting the invitation as being—

"a great honour intended towards ourselves, in respect whereof we yield with all good will to that which your honourable letters import, as your kindness and the bond of our ancient amity and league, requireth and deserveth.

"Your assured friend,
"THE STATE OF TEMPLARIA.

"From Templaria, the 18th of December, 1594."

Everything passed off successfully on the first night. It is not necessary to follow the proceedings, which are set out at considerable length, but speeches were prepared by the Prince's attorney and solicitor, and these gave the Prince a list of his territories which have to do homage. A few examples must suffice. Alfonsio de Stapulia and Davillo de Bernardia (Staple and Barnard's Inns) had to render a coronet of gold yearly, and five hundred millions sterling. Then followed Morotto Maraquillo de Holborn, one Lucy Negro, Abbess of Clerkenwell, &c., with here and there a somewhat stilted joke not always of the choicest description. Then followed a general pardon, except crimes intended to be omitted, followed by an exception of every crime that could be thought of set out in great detail, with a final and general exception of all manner of offences, &c. whatsoever. The final exception from the pardon being "except all and all manner of offences, pains, penalties, mulcts, fines, amercements, and punishment, corporal and pecuniary whatsoever." The pardon being read, there was a short speech, and the night ended with dancing. I think it is very possible that a good deal of this elaborate nonsense was Bacon's. There is the same doubtful wit and low comedy ideas which, I think, we see in the passages between Escalus and the clown, already referred to. But one hesitates to express any strong opinion on it.

It is not necessary to follow further all these somewhat stilted jokes, the blazoning of the Prince's arms, the speech of the attorney-general, the homages and tributaries of the prince, with fanciful names for Staple and Barnard's Inns, High Holborn, &c.

On the second night, however, a *fiasco* took place. The ambassador from the Temple[1] with his train

---

[1] Inner Temple.

came, but also came many others. For the account tells us that after the ambassador had been duly received and placed in a chair beside his highness—

"That there was something to be performed for the delight of the beholders, there arose such a disordered tumult and crowd upon the stage, that there was no opportunity to effect that which was intended: there came so great a number of worshipful personages upon the stage that might not be displaced, and gentlewomen whose sex did privilege them from violence, that when the prince and his officers had in vain, a good while, expected and endeavoured a reformation, at length there was no hope of redress for that present. The lord ambassador and his train thought that they were not so kindly entertained as was before expected, and thereupon would not stay any longer at that time, but, in a sort, discontented and displeased. After their departure the throngs and tumults did somewhat cease, although so much of them continued as was able to disorder and confound any good inventions whatsoever. In regard whereof, as also for that the sports intended were especially for the gracing of the Templarians, it was thought good not to offer anything of account, saving dancing and revelling with gentlewomen; and after such sports, a Comedy of Errors (like to Plautus his Menechmus) was played by the players. So that night war begun and continued to the end in nothing but confusion and errors; whereupon, it was ever afterwards called 'The Night of Errors.'"

This departure of the Inner Temple ambassador with his following, for we are told he "came very gallantly appointed and attended by a great number of brave gentlemen," was no doubt felt by the Prince and whoever were the real mover or movers in getting up the entertainment, to be a real misfortune; and as some one had to be made liable, a prosecution was instituted upon some one whose name is not disclosed, but to whose identity we have certain clues, which make it not improbable that the person who was sought to be made liable for all the confusion was Bacon. The account, which must speak for itself, is as follows :—

This mischanceful accident sorting so ill to the great prejudice of the rest of our proceedings was a great discouragement and disparagement to our whole state; yet it gave occasion to the lawyers of the Prince's Council, the next night after revels, to read a Commission of Oyer and Terminer, directed to certain noblemen and lords of His Highness's Council, and others, tl t they should enquire, or cause enquiry to be made, of some great disorders and abuses lately done and committed within His Highness's dominions of Purpoole, especially by sorceries and inchantments, and namely, of a great witchcraft used the night before, whereby there were great disorders and misdemeanours, by hurly-burlies crowds, errors, confusions, vain representations and shows, to the utter discredit of our state and policy.

The next night, upon this occasion, we preferred judgments thick and threefold, which were read publickly by the Clerk of the Crown, being all against a *sorcerer or conjurer* that was supposed to be the cause of that confused inconvenience Therein was contained: *How he had caused the stage to be built, and scaffolds to be reared at the top of the house, to increase expectation. Also how he had caused divers ladies and gentlemen, and others of good condition to be invited to our sports, also our dearest friend, the State of Templaria, to be disgraced and disappointed of their kind entertainment deserved and intended, Also that he caused throngs and tumults, crowds and outrages, to disturb our whole proceedings. And lastly, that he had foisted a company of base and common fellows to make up our disorders with a play of Errors and Confusions;* and that that night had gained to us discredit, and itself a nickname of errors. All which were against the Crown, and dignity of our Sovereign Lord and Prince of *Purpoole.*

Under colour of these proceedings were laid open to the view all the causes of note that were committed by our chiefest statesman in the government of our principality, and every officer in any great place that had not performed his duty in that service was taxed hereby, from the highest to the lowest, not sparing the guard and porters, that suffered so many disordered persons to enter in at the court gates; upon whose aforesaid indictments the *prisoner* was arraigned at the bar, being brought thither by the Lieutenant of the Tower (for at that time the stocks were graced with that name); and the sheriff impannelled a jury of twenty-four gentlemen, that were to give their verdict upon the evidence given. The prisoner appealed to the Prince, his Excellency, for justice, and humbly desired that it would please his Highness to understand the truth of the matter by his supplication, which he had ready to be offered to the Master of the Requests. The Prince gave leave to the Master of the Requests that he should read the petition, wherein was a disclosure of all the knavery and juggling of the attorney and solicitor, which had *brought all this law stuff* on purpose to bind the eyes of his Excellency and all the honourable Court there, going about to make them think that those things which they all saw and perceived sensibly to be in very deed done, and actually performed, were nothing else but vain illusions, fancies, dreams, and inchantments, and to be wrought and compassed *by the means of a poor harmless wretch that never had heard of such great matters in all his life:* whereas the very fault was in the negligence of the Prince's Council, Lords and Officers of his State, that had the rule of the roast, and by whose advice the Commonwealth was so soundly misgoverned. To prove these things to be true, he brought divers instances of great absurdities committed by the greatest; and made such allegations as could not be denied. These were done by some that were touched by the Attorney and Solicitor in their former proceedings, *and they used the prisoner's names* for means of quittance with them in that behalf. But the Prince and Statesmen (being pinched on both sides by both the parties) were not a little offended at the great liberty that they had taken in censuring so far of his Highness's government; and *thereupon the prisoner was freed and pardoned*, the Attorney, Solicitor, Master of the Requests, and those that were acquainted with the draft of the petition, were all of them commanded to the Tower, so the Lieutenant took charge of them. And this was the end of our law-sports concerning the "Night of Errors."

When we were wearied with mocking thus at our own follies, at length there was a great consultation had for the recovery of our lost honour. It was then concluded, that first the Prince's Council should be reformed, and some graver conceipts should have their places to advise upon those things that were propounded to be done afterward. Therefore, upon better consideration there were divers plots and devices intended against the Friday after New Year's Day being the 3rd of January, and to prevent all unruly tumults, and former inconveniences, there was provided a watch of armed men to ward at the four ports; and whifflers to make good order under the four Barons, and the Lord Warden to over-see them all; that none but those that were of good condition might be suffered to be let into the Court. And the like officers were everywhere appointed.

The result of this new arrangement for preventing the overcrowding was that the Temple guests came back again, and the Prince held an investiture of the knights of Helmet (his crest it may be remembered), and afterwards made a set speech to his councillors, six of whom replied to him.

The second entertainment took place on the 3rd January night, before a considerable number of noblemen, "knights, ladies, and very worshipful personages." Graius and Templarius came in lovingly arm in arm, and offered incense at an altar to the goddess of Amity, but the smoke was troubled, &c. Finally, the goddess was appeased, and the pair declared perfect friends, as the account says,—

"as ever were Theseus and Perithous, Achilles and Patroclus, Pylades and Orestes, or Scipio and Lælius, and therewithal did further divine that this love should be perpetual.

*   *   *   *   *   *

"Thus was this show ended which was devised to that end, that those that were present might understand that the unkindness which was growing betwixt the *Templarians* and us, by reason of that former 'Night of Errors,' and the uncivil behaviour wherewith they were entertained, as before I have partly touched, was now clean-rooted out and forgotten," &c.

The Prince then proceeded to invest the Templarians and several others with the Knighthood of the Helmet, an order of his own institution.

After being duly invested, Helmet, his highness's king-at-arms, stood before the Prince in his surcoat of arms, &c., and made his speech, and the king-at-arms read the articles of the order, which are of a quaint and humorous turn, such as—

"ITEM.—No knight of this Order shall be inquisitive towards any lady or gentlewoman, whether her beauty be English or Italian,[1] or whether with care taking she have added half-a-foot to her stature; but shall take all to the best. Neither shall any knight of the aforesaid Order presume to affirm that faces were better twenty years ago than they are at this present time, except such knight have passed three climacterical years," &c.

Then followed concert music and a banquet, and afterwards the Prince addressed his six councillors in a speech, which is set out at length, to which they replied in six long speeches, the first advising war, the second philosophy, &c.

These speeches, which are too long to give here, are, no doubt, couched in a more serious vein than the various matters which are set out before. We no

---

[1] Because cosmetiques were supposed to come from Italy.

longer have the somewhat bold allusions to the virtue of the fair maids of Islington, &c., to the habits of Lucy Negro, Abbess of Clerkenwell, but we have the didactic epistles which Bacon so much delighted in. From the speech of the first councillor, an extract may give the reader an idea of their style.

The first councillor advising the exercise of war—

Most Excellent Prince,

Except there be such amongst us, as I am fully persuaded there is none, that regardeth more his own greatness under you, than your greatness over others, I think there will be little difference in the chusing for you a goal worthy your vertue and power. For he that shall set before him your magnanimity and valour, supported by the youth and disposition of your body; your flourishing Court, like the horse of Troy, full of brave commanders and leaders; your populous and man-rife provinces, overflowing with warlike people; your coffers, like the Indian mines, when that they are first opened; your store-houses are as sea-walls, like to Vulcan's cave; your navy like to an huge floating city; the devotion of your subjects to your crown and person, their good agreement amongst themselves, their wealth and provision; and then your strength and unrevocable confederation with the noble and honourable personages, and the fame and reputation without of so rare a concurrence, whereof all the former regards do grow; how can he think any exercise worthy of your means, but that of conquest? for, in few words, What is your strength, if you find it not? Your fortune, if you try it not? Your virtue, if you shew it not? Think, excellent Prince, what sense of content you found in yourself when you were first invested in our state; for though I know your Excellency is far from vanity and lightness, yet it is the nature of all things to find rest when they come to due and proper places. But be assured of this, that this delight will languish and vanish; for power will quench appetite, and satiety will endure tediousness. But if you embrace the wars, your trophies and triumphs will be as continual coronations that will not suffer your glory and contentment to fade and wither. Then, when you have enlarged your territories, ennobled your country, distributed fortunes good or bad, at your pleasure, not only to particulars, but to cities and nations, marked the computations of times with your expeditions and voyages, and the memory of places by your exploits and victories in your later years, you shall find a sweet respect into the adventures of your youth, you shall enjoy your reputation, you shall record your travels, and after your own time you shall eternize your name, and leave deep footsteps of your power in the world.

Such were the proceedings that took place, but the benchers and ancients evidently thought they had lasted long enough. Term was coming on, and the hall was wanted, and it was ordered to be cleared, much to the disgust of the would-be revellers, who did not seem to recognise the truth of the adage that " Enough is as good as a feast."

"The purpose of the gentlemen was much disappointed by the readers and ancients of the house by reason of the term; so that very good inventions which were to be performed in public at his entertainment into the house again, and two grand nights which were intended at his triumphal return, wherewith his reign had been conceitedly determined, were by the aforesaid readers and governors made frustrate, for the want of room in the hall, the scaffolds being taken away and forbidden to be built up again (as would have been necessary for the good discharge of such matter), thought convenient; but it showed rather what was performed than intended."

The result was, that though the sports were carried on till Shrove Tuesday, they were outside the hall at Greenwich and elsewhere as already stated.

It is, I think, to be noticed in this account of the proceedings, that the officers are named as well as the guests who came on the 5th of January, among whom were the Lord Keeper, the Earls of Shrewsbury, Cumberland, Northumberland, Southampton and Essex, so that there was no general desire to conceal the identity of the different persons. Yet when we come to the mock trial,[1] the defendant's name is not given, but he is spoken of as a *sorcerer or conjurer* who had caused the stage to be built and the scaffolds to be reared to the top of the house to increase expectation, and had caused divers ladies and gentlemen to be invited to our sports, &c.; and lastly, that he had foisted a company of base and common fellows to make up our disorders with a play of errors and confusions, &c., being careful to mention it was like to Plautus his Mænechmus, " all of which were against the crown and dignity of our Sovereign Lord the Prince of Purpoole "—probably a quotation from the indictment. Now these trials between members of the Bar have been carried down to our own day. The old Home Circuit had an attorney specially appointed for prosecuting so-called delinquents, and considerable wit was often shown in the proceedings. Looking at the various other documents set out at full length in the account, the pardon, &c., it is curious that the indictment, which no doubt was facetiously drawn, and the defendant's reply, are not given. I think it may be that the defendant did not wish his identity disclosed, which the setting out of these documents *in extenso* might have done. But whoever he was, he was the introducer of the players and Shakespeare's play; he had the stage put up, for which he would require the permission of the benchers. Bacon was an ancient of the Inn, and therefore a person of some

---

[1] Page 279.

authority. If another than the person who introduced the players wrote the account we are considering, he probably would have given us the defendant's name, and set out the indictment and the defence, especially as the result of the trial was that the defendant alone was acquitted, and the prosecuting counsel and others concerned were sent to the Tower (the stocks). If this defendant was the author of the account, then the compliment to Elizabeth points to Bacon. And this, I think, is confirmed by the description given of the defendant as being a sorcerer or conjurer, which is the character Bacon's namesake, Friar Bacon, bore, which might well have led to his being so described; so that there seems to be a chain connecting the writer of the account with the defendant, who was termed a sorcerer, and both with Bacon; and that it was to the latter the introduction of the play and the building of the stage, &c., were due. It is almost impossible to see how this could have been done without bringing him into direct communication with Shakespeare as author of the play.

Be this as it may, if Mr. Spedding is correct in saying that the speeches made on the 3rd of January were Bacon's, we have an entertainment begun, as it were, by Shakespeare and his play, and continued by Bacon and his speeches; and, therefore, I think it is not unreasonable to suppose that the two, at least, knew of each other's existence at this time.

I have set out at some length the extracts from the account we have of the "Gesta Grayorum" of 1594, and pointed out the inference which, I think, may be drawn, *i.e.*, that Bacon was the prime mover, the one who caused the stage to be built, and introduced the players into Gray's Inn Hall, as showing the probability of his being in direct connection with Shakespeare and the company of players to which he belonged. And I think if there was some one who was assisting Shakespeare in the authorship of the plays, as well as in their production when written, that it was not unreasonable to suppose that he who did the one may have done the other. The "Comedy of Errors," though full of many absurdities, has also very many legal expressions and ideas, which, if my view of Shakespeare's ignorance of the law be correct, must have been furnished to him by some one. That this person was Bacon, is to my mind somewhat confirmed by the fact that the "Promus," to which reference has already been made, was commenced at about this time, for it is dated on the top of the page, 5th December, 1594. At this time Gray's Inn Hall was probably being prepared for the "Comedy of Errors." And whatever may be said of Mrs. Potts' attempts to connect the various sentences with passages in Shakespeare's works, this collection of "wise saws" is just such a work as Bacon may have commenced if he had made up his mind to assist Shakespeare with his playwriting. If, on the other hand, Bacon was a perfect stranger to Shakespeare and his works, then we have this remarkable coincidence, that Bacon at the time Shakespeare, who had been assisted by some legal friend, found his way with his play upon a stage in Gray's Inn Hall, Bacon commenced a work which, to some at least there seems almost conclusive evidence, was in many cases used for the subsequent writings of Shakespeare and his unknown friend.

Evidence must not be treated piecemeal. At present I have only shown one matter that cannot well be questioned, and that is, Bacon was in some way or other, in 1594, mixed up with the earliest known production of any play said to be by Shakespeare. I now propose to pass over about twenty-nine years and show what evidence there is which connects Bacon with the production of the Folio in 1623. I think if I can show that there is strong ground for believing that he was connected with that, we shall then have some connection shown between the first and last production of Shakespeare's plays, the Alpha and Omega of our inquiry. There are certain small matters already referred to in the interval which are nothing if they stood alone, but I think are of value as connecting links. I illustrate this to my own mind by the example of a traveller exploring the site of an ancient city. If he can discover traces of a gate at one place, and traces of another gate some distance off, then small objects, such as occasional wrought stones, &c., which would prove nothing of themselves, would, if they lay between the two supposed gates, be strong evidence of the city that was supposed to exist between them. So, if I have established that some one must have assisted Shakespeare, and show that when his first play was produced Bacon was on the spot, apparently taking an active part in its production, and that there is good reason for believing that Bacon took an active part in the production of the Folio of 1623, then I think the small incidents that took place in this interval of time may prove of weight as showing that there was a more or less continuous connection between the two during the period of 1594 to 1623.

CHAPTER IX.

BACON AND THE FOLIO OF 1623.

THERE are many circumstances that connect Bacon with the publication, in 1623, of the first folio of Shakespeare's plays. At this period Bacon had been sentenced by the House of Lords, and deprived of his offices, including the Lord Chancellorship. He was not only in want of money, but of employment, as his letters to the king tell us. And if he had assisted Shakespeare some years before, but had set aside his play-writing on the accession of James in 1603, and turned his attention to politics, and ambition, he might be well expected to return to his literary labours when he found his professional life closed. This is, of course, arguing in a circle, as it assumes that he did assist Shakespeare in order to prove that he did so. But, as I have said before more than once, there are many circumstances connected with Shakespeare and his works which may lead to several conclusions, one of which is that Bacon assisted him, and the publication of the Folio collection of his plays, many of which had never before been published — some fourteen, I think—at this period may be accounted for by the fact that at this time Bacon was out of employment. This might be a mere coincidence. But it is considerably strengthened by the presence in the

Folio of the play of "Henry VIII.," which seems to point to Bacon as being its part author.

The reasons for this conclusion may be thus stated—
1. It is a legal play.
2. It contains the special knowledge that Bacon alone would possess.
3. It has been altered from a merry licentious play to a sad and serious one.
4. This alteration appears to have been made by Jonson, who was assisting Bacon.
5. There appears to be no reason why Jonson should have touched this particular play, except to give Bacon an opportunity of calling attention to his own sorrows.
6. This view is confirmed by Bacon's own letters.

"Henry VIII." a legal Play.

The play of "Henry VIII." is classed by Lord Campbell among those which show no legal knowledge, but I think wrongly so. I think there will be found in the play many more traces of legal knowledge than are in some of the plays he has given extracts from. Thus, the Queen, when she is confronted with Wolsey, makes her challenge that he, being her enemy, shall not be her judge, and says:—

> I utterly abhor, yea, from my soul,
> Refuse you for my judge.

This she repeats—

> I do refuse you for my judge; and here,
> Before you all, appeal unto the Pope,
> To bring my whole cause before his Holiness,
> And to be judged by him.

Of course, all this is history; but it has been pointed

out by Sir William Blackstone, that abhor and refuse are technical terms of the canon law, *Detestor* and *Recuso*. These words are given in Hollinshed, but not as words of art, but rather the redundant expressions of an angry woman. And I think it required as much technical knowledge to have selected the proper words to use as it would be for a dealer to pick out real stones from imitations.

The sentence from Hollinshed is as follows—

Here is to be noted that the queen, in the presence of the whole Court, most grievously accused the Cardinal of untruth, deceit, wickedness, and malice, which had sown dissension between her and the king, her husband; and therefore openly protested that she did utterly abhor, refuse, and forsake such a judge, as was not only a most malicious enemy to her, but also a manifest adversary to all right and justice, and therewith did appeal to the Pope, committing her whole cause to be judged by him.

I do not think anyone, not being a lawyer acquainted with the canon law, reading this passage would have known the words "abhor" and "refuse" to be proper legal expressions. It may be that they were copied into the play in ignorance of this fact, but they follow the word "challenge," which had just been used in its proper technical sense, and is not found in the extract from Hollinshed. There are numerous other expressions and ideas which savour of the law. Thus, Buckingham is properly arrested by a sergeant-at-arms by Brandon's orders—

Brandon. Your office, sergeant, execute it.
Serg. Sir,
My lord the Duke of Buckingham, and Earl
Of Hereford, Stafford, and Northampton, I
Arrest thee of high treason, in the name
Of our most sovereign king.

Buckingham says—

> It will help me nothing,
> To plead mine innocence.

In the next scene the king, when he has heard the witnesses, says—

> He is attach'd;
> Call him to present trial: if he may
> Find mercy in the law, 'tis his; if none,
> Let him not seek 't of us.

This is very similar to the arrest of Scroop and the others in "Henry V.,"[1] when they are arrested to the answer of the law.

We find Wolsey, when he is accused of issuing illegal commissions, says—

> I have no further gone in this, than by
> A single voice; and that not passed me, but
> By learned approbation of the judges.

Referring to the practice of taking the advice of the judges by Parliament, &c. And the king asks—

> Have you a precedent
> Of this commission?

When he gets no answer, says—

> To every county,
> Where this is questioned, send our letters, with
> Free pardon to each man that hath denied
> The force of this commission.

Lovel, describing the dismissal of the young nobles from court, their French manners having offended the king, says—

> They may, *cum privilegio*, wear away
> The lag end of their lewdness and be laughed at.

---

[1] Act II. Scene II., *ante*.

The scene where Buckingham comes back from his trial is correctly described.

Wolsey defends his conduct to the queen—

> How far I have proceeded,
> Or how far further shall, is warranted
> By a commission from the consistory,
> Yea, the whole consistory of Rome.

Campeggio states the difficulty the Court are in by the queen's refusal to attend, having appealed to Rome—

> The queen being absent, 'tis a needful fitness
> That we adjourn this court till further day:
> Meanwhile must be an earnest motion
> Made to the queen, to call back her appeal
> She intends unto his holiness.

The queen says—

> That comfort comes too late;
> 'Tis like a pardon after execution.

Perhaps one of the most interesting scenes to be found in this play, as showing the familiarity of the legal friend with one branch of the law, is where Wolsey introduces Campeggio to the king. In the play he is called Campeius, the name given both in Hall and Hollinshed, Cavendish uses the Italian form. Wolsey explains that the king has given a precedent of wisdom by committing his scruples about the marriage to Christendom, so that all must, even the Spaniard, confess the trial just and noble.

> All the clerks,
> I mean the learned ones, in christian kingdoms
> Have their free voices; Rome, the nurse of judgment,
> Invited by your noble self, hath sent
> One general tongue[1] unto us, this good man, &c.

---

[1] I suppose as the mouthpiece of Christendom.

Campeggio says :—

> To your highness' hand
> I tender my commission; by whose virtue
> (The court of Rome commanding), you, my lord,
> Cardinal of York, are joined with me, their servant,
> In the impartial judging of this business.

All this is in due form and might perhaps have been learned from history, but I think it requires a legal training to express so shortly what is necessary and no more. The next expression is very curious, Wolsey tells the King that the Queen is entitled to legal assistance.

> I know your Majesty has always loved her
> So dear in heart; not to deny her that
> A woman of less place might ask by law,
> *Scholars*, allowed freely to argue for her.

The word "scholars" is a word that requires some explanation, which I think to be this. In England we have the common law, which is paramount; but in addition there were the civil law and the canon law. These two have often been confused, but they are quite distinct. Mr. Lewis Dibden, in his work on Church Courts,[1] says :—

I gather that the distinction between Canon and Civil Law was as marked at Oxford as at Cambridge, so that there does not seem to be the slightest ground for confounding civilians with canonists.

Perhaps the strongest proof of this marked distinction between the two systems is to be found in the very different manner in which they were treated in our Universities at the Reformation. While canon law was interdicted, civil law was not interfered with. The material support which the former lent to the papal usurpation is a sufficient reason for its disfavour. On the other hand, the freedom of the civil law from

---

[1] Page 57.

any special connection with the Romish Church seems not only to account for its toleration, but to be the necessary explanation of an otherwise meaningless inconsistency. When the Church of England was liberated from the bondage of Rome, it no longer required to be preserved within it a knowledge of the Decretals and Bulls of pontifical and canon law; but for matters of probate and administration, as well as those dealt with in the Admiralty Court, Roman civil law, which had always regulated them, was yet required and was therefore still maintained. It would be difficult to illustrate the divergence between canon and civil law more forcibly than by a simple statement of well-known historical facts.

Henry VIII., in 1535, by one of the celebrated royal injunctions of that year, commanded the Universities to cease teaching, examining, or granting decrees in canon law (the greater part of which was swept away by the removal of the papal authority). The order which was sent to Cambridge is still extant, and it is supposed that a similar one went to Oxford.

If, therefore, persons could not get a degree given to them in canon law, they must have remained scholars, and I think this may have been the reason the word is used in the play, the trial before the two Cardinals being under the canon law. If this be so, it affords us another example of the law in Shakespeare's plays being the law as it was in his time, for the trial took place in 1529, and, as we see, Henry's injunction was not till 1535, so that Wolsey used the word in that curious spirit of prophecy which I have before noticed in the legal knowledge displayed in the plays; afterwards Wolsey describes the *scholars* thus :—

> You have here, lady,
> (And of your choice) these reverend fathers; men
> Of singular integrity and learning;
> Yea, the elect of the land, who are assembled
> To plead your cause.

Wolsey then points out that, being represented by counsel, she must act through them.

> It shall therefore be bootless
> That longer you desire the Court: &c.

Campeggio supports Wolsey's ruling—

> His grace
> Hath spoken well and justly. Therefore, madam,
> It's fit this royal session do proceed,
> And that without delay, *their*[1] arguments
> Be now produced and heard.

But the queen is not to be silenced, and insists on speaking for herself, notwithstanding she has counsel, and, as we have seen, challenges Wolsey as judge, uses the proper expressions, herself gives notice that she appeals to Rome, and sweeps out of Court, leaving the Court to a certain extent powerless, so that it has to be adjourned.

All this is, as I have said, history, but it is told as a lawyer would tell it, and not, I think, as a layman inexperienced in the practice of the Courts would. The more one reads this play the more one is struck with the evidence of legal training it displays wherever such legal knowledge is required, but not otherwise. As I have said before, in some of the plays the law is often dragged in for the purpose of display; but all that is connected with the law is told in this play in a lawyer-like manner. There are no doubt other examples, but I think enough has been adduced to show that "Henry VIII." is one of the legal plays, and it is difficult to understand how Lord Campbell could have found no traces of legal knowledge in it.

It seems to me, therefore, that this play shows the

---

[1] *Her counsel's.*

progress of Shakespeare's legal friend. In the earlier plays written some thirty years before, the law is made the vehicle for jesting; the student airs his knowledge; he is often grotesque, he makes Venus in her baffled passion talk of English common money bonds. There is nothing of this in "Henry VIII."; the law is used in a grave and solemn manner, and more particularly we find not the mere lawyer, but one who has, as we shall see, an intimate and familiar knowledge of the manners and customs belonging to the Chancellorship, in fact just that information which Bacon could best have supplied if he were assisting Jonson to write up this play for the press about 1622-3. As this is to my mind the peculiar feature of this play, it may not be out of place to call attention to both Bacon and Wolsey's position with regard to the Lord Chancellorship. Both had been deprived of it; but while Wolsey was to the Protestants an enemy to be humbled, Bacon was to all a criminal to be punished.

Wolsey had lost it because he could not get Campeggio to give a decision. We now know that the latter had pledged himself in a letter to the Pope not to do so; this was before he ever came to England, and Wolsey had remonstrated with him upon this matter without success, and had pointed out to him what would be the consequences if the king did not get the divorce. The following extracts from Campeggio's letters may be interesting, as showing the real position taken up by Wolsey. Before coming to England, Campeggio explains his position to the Pope's secretary Salviati—

As to not binding myself or giving any promise, His Holiness may trust to my fidelity. Neither with all his kingdom, nor with all his treasure, will he [the king] be able to cause me to deviate from my duty. I will be careful, when speaking with him, not to promise any sentence. If you mean to say that I am to do nothing whatever without informing the Pope, I do not see how, in case it should be impossible to shake the king's opinion, the *trial* can be avoided without scandal. They would think I had come to hoodwink them and might resent it. You know how much that would involve. But so far as the sentence itself is concerned, I will observe all your instructions; and they shall never learn my opinion until I am about to give judgment—that is to say, if the cause should proceed so far.

Campeggio in a letter states how he tried to convince Wolsey and the result which followed.

But though I spoke with my utmost power, I could not the least move his Lordship [Wolsey] from his opinion. He alleged that if the king's desire were not complied with, fortified and justified as it was by the reasons, writings, and counsels of many learned men who feared God, *the speedy and total ruin would follow of the kingdom, of his lordship, and of the Church's influence in this kingdom.*

* * * * *

I have no more moved him [Wolsey] than if I had spoken to a rock. His objections were always founded upon the invalidity of the marriage and upon the *instability of the realm* and the succession.

* * * * *

In my last conversation with his lordship, he said, and repeated many times, in Latin: Most Reverend Lord, beware lest, in like manner as the greater part of Germany, owing to the harshness and severity of a certain Cardinal, has become estranged from the Apostolic See and from the Faith, it may be said that another Cardinal has given the same occasion to England, with the same result. He [Wolsey] often impresses upon me that if this divorce is not granted, the authority of the See Apostolic in this kingdom will be annihilated. And he certainly proves himself very zealous for its preservation, having done, and still doing, for it very great services, *because all his grandeur is connected with it.*"

This letter was signed 28th October, 1528; we shall see by that day twelvemonth Campeggio had refused to give sentence, and Wolsey's fall was imminent.

It appears that Campeggio put off the matter as long as he could, but finally the king and queen were summoned to appear before the Cardinals on the 18th June, 1529, between the hours of 9 and 10. The Queen, however, as stated in the play, appealed to Rome, and after that, we are told, appeared no more.

In his letters, Campeggio incidentally mentions that on the 4th June "we are still wearing our winter clothing and using fires as if it were January." Generally, he seems to have objected to the country and the people as well as the climate. He was hustled, as it were, into proceeding with the trial. Unfortunately the story as told by him is not complete, as his letters appear to have been intercepted by the king, and we have only copies of those which got through to Rome. We learn, however, that by the 7th October, he had said farewell to the king, and he was going to More "where Wolsey had a very fine palace"; and he left England on the 26th October, and on the 5th November he writes from Paris to Salviati, the Pope's secretary—

Immediately after my departure from London the designs against the Cardinal of York commenced to develop with great violence, so that before I crossed the sea[1] I learned they had deprived him of the seal and of the management of

---

[1] This was not so, for we learn from Cavendish that Wolsey sat in Westminster Hall on the first day of Michaelmas term (2nd November), and was deprived of his seal on the 4th. Cavendish says he waited at home the next day after Saturday (*i.e.*, the 3rd), and the dukes came to ask for the seal on the 4th, but having no written authority from the king, had to come back again.

all affairs and of a great part of his servants, and an inquiry was being made respecting his money and other possessions, with very evident signs of his tending to ruin. He has done nothing in the past, so far as ecclesiastical matters are concerned, to merit such disgrace. And, therefore, it may be thought his majesty will not go to extremes, but act considerately in this matter, as he is accustomed to do in all his actions.

We learn further from the State Papers that Wolsey was indicted on the 9th October, 1529, for obtaining bulls to be made legate, contrary to 16 Rich. II.; and on the 27th October he appeared by two attorneys, who stated that he was not aware that he had committed any offence, but threw himself on the king's mercy; and the judgment was that he was to be out of the king's mercy, and forfeit all lands and goods.

It is to be noticed that even Campeggio expects that the king would act considerately, and we shall see that Wolsey shared this opinion, and that although he allowed him to be deprived of his possessions, the seal, &c., the king did not desert him, but tried to help him as far as Anne would let him.

If any one takes the trouble to read Cavendish's "Life of Wolsey," he will find that though Wolsey lost the seal, he did not until quite the last lose the friendship of the king. Anne Boleyn was his enemy: the king was in love with her, and Wolsey was sacrificed to her enmity. But his plate, &c., was for the most part returned to him. Lord Campbell says he received a general pardon on giving up some of his preferments. He had a large retinue of servants; the king sent his own physicians to him when he was ill, and ordered them not to take any fees, and found him money to set out for his archbishopric in York; and it was not until he made preparations for his installation as Archbishop of York that the king ordered his arrest. He went so far, Lord Campbell says, as to ask the king to lend him some special robes, seized by the Crown officers with the rest of his goods, which he was accustomed to wear on great occasions. But even then every consideration was shown him; he stayed eighteen days with Lord Shrewsbury, who, it appears, was commanded by the king by letters received daily, to entertain him "as one that he [the king] loveth and highly favoureth." But when the Constable of the Tower appeared to bring him up to London, Wolsey lost heart. In vain Cavendish tried to re-assure him. "Well, well then," quoth he, "I perceive more than ye can imagine or do know; experience of old hath taught me." The common report was that he took poison, but whether that be so he died shortly after, not having got far on his journey, and so escaped the Tower and, it may be, the block. It is true that just before he died, he, according to Cavendish, made use of the memorable words we find in the play, addressing the Constable of the Tower :—

"Well, well, Master Kingston," quoth he, "I see the matter against me, how it is framed; but if I had served God as diligently as I have done the king, he would not have given me over in my grey hairs. Howbeit, this is the just reward that I must receive for my worldly diligence and pains that I have had to do him service, only to satisfy his vain pleasure, not regarding my godly duty."[1]

I think this is the first and last complaint he made against the king, if he did make it, for I think

---

[1] Page 250.

Cavendish wrote up some of his speeches, and it may have been the latter's embellishment. But up to the hour of his death he always seemed to recognize that the king was forced to treat him as he did; for instance, when he was leaving York House his treasurer, Sir William Gascoigne, said :[1]—

"Sir, I am sorry for your Grace, for I understand ye shall go straightway to the Tower."

"Is this the good comfort and counsel," quoth my lord, "that ye can give your master in adversity? It hath been always your natural inclination to be very light of credit, and much more lighter in reporting of false news. I would ye should know, Sir William, and all other such blasphemers, that it is nothing more false than that, for I never (thanks be to God) deserved by no ways to come there under any arrest, although it has pleased the king to take my house ready furnished for his pleasure at this time," &c.

And when he was asked by Cavendish why he confessed himself guilty on the præmunire,

"Wherein ye might full well have stood in the trial of your case;"

(the king's learned counsel, it appeared, had expressed an opinion that, his case well considered, he had great wrong), Wolsey explained his reasons, which were that his enemies, having made the king take up their quarrel, it was no use opposing him, and by his submission, he said—

"The king, I doubt not, had a great remorse of conscience, wherein he would rather pity than malign me."

He then referred to Anne as the "night crow" who would, if he had been stiff-necked, have "called continually upon the king in his ear," that with the

---

[1] Page 142.

help of her assistance, he would have obtained sooner the king's indignation than his favour;

"And his favour once lost (which, I trust, at this present I have) would never have been by me recovered,"

and therefore he thought it better to lose his goods and dignities and keep his favour, and concluded by saying—

"I understand the king hath received a certain prick of conscience, who took to himself the matter more grievous in his secret stomach than all men knew. For he knew whether I did offend him therein so grievously as it was made or no, to whose conscience I do commit my cause, truth, and equity."

This, I think, shows the trust Wolsey had in the king's personal friendship. And if Chapuy's account, which he sent to his sovereign Charles V., is to be accepted, it was this very friendship of Henry's that ultimately led to Wolsey's arrest—

"Eight days ago the king gave orders for the Cardinal to be brought here; on which the Cardinal remained for some days without food, hoping rather to finish his life in this way than in a more shameful one, of which he had some fears. He has been taken ill on the road, and has not arrived. It is said he is to be lodged in the same chamber in the Tower where the Duke of Buckingham was detained. The cause of his arrest is a mere conjecture. A gentleman told me that a short time ago the king was complaining to his council of something that was not done according to his liking, and said in a rage that the Cardinal was a better man than any of them for managing matters; and repeating this twice, he left them. The duke, the lady, and the father have not ceased since then to plot against the Cardinal; especially the lady, who does not cease to weep and regret her lost time and her honor, threatening the king that she would leave him,—in such sort that the king has had much trouble to appease her; and though the king prayed her most affectionately, even with tears in his eyes, that she would not speak of leaving him, nothing would satisfy her except the arrest of the Cardinal. It was pretended that he had written to Rome to be reinstated in his possessions, and to France for its favor, and was returning to his ancient pomp, and corrupting the people."

Of course, Wolsey did not know that it was the jealousy of Anne Boleyn and the Duke of Norfolk, that was the immediate cause of his being arrested. The world and, perhaps, he himself attributed it to his ostentatious preparations for his installation as Archbishop of York. But whatever the cause was, the appearance of the Constable of the Tower was a stern reality, which caused Wolsey for the first time to give way to despair.

Although Cavendish and others tell us this, we find in the play the king is made as much Wolsey's enemy as Anne herself was. We have this fact, then, that up to a certain point the author follows Cavendish, and then departs from him: the question is, why? That "Henry VIII.," as far as Wolsey is concerned, is, for the most part, based on Cavendish, the following examples will show. Let us take, for instance, the scene where the two cardinals visit Catherine to persuade her—

"To leave her case entirely in the king's hands, which would be much better to her honour than to stand the trial of law and to be condemned, which would seem much to her slander and defamation."

The scene between the queen and the cardinals very closely follows Cavendish's account, where she says—

Alack, my lord, I am very sorry to cause you to attend upon me. What is your pleasure with me?—*Cavendish.*

What are your pleasures with me, reverend lords?—*Shakespeare.*

If it please you, quoth the cardinal, to go into your privy chamber, we will show you the cause of our coming.—*Cavendish*.

May it please you, noble madam, to withdraw into your private chamber, we shall give you the full cause of our coming.—*Shakespeare*.

The Queen, both in the play and according to Cavendish, asks them to speak openly before her folk, upon which Wolsey commences to speak in Latin, when she beseeches him to speak in English; Wolsey then explains his errand, which is to know how she may be disposed to do, in the matter between the king and herself. For which she thanks them for their good wills, and then follows her complaint that she has been at work among her maids and is not prepared to answer so weighty a matter, &c., and finally she takes them to her private chamber, when the scene ends in the play, and Cavendish says :—

"We, in the other chamber, might sometimes hear the queen speak very loud, but what it was we could not hear."

So with the scene when the two dukes ask Wolsey to give up the seals and to depart unto Asher, a house belonging to the See of Winchester, Wolsey asks what commission they had to give him such a commandment. They replied :—

"That they were sufficient commissioners in that behalf, having the king's commandment by his mouth so to do."

These expressions are to be found in the play, and so is Wolsey's statement that the seal was delivered to him by the king himself to enjoy during his life, for which he had the king's letters patent to show, Cavendish said, which matter was greatly debated between the dukes and him, with many stout words between them. In the play we have the quarrel gone into fully. But no one can, I think, doubt that the author of the play worked up some of his scenes, and took some of his dialogue, directly from Cavendish. Reference is made in the scene to the articles which had been preferred in Parliament against Wolsey, and also to the prosecution in the præmunire matters, which did not take place till afterwards, but are all referred to in Cavendish. So far the author of the play has followed Cavendish, but when we come to his "farewell to greatness," we find he is no longer followed; but we seem to have not Wolsey but Bacon on the stage.

With Bacon all was different; he had been sentenced by his peers, as we shall see; deprived of his chancellorship, all he had; declared incapable of holding office again, and banished from the court. He may have thought the king ought to have shielded him, but Wolsey knew Henry was doing all that Anne and her party would allow him to do. Is it a coincidence then, that in the play the king is made as much Wolsey's enemy as Anne was, and Wolsey is made to utter his farewell to greatness, &c.? It may have been done for dramatic effect. It may have been that Bacon desired to excite sympathy for himself. It is like so much of what we find in Shakespeare, capable of two explanations, one of which is Bacon. And if the Athenians were right in choosing Themistocles, because each general put himself first and Themistocles second, so it is not unreasonable to give some weight to the fact that there is so much which may be explainable by Bacon being the person who assisted in the legal play, though each incident may be explained some other way. It is the accumulation of these coincidences which constitute circumstantial evidence, and we shall see there are a great many extraneous facts besides the internal evidence which points possibly to Bacon.

There are several incidents in the play of "Henry VIII." which, I think, derive a new interest if we are of opinion that the play is partly Bacon's; though they do not amount to evidence that it was so, they illustrate what, perhaps, passed through his mind. We learn from Cavendish that an inventory was made of Wolsey's goods when he left York Place to go to Asher. This inventory is to be found in the State Papers, and includes not only his plate, linen, silks, &c., but also his robes and vestments, and even two dresses, one with *false* pearls for the Virgin, and a coat for her son. Cavendish gives a general account of a number of rich stuffs, "of silk in whole pieces of all colours," and "velvet, satin, damask, cuffa, taffeta, grograine, sarcanet, and of others not in my remembrance, and a thousand pieces of fine holland cloth; the walls of the gallery were hanged with cloth of gold, and in one room was set nothing but gilt and gold plate, in another silver, &c." Now, in the play this inventory is supposed to be left by Wolsey amongst some papers he had given to the king, together with a letter from Wolsey to the Pope, &c. These two documents were supposed to have turned the king against Wolsey. This is all the author's imagination, as it was not till after his fall that the inventory was made; in fact, almost the last words of Wolsey in the play are:—

> Prithee, lead me in:
> There take an inventory of all I have,
> To the last penny; 'tis the king's, &c.

The author, as I have said, makes the inventory

one of the causes of Wolsey's fall, and Henry is made to enter reading the schedule, saying :—

> What piles of wealth hath he accumulated
> To his own portion! and what expense by the hour
> Seems to flow from him? How, i' the name of thrift,
> Does he rake this together?

The king must have known all about Wolsey's plate and linen, he had too often enjoyed his hospitality not to do so. But Bacon, who spent as much as he got, lawfully and unlawfully, who gave usually 2*l.* to a servant who brought him a present of a stag, about 16*l.* of our money, as his own accounts show, may well have been surprised how Wolsey could have got together all this wealth, and it may have been his own expression when he makes the king ask "How in the name of thrift does he rake this together?".

The Mace.—I do not know whether the author was right when he had the sword and mace carried before Wolsey when he went with Campeggio to open the Legatine Court at the Blackfriars. Cavendish is silent as to the ceremony of the opening of this Court, and unless there is some account preserved amongst the State Papers which I have not seen, the long stage direction at the commencement of Act II. scene 4, in which the procession to the Court is given, must have been written by someone who knew something about this kind of ceremony, and what was likely to be done. We know the mace is carried into the ordinary courts when the Lord Chancellor sits, but then he sits there as Lord Chancellor. But in the play he sits as Legate from the Pope, and I should have thought the mace would not have been there. But, no doubt, Wolsey would do as he pleased, and whatever he did would, if known, be a precedent if ever a similar court were held. So the Lords, when they considered how Bacon was to be tried, passed a resolution that the mace was to be shown to him, but not carried before him, which terrible insult Bacon escaped by going to bed and saying he was sick. But, I suppose, if ever a Lord Chancellor should have to be tried by his peers, this old resolution would be considered a precedent. Bacon was, therefore, well acquainted with the circumstances under which the mace should accompany the Chancellor, and if it is by his authority that the play says it is to be carried even into a Legatine ecclesiastical court, probably it was so. But I do not think Shakespeare or Jonson could have known anything about the subject, and finding that Cavendish was silent on the point, I find difficulty in believing that they would have had the audacity to evolve all the procession as it is given us, from their own self-consciousness.

The second matter which, to my mind, seems to point to Bacon, is the attention the author gives to the details of Wolsey's position *as Chancellor*, at the same time other details are treated carelessly. It must be remembered that though Wolsey was Chancellor, this was only an incident of his position. Many other ecclesiastics had been Chancellor, and had to resign the seals, and then received them again, and again had lost them. Campbell in some cases says as many as four or five times, and he also says,[1] speaking of Wolsey,—

Not only historians, but his own biographers, in describing the politician and the churchman, almost forget that he ever was Lord Chancellor.

---

[1] "Lives of the Chancellors," vol. I, p. 499.

Campeggio says:—

"All Wolsey's grandeur was connected with the church."

Cavendish says Wolsey asked the Duke of Norfolk to wash with him; but the latter desired to have him excused, and said :[1]—

"That it became him not to presume to wash with him any more now than it did before in his glory."

"Yes, forsooth," quoth my Lord Cardinal, "for my authority and dignity legatine is gone, wherein consisted all my high honor."

"A straw," quoth my Lord of Norfolk, "for your legacy, I never esteemed your honor the more or higher for that, but I regarded your honor, for that ye were Archbishop of York and a Cardinal, whose estate of honor surmounteth any duke now being within this realm, and so will I honor you and acknowledge the same, and bear you reverence accordingly."

Not a word about the chancellorship.

With Bacon all this was different. He was Lord Chancellor and nothing more, when he lost that by the sentence of his peers, and was deprived of the right of holding any other office, and banished from the Court, he had lost everything. It was indeed with him—

Farewell, a long farewell, to all my greatness!

To him the chancellorship was the paradise from which he was banished; and I now propose to point out, if it be true, as Campbell puts it, that people seem to forget Wolsey was a Chancellor; it is not so in the play of "Henry VIII.," where his office and all its attendant accessories are well thought out, whilst his cardinalship is comparatively neglected, as well as the ceremony and state of other personages.

Cavendish tells us that Wolsey—

"Had two great crosses of silver, whereof one of them was

---

[1] Page 164.

for his archbishopric, and the other for his legacy, borne always before him whithersoever he went or rode, by two of the tallest and comeliest priests that he could get within all this realm";

and when he went to Westminster,

"there was always borne before him first, the Great Seal of England, and then his Cardinal's hat, by a nobleman or some worthy gentleman right solemnly bareheaded, and also the two crosses of silver and two great pillars of silver, and his pursuivant-at-arms with a great mace of silver gilt."

Now Cavendish was a servant of Wolsey as Cardinal rather than Lord Chancellor, and he does not seem to have considered who carried the seal. But Lord Campbell says:[1]—

When he [the Chancellor] appears in his official capacity in the presence of the sovereign, or receives messengers from the Commons at the bar of the House of Lords, he carries the purse himself; on other occasions it is carried by his purse-bearer, and lies before him as an emblem of his authority.

As we have seen, when he attended the Chancery Court he had his mace. But Wolsey also had his crosses and pillars and his Cardinal's hat, and also, we have from Cavendish, men carrying battle-axes. Let us see how the stage directions are with regard to Wolsey. He first appears on his road to attend the king in the council chamber, and he crosses the stage.

[*Enter* Cardinal Wolsey (*the purse borne before him*), *certain of the Guard, and two Secretaries with papers.*]

Not one word about the crosses which Cavendish

---

[1] "Lives of the Chancellors," vol. I, p. 27.

tells him were borne before him wherever he went, and the Cardinal's hat is, apparently, left at home. No doubt this is a small matter; but it is only small matters that we can expect to reveal the secret, if there be one. We do not find on other occasions Shakespeare takes special notice of the fact that one of his characters is Lord Chancellor. In the first part of "Henry VI." we have the quarrel in Parliament between Beaufort, the Bishop of Winchester, and the Duke of Gloster. Beaufort was at the time Lord Chancellor, and when the peace was patched up between them, Lord Campbell said it was one of the conditions that Beaufort should resign the seals. Yet the fact is not mentioned, and, as far as I can see, there is nothing to show that Beaufort was the Chancellor; it was not material to the play; nor more was Wolsey's chancellorship to the play of "Henry VIII.," except so far as the incident of demanding the seals made it so. His part was played as Cardinal and Legate, not as Chancellor, and, therefore, it seems to me that an ordinary historian or dramatist would not have laid this stress on what was only an incident of his career, and ignored what was essential. But it has been said that this play is more of a pageant than an ordinary drama, if so, still more it seems that an ordinary author would have omitted the purse but mentioned the hat, "solemnly carried by a nobleman, bareheaded," though Bacon may have been biased by the memory of what he had been. We shall see this attention to the one side of Wolsey's position, and the neglect of, or indifference to, the more important rank still further shown in the subsequent scenes. I do not know whether a cardinal, who was also a chancellor, would or would not have his crosses and hat, &c., when he went to attend the king, but I think that an ordinary writer if he mentioned the one would have done so with the other. Scene 2 is the council chamber, but no directions are given, one way or the other, as to any of the accessories of either the king, queen, or cardinal. In the banquet scene we find only " Enter Wolsey attended," and the same when Wolsey introduces Campeggio to the king. But in the trial scene we shall see attention is paid to Wolsey and his purse, mace, &c., but the insignia of the rest is ignored. We have trumpets, &c., vergers, scribes, Archbishop of Canterbury, sundry bishops, next them, with some small distance, a gentleman bearing the Purse, with the Great Seal, and a Cardinal's Hat. Apparently one person has to carry both. The modern custom is that the Purse is carried on a cushion, and requires both hands, so it is difficult to see how the gentleman carried the hat, unless he wore it, which would not satisfy Cavendish's description of carrying it solemnly, bareheaded. Then came the two priests with the two crosses and the silver mace, then the two Cardinals, and two noblemen with the Sword and Mace; all this is for Wolsey; we have his crosses and his hat. But the Archbishop of Canterbury had a cross, for, Cavendish tells us, it was because the Archbishop of Canterbury, as Primate of All England, insisted upon Wolsey "abating the advancing of his cross in the presence of the cross of Canterbury," and, as Wolsey's pride could not stand this; he got himself made Cardinal and Legate, "to be superior in dignity to Canterbury rather than to be either obedient or equal to him." So Campeggio, as a Cardinal and Legate, was entitled to a cross; and even if he left that at Rome he must have had a cardinal's hat. So that whilst we have the purse, mace, &c., accurately given, we have only two crosses instead of four, and one hat between the two Cardinals. When we come to the king and queen we have no details given, only we are told they "came with their trains." We have no more details given about Wolsey, except that when Cromwell sees him after his fall, he says—

> Sir Thomas More is chosen
> Lord Chancellor in your place.

Now Bishop Williams was made chancellor when Bacon was dismissed, and he had not shown himself very complaisant to Bacon. He had, I believe, stopped the publication of his "Henry the VII." for a while, and delayed his pardon. Now if there was one thing Bacon liked, it was giving flattery; and if it ever were whispered that he had anything to do with the play, he may have thought the following speech by Wolsey would not do any harm if Williams might chance to take it to himself.

Wolsey replies to Cromwell's information about Sir Thomas More—

> That's somewhat sudden:
> But he's a learned man. May he continue
> Long in his highness' favour, and do justice
> For truth's sake, and his conscience; that his bones,
> When he has run his course, and sleeps in blessings,
> May have a tomb of orphans' tears wept on 'em!
> What more?

Cromwell tells him—

> That Cranmer is return'd with welcome,
> Install'd Lord Archbishop of Canterbury.

Wolsey only answers—

> That's news indeed.

One would have thought the fact that the Protestant Cranmer was to succeed him would not have been treated in such a cavalier fashion by Wolsey, who, if anything, was a staunch Romanist; but throughout the play it is the chancellorship that is principally considered, and not the churchman.

In the coronation scene, when More was chancellor, we have the same attention to the purse and mace, and indifference to other persons, this time it is the Lord Mayor.

The Order of the Procession.—This is taken with some alteration from Hall. The monks of the abbey are turned into choristers. The Duke of Norfolk was in France, and his brother represented him, &c.

A lively flourish of trumpets; then enter—
1. Two judges;
2. Lord Chancellor with the purse and mace before him;
3. Choristers singing;
4. Mayor of London bearing the mace, &c.

Now the chancellor had, as we have seen, on certain occasions to carry the purse himself. But it is hard to make the Lord Mayor carry his own mace. Sir Steven Peacock, who was mayor when Anne Boleyn was crowned, had worked very hard and been of great service in collecting funds, &c., for the coronation. This was Cromwell's great device, for he hoped by the magnificence of the ceremony to reconcile England to the change in religion, and he had forced contributions from all parts and a good deal from the City with the help of the Lord Mayor, and the latter, no doubt, attended in great state, and if he or some ex-lord mayor had written or assisted to write this play, he might as well have described his own part as—

>   *Enter—*
> 1. The Common Serjeant.
> 2. The Recorder.
> 3. The City Remembrancer.
> 4. The City Marshal.
> 5. The Mace and Sword borne by the proper Officers.
>   THE LORD MAYOR.
>   *   *   *   *   *
>   The Lord Chancellor with the Seals in his Pocket,
>   &c., &c.

The last time the Lord Chancellor is referred to, we have the inside of the council chamber, with the chancellor in the second chair, the archbishop outside. This follows the story told in "Fox's Book of Martyrs." There is a dispute between Cromwell and Gardiner which the chancellor stops, and then in due form he puts the question to the council as to Cranmer's being sent to the Tower, as Bacon no doubt often had put the question from his seat. It is difficult for one who is not a privy councillor, to know whether this scene is correctly drawn or not, but apparently it is described by one who knew, as the speech of the chancellor shows; addressing Cranmer, he says:—

> Then thus for you my lord. It stands agreed,
> I take it, by all voices, that forthwith
> You be conveyed to the Tower a prisoner;
> There to remain, till the king's further pleasure
> Be known unto us: Are you all agreed, lords?
>
> *All.* We are.

It is no doubt a matter of opinion only, but it seems to me that not only are there traces of that legal knowledge and acquaintance with our law courts and their proceedings which we find in so many of the other plays, but that this knowledge extends more particularly in the play to the chancellorship and its surroundings, which are dealt with and brought into the play to the neglect of other and equally important details; and that it would not be an unfair inference, if the authorship of this play had to be discovered, if we attributed it in part to some one who joined with legal training an intimate acquaintance with the habits and customs of the chancellor. And I think that as Bacon was the only living lawyer who, at the time the Folio was published in 1623, was or had been Lord Chancellor, if we are looking for some one who might have assisted the author, we might fairly select him; and I think this view will be in some measure supported if we see what are the surrounding circumstances connected with this play.

CHAPTER X.

THE HISTORY OF THE PLAY OF HENRY THE EIGHTH.

IN the previous Chapter, I have collected the passages in " Henry VIII.," which, in my opinion, show that the author was assisted by some legal friend, who was not only a lawyer, but one who showed a special and intimate knowledge of the chancellorship; and as the person who would best fulfil these conditions was Bacon, it seemed not unreasonable to suppose that he might have assisted in the authorship of this play. There are, in addition, several circumstances connected with its history, so far as we can ascertain it, which, I think, support this view.

The play of " Henry the Eighth " occupies a very peculiar position, it is the only one attributed to an author other than Shakespeare. Doubts have been suggested whether Shakespeare wrote " Titus Andronicus," the first part of " Henry VI.," &c., the first of these plays not being considered to be in Shakespeare's style. But " Henry VIII." would be gladly admitted to be Shakespeare's were it not that the commentators have nearly all agreed that it has been altered, or some say tampered with, by Jonson. The reasons for which opinion I will refer to in their place.

As far as we can ascertain the facts connected with this play, they appear to be these, Cavendish gives us

HISTORY OF THE PLAY OF HENRY THE EIGHTH. 259

a description of how the king visited Wolsey at York House, in the midst of an entertainment he was giving.

"I have seen the king suddenly come in thither in a mask, with a dozen of other maskers, all in garments like shepherds, made of fine cloth of gold and fine crimson satin paned, and caps of the same, with visors of good proportion of visnomy; their hair, and beards, either of fine gold wire, or else of silver, and some being of black silk, *having sixteen torch bearers* besides their drums, and other persons attending upon them, with visors, and clothed all in satin, of the same colours. And at his coming, and before he came into the hall, ye shall understand, that he came by water to the water-gate, without any noise; where *against his coming*, were laid charged many *chambers*, and at his landing they were all shot off, which made such a rumble in the air that it was like thunder.

The ladies are alarmed, but Wolsey reassures them, and sends the chamberlain and controller to see who they are, and he reports the arrival of some noblemen and strangers at his (Wolsey's) bridge, as ambassadors from some foreign prince. The Cardinal says, "I shall desire you, because ye can speak French, to encounter and receive them," &c. Now, all this is closely followed in the play. The only difference is that, perhaps by design, Wolsey picks out Sir Edward Neville for the king. In the play, in one of the voluminous stage directions, we find not only the king and his twelve maskers, but also the sixteen torch-bearers, so closely does the author follow Cavendish. I think Shakespeare, the actor and stage-manager, would not have crowded his already very full scene with so many supernumeraries. For it must be remembered that there was the Cardinal *attended*, the guests, the banqueting table; then the king and his companions, who had to march before Wolsey and salute him; and the sixteen torch-bearers one would have thought would be rather in the way on a small stage. But to return to the history. It appears from Cavendish that Wolsey knew of the visit, as he had the chambers ready loaded. The word chamber is no longer used for the name of a piece. But every gun has, as we know, its chamber where the powder goes, besides the body of the gun and the muzzle. These chambers, therefore, I suppose, were what a gun would be if all the rest were cut away: something like small mortars.

Now, we learn from outside sources, that on the 29th June, 1613, the Globe Theatre was burned down, the cause of the fire being attributed to the discharge of the pieces (chambers) that were used to give effect to the coming of the king to Wolsey's house.[1] Sir H. Wotton, in his letter of 2nd July, 1613, speaks of a *new play* acted by the king's players at the Bankside, called "All is true," and of "certain cannons shot off at the king's entry to a masque at the Cardinal Wolsey's house." And in an MS. letter of Thomas Larkin to Sir Thomas Pickering, dated "London, this last day of June," 1613, the fact is thus related—

"No longer since than yesterday, while Burbage and his companie were acting at the Globe the play of Henry VIII., and there shooting of certain chambers in way of triumph, the fire catched," &c.

Now, as we have seen, this incident is in the present play (Act I. Scene 4), where we find that when the king is approaching York House, the stage direction is—

Drum and trumpets within; chambers discharged.

---

[1] Variorum Edition, vol. xix. p. 307.

HISTORY OF THE PLAY OF HENRY THE EIGHTH.

If these chambers were like mortars, fired upwards, it is easy to understand how the burning wads might fly upwards into the thatched roof. The presence of this incident in both plays for a long time led the commentators to suppose that the two plays were identical. But Dr. Johnson was the first, I believe, to point:—

That neither the Prologue nor Epilogue to this play is the work of Shakespeare, "*non vultus non color*." It appears to me very likely that they were supplied by the friendship or officiousness of Jonson, whose manner they will be perhaps found exactly to resemble.[1]

This suggestion once made appears to have been universally adopted, Malone and Farmer both expressing the same opinion. In fact, Farmer goes further, and said,[1] "I think I now and then perceive his hand in the dialogue." Subsequent writers have carried this idea of Jonson's interference still further. It has been shown, the versification is not Shakespeare's, but of a later style. Mr. Halliwell, speaking "of the immoderate use of lines with the hyper-metrical syllable," says,[2] in an illustrative note—

"There are several critics who take another view," (*i.e.*, that Shakespeare "had suffered himself to be influenced by this disagreeable innovation,"[3]) "and, relying in a great measure on metrical percentages, would have us redolent with this peculiarity, it must have been written by one or the other of those later cotemporaries of Shakespeare who were specially addicted to its use."

Though, as if to show the absurdity of this view, he points out that, by this process of reasoning, Wolsey's

---

[1] Variorum Edition, vol. xix. p. 499.
[2] Second Edition, p. 164.
[3] Page 304.

farewell to greatness, the last speeches of Buckingham, the death scene of Katherine, the speech between Wolsey and Cromwell, and Cranmer's prophecy must be eliminated. In fact, he shows if this test be true, that it is not right to say that Jonson or some one besides Shakespeare tampered with the text, but he actually wrote or re-wrote it. And this is the view taken by Mr. Knight, who says, speaking of this play :—

A theory has been set up that Jonson *tampered* with the versification. We hold this notion to be utterly untenable, for there is no play of Shakespeare's which has a more decided character of unity, nor one from which any passage could be less easily struck out.

Now this "character of unity" which Mr. Knight attributes, and I think correctly, to this play, may be evidence that there has been no partial alteration of the text. And this is confirmed by what Mr. Halliwell says if the test be correct, that nearly all the principal speeches must be considered not Shakespeare's. But this by no means proves that Jonson did not write it as a whole.

I think whatever view is taken upon the further evidence I propose to bring forward to show that Jonson did in fact write or re-write this play, that it must be admitted that the idea is not a new one, nor one that has arisen from a desire to show Bacon assisted Jonson; but that the opinion of many critics has been to show that Jonson did work on the play, founded upon reasons which, if true and are carried to a logical conclusion, establish that practically Jonson was the author of it.

There are, in addition to the authorship of the Prologue and Epilogue and the versification, other reasons which have been brought forward as showing that this play is not Shakespeare's. Thus Steevens says of the line,[1]

    Nor.   One, certes, that promises no element.

"It is remarkable that, in the present instance, the adverb certes must be sounded as a monosyllable. It is well understood that old Ben had no skill in the pronunciation of the French language, and the scene before us seems to have had some touches from his pen. By genuine Shakespeare, certes is constantly employed as a dissyllable."

There are also the Latinisms, which are a peculiarity of Jonson's, and the elliptical expressions, "with which," Mr. Knight says, "the play abounds." But it seems to me two especial points have been overlooked, (a) The general poverty of the language; and (b) the numerous stage directions. The former showing in my view that the work is not by Shakespeare, the latter that it is by Jonson.

    (a) *The Poverty of the Language.*—Mr. Knight says[2] "The elliptical construction and the licence of versification brought the dialogue, whenever the speaker was not necessarily rhetorical, closer to the language of common life." I think this is a very favourable way of stating it; there are no doubt fine passages in the play, but the bulk of the text is very commonplace. Take Norfolk's description of the Field of Cloth of Gold.

    Buck.   I was my chamber's prisoner.
    Nor.   Then you lost
       The view of earthly glory. Men might say,

---

[1] Variorum Edition, vol. xix. p. 315.   [2] Page 431.

> Till this time, pomp was single ; but now married
> To one above itself. Each following day
> Became the next day's master, till the last
> Made former wonders *it's*.[1] To-day, the French,
> All clinquant, all in gold, like heathen Gods,
> Shone down the English, &c.

Compare this very bad prose, for it has no pretence to be called poetry, with Shakespeare's description of Cleopatra :—

> The barge she sat in, like a burnished throne,
> Burned on the water: the poop was beaten gold ;
> Purple the sails, and so perfumed, that
> The winds were love-sick with them; the oars were silver;
> Which to the tune of flutes kept stroke, and made
> The water, which they beat, to follow faster,
> As amorous of their strokes, &c.

I think hardly anyone could suppose these two descriptions were the work of the same person. No doubt Jonson could write very beautiful poetry, and some of his verses are all that could be wished. It may, therefore, be asked why he wrote such wretched prose here; the answer I give is, because he was doing what he was not accustomed to do, *i.e.*, putting English history into blank verse.

(b) *The Stage Directions in "Henry VIII."*—I think it is universally admitted that the stage directions in "Henry VIII." are most elaborately set out. Now any one who turns to Jonson's "Masques" must recognize, I think, where these stage directions come from. We have most of Jonson's "Masques," written by himself, and in them we find he has carefully set out a kind of note of the dances and pantomime which

---

[1] This is simply atrocious.

took place, *e.g.*, the following is taken from the "Golden Age Restored"[1]:—

> The EVILS *enter for the Antemasque and* DANCE *to two drums, trumpets, and a confusion of martial music. At the end of which* PALLAS *re-appears showing her shield. The Evils are turned to statues.*

In "Henry VIII." we find similar descriptions of the movements the author required. To take a short example, when Katherine is called before the Court, the stage direction is—

> *The Queen makes no answer, rises out of her chair, goes about the Court, comes to the King, kneels at his feet, then speaks.*

There are many others, one of the best known is the description of the vision. It is well known[2] that it was not Shakespeare's custom to write these directions, he sometimes gave the cue for them in the text, but working with his fellow players, he could arrange what is technically called "business" on the stage itself. But Jonson's "Masques" were written for amateurs, the Queen and her ladies, and he appears to have acquired the habit of writing out these stage directions at great length. But in the Folio of 1623, I think we shall find that "Henry VIII." is the only play that has these copious instructions. There are the ordinary exits and entrances, and sometimes a short note, as "Witches dance and vanish." Jonson in his plays, as we have them in the Folio and Quarto, did not write out these directions at length, any more than Shakespeare did. But he had for a long time devoted himself to writing masques, and there, as I have said, we have ample proof of his practice.

---

[1] Vol. 3, p. 102.   [2] P. 289, *post*.

The special knowledge, &c., contained in the Play.—It is not advisable to enter into more subjects which are likely to be disputed than are necessary. I think, therefore, the play of "Henry VIII." may be, at least, taken as a play that it is supposed Jonson in some way interfered with; that by many he is supposed to have written the Prologue and Epilogue, and in some places to have tampered with or written the text; whether he did so in 1613 or 1614, when the new Globe was opened, as some suppose, or not, is immaterial, because if the play was one for which he was in any way responsible, it is not unreasonable to suppose that he may have revised it when he was preparing it for the press. And when we come to the play itself, I think we shall see that there is evidence that some revision must have taken place after Bacon's fall, and I also think there can be but little doubt that Bacon helped him. And the reasons I have for saying this, is, the knowledge displayed in this play, not only of law, but of all the ceremony that surrounds a Lord Chancellor, whether in Court or in the Council Chamber, and because we have not Wolsey as he truly was, but altered to resemble Bacon.

The Prologue.—The Prologue, if read in one way, supports in a very remarkable manner the view that Jonson altered or tampered with the text of the play. It commences with—

> I come no more to make you laugh; things now,
> That bear a weighty and a serious brow,
> Sad, high, and working, full of state and woe,
> Such noble scenes as draw the eye to flow,
> We now present. . . . .
>   Only they,
> That come to hear a merry, bawdy play,

HISTORY OF THE PLAY OF HENRY THE EIGHTH. 267

> A noise of targets; or to see a fellow
> In a long motley coat, guarded with yellow,
> Will be deceived.

If we refer to the account in verse of the burning of the Globe in 1613, these latter words apparently refer to the play as it was in those days. We see that it had the same scene, with the discharge of the chambers when the king came to Wolsey's house; but we also learn that there was an important part played by the Fool.

Wolsey had a fool in his house (whom he gave to the king), who was so attached to Wolsey that it was necessary to send six yeomen to conduct him to the king. Campbell says of this incident:[1] "A fool was so necessary to the establishment of a Lord Chancellor, that we shall find one in the household of Sir Thomas More"; adding, with playful sarcasm, "It is very doubtful when lord chancellors ceased to have about them any such character." Now, that this or some other fool played a principal part in the play of 1613, is shown by the following lines :—

> Out runne the knightes, out runne the lordes,
>   And there was great adoe;
> Some lost their hats, and some their swords,
>   Then out runne Burbage too;
> The reprobates, though drunk on Monday,
>   Prayed for the fool and Henry Cundye.
> *Refrain.* Oh, sorrow, pittiful sorrow! and yett all this is
>   true!

The commentators seem to think that the last line means that Cundye played the part of the fool. I do not see why. But it is evident that whoever played

---

[1] "Lives of Chancellors," vol. 1, p. 489.

this part, it was of sufficient importance to be mentioned with the name of Burbage, &c. Now in the 1623 play, this part is wanting, and the author of the Prologue says in words that those who came there to see him would be deceived. Why should they come there to see him if they did not think they were about to see the play of 1613, in which he appeared? And it was in consequence, so it seems to me, of the old play being altered and having lost its character of a merry licentious play, and being now sad, high, and working, full of state and woe, that the Prologue was written to prevent the audience being disappointed and perhaps noisy. It seems, therefore, in one view, at all events, of the Prologue, that it states in effect that the old play has been altered, and as we find evidence of Jonson's handiwork in the text, and the Prologue is generally admitted to be written by him, the natural conclusion is that he altered the play, and takes care in his Prologue to warn the audience that he has done so.

If this be so, it is immaterial to inquire whether the 1613 play, which is described as a new play, was Shakespeare's or not. Shakespeare had by 1613 retired, as far as we know, and was living at Stratford. He is not mentioned as being at the representation; but however this may be, if we have the fact that Jonson altered the play of 1613, we have these questions to consider: Why did he do it? how did he do it? and when?

The answer to the first question, if he did it, is, I think, because of his friendship with Bacon. I can think of no other reason why he should alter Shakespeare's work, or introduce his own as Shakespeare's. He has told us that he loved Shakespeare this side of idolatry, but in reality he was to the last intensely jealous of him. Years after Shakespeare was dead, and Bacon too, in 1629 Jonson produced his "New Inn" —a play deservedly damned on its first night. It was not allowed to be finished. In many ways he attempted to copy Shakespeare's method; we have a girl masquerading as a boy, and then appearing as a girl, &c. Jonson thereupon wrote an ode to himself, in which he tries to derive comfort from the fact that the critics were all wrong.

> Come, leave the loathed stage,
>   And the more loathsome age,
> Where pride and impudence in faction knit,
>   Usurp the chair of wit;
> Indicting and arranging every day,
>   *Something they call a play.*[1]
>
> *   *   *   *   *
>
> If they love lees, and leave the lusty wine,
> Envy them not their palates with the swine.
>
> *No doubt some mouldy tale,*
>   *Like Pericles, and stale*
> As the shrieve's crusts, and nasty as his fish,
>   Scraps out of every dish,
> Thrown forth and raked into the common tub,
>   May keep up the pay club :
> These sweepings do as well
>   As the best ordered meal,
> For who the relish of these guests will fit,
> Needs set them but the other's basket of wit.

I think these lines, which clearly point to Shakespeare, show that his old feeling of jealousy was still there, and though Dr. Johnson speaks of friendship or officiousness, I think it is difficult to realise that

---

[1] Bethell's "What you are pleased to call your Mind," is not so original as one supposes.

Jonson would re-write a play like "Henry VIII." and give Shakespeare the merit of it, either from officiousness or friendship, as far as Shakespeare was concerned. But with Bacon it was different; Bacon had often got Jonson to write masques for him, and we know that down to the last Jonson had the highest admiration for the great man, who no doubt had won his heart by what in those days would be called his gracious condescension.

Now, with regard to the friendship existing between Bacon and Jonson, I have already shown that this was so,[1] when Bacon was Chancellor, and even then was of old date, and Jonson tells us it was renewed after Bacon's fall. His well-known words are:—

My conceit to his person was never increased towards him by his place or honours, but I have and do reverence him for his greatness that was only proper to himself, in that he seemed to me ever by his work, one of the greatest of men and most worthy of admiration that had been in many ages. In his adversity I ever prayed that God would give him strength; for greatness he could not want. Neither could I condole in a word or syllable for him as knowing no accident could do harm to vitiate, but rather help to make it manifest.

The next question is, How did Jonson do it unless with the assistance of some legal friend as Shakespeare had in some of his plays? Where did Jonson get that intimate knowledge of trial for treason, the constitution of the papal courts and their procedure, the inner mystery of the council chamber and all its ceremony, unless he also had a legal friend? If so, who was his legal friend? The only one we know of is Bacon. This may be another coincidence. Besides,

---

[1] *Ante*, p. 171.

there is nothing in Jonson's writings that shows he was capable of constructing a play like "Henry VIII." Compare the arrangement of the scenes in the play and the general plot, if we may use the word, for an historical drama, with that of the "New Inn." I do not think there is any reason to suppose Jonson capable of re-writing the play, as it must have been, changing it from a merry to a serious drama without aid.

The last question is, When did he do this? It must have been after 1613 if he altered the play of that date: we have no other information. If the earlier play was Shakespeare's, Jonson would hardly have tampered with it during Shakespeare's lifetime, *i. e.*, before the 23rd April, 1616. And Bacon would not have had the great experience of having filled the highest position his profession offered him and of having lost it. In fact, I do not believe Bacon himself was able to write, or help to write, such a play before he had had and lost all. He was, to mention only one thing, too busy, too full of the pride and pomp of place, I think, to take to the serious work of writing such a work. And to conclude what I have to say about this play, when we come to Spedding's history of Bacon's career after his fall, we shall find evidence of his being at work upon what was, I think, this very play.

CHAPTER XI.

CIRCUMSTANCES WHICH CONNECT BACON WITH THE PUBLICATION OF THE FIRST FOLIO IN 1623.

I THINK I have collected a considerable number of circumstances connected with the publication of the first folio which warrant the belief that the legal friend who assisted Shakespeare was no other than Bacon, and I think this belief will be considerably strengthened when we consider the story of Bacon's life after his fall as told by Mr. Spedding in his seventh volume of "Bacon's Letters and Life."

As soon as Bacon found that he was to be prosecuted in earnest, and neither the king nor Buckingham could prevent his trial, he appears for a short time to have thought of death, and Mr. Spedding gives us his will drawn up in haste dated the 10th April, 1621,[1] and also a psalm, which our author says was composed certainly before the 18th April and, probably, at the date of the will.[2] But this seems to have passed away, and he made notes of the judgment that had been passed upon persons who had received bribes like he had. These notes, which have come down to us, were probably copied and handed to

---

[1] Spedding, p. 228.
[2] Page 227.

Lord Hunsdon as a kind of brief, for we find, in the notes of the proceedings in the Lords, the following—

"Hunsdon delivered some notes of judgments against Poole, Thorpe, &c., read, and he received the notes back again."

This agrees with Bacon's notes which commence with notes upon Michal de la Pole's case and then observations upon Thorpe's case. But it was of no avail, and sentence was duly passed upon him—

1. A fine of 40,000*l*.
2. Imprisonment in the Tower during the king's pleasure.
3. To be for ever incapable of any office, place, or employment in the state or commonwealth.
4. Never to sit in Parliament, nor come within the verge of the Court.

This judgment was delivered on the 3rd May, 1621, and no doubt was a very severe one. We have nothing to do with the merits of the case, but only to trace what was Bacon's life subsequent to this date. His political and professional careers were brought to an abrupt termination; but after a short—very short—detention in the Tower, not more than a few days, we find him writing in Latin to the Spanish ambassador, that—

Age, fortune and even my genius call me, that, leaving the theatre of civil affairs, I may give myself to letters and instruct the actors themselves and serve posterity.[1]

Mr. Spedding tells us the true information of Mr. Bacon's years is to be looked for in his books. But all that I can learn from Mr. Spedding that he actually produced after this date was the "History of Henry the VII." and two volumes or parts of his "Natural History," not very much work for a man of his active powers of composition, especially when we

---

[1] Page 285.

find, as I think we shall, that the "Henry VII.," the more important of the two, was an old manuscript that had been lying about Bacon's chambers for perhaps many years.[1] I pass over his correspondence with Buckingham and others with regard to his being allowed to live in London, from which he was precluded by the fourth article of his sentence, viz., his exclusion from the verge of the court; and how he managed to turn the fine of £40,000 into a blessing in disguise by having it assigned by the king to persons nominated by himself. Thus the king not only forbore to enforce it, but it served as a protection to Bacon against his own creditors, as the outstanding fine being unsatisfied was in the nature of a judgment over his property. But I propose to come to the 8th October, 1621, when he states in the draft of a letter which he has left us in his own handwriting addressed to the king :—

To the King,

It may please your most excellent Majesty,

I do very humbly thank your Majesty for your generous remission of my fine. I can now (I thank God and you) die and make a will.

I desire to do, for the little time God shall send me life, like the merchants of London, which, when they give over trade, lay out their money upon land. So, being freed from civil business, I lay forth my poor talent upon those things which may be perpetual, still having relation to do you honour with those powers I have left.

I have therefore chosen to write the reign of King Henry the Seventh who was, in a sort, your forerunner, and whose spirit as well as whose blood is dualled upon your Majesty.

I durst not have presumed to entreat your Majesty to look

---

[1] *Post.*

over the book and correct it, or at least to signify what you would have amended. But since you are pleased to send for the book, I will hope for it.

There is no evidence that this letter was ever sent. We have many drafts of letters, some of which I may have to refer to, which there is reason to believe represent only what Bacon would have said or written, not what he did, rather notes of what he intended upon certain contingencies happening. But however this may be, whether the king had desired to see the work, or we only have what Bacon would have written if he had so desired, I think there is sufficient evidence that the work was in existence as early as 8th October, 1621.

Now this work Mr. Spedding[1] describes as—

"A work which, done under every advantage, would have been a rare specimen of skill, diligence, and spirit in the workman; but for which—begun as it was immediately after so tremendous an overthrow, and carried on in the middle of so many difficulties in the present and anxieties for the future—it would be hard to find a parallel."

Again he speaks of it as "A work of this order being the first-fruit of a single long vacation," &c. And I think Bacon's own words would suggest that he had at least recently written the work; but I do not think this was the case. I quite agree with all that Mr. Spedding has said of it, and the high eulogium he has put upon it, *i.e.*,

"As a study of character in action, and a specimen of the art of historical narrative, it comes nearer to the merit of Thucydides than any English history that I know."

---

[1] Page 302.

But I do not think it was written as a new work at this time for reasons I shall give hereafter.

Whenever the "History of Henry VII." was written, it is to be noticed that the play of "Henry VIII.," taken in connection with it, completes the plays which otherwise end with "Richard III.," so that, taking the two former with the others, we have a continuous covering of English history from Richard II. to Henry VIII.

Now we find from the documents, which have come down to us, and are to be found in Vol. VII. of Spedding's "Bacon," that early in 1622 (March, 1621-22) Bacon had written[1] in Greek characters notes for an interview that he hoped might take place with the king. Amongst them we find that he intended to propose to the king that his pen should be employed actively in recompiling the laws, &c., or contemplatively going on with the story of Henry VIII. This, I believe, is the earliest notice we have that Bacon contemplated writing or telling the story of this king. It appears that at this time the manuscript of "Henry VII." had been returned by the king, and had been printed, and was ready, and was out before the end of March, and might be bought for six shillings; and in due course copies were sent to the king and Duke of Buckingham, and afterwards to the Queen of Bohemia. But we hear nothing of "Henry VIII." except incidentally.

Thus, Mr. Spedding tells us that on the 10th January, 1622-23, Sir T. Wilson reported to the king that Bacon had applied to him for such papers as he had in his custody relating to Henry VIII.'s time.

---

[1] Page 352.

And that on the 10th February Sir T. Wilson had been directed by the king to supply him [Bacon] with any papers he might require. And that it was generally believed that Bacon was writing the life of Henry VIII. appears by an extract Mr. Spedding gives us from a letter written by Chamberlain on the 10th February, 1622-23 :—

That Lord [Bacon] busies himself about books, and hath set out two lately, "Historia Ventorum" and "De Vitâ et Morte," with promises of more. I have not seen either of them because I have not leisure ; *but if the life of Henry VIII., which they say he is about*, might come out after his own manner, I should find time and means enough to read it.

Bacon in a letter to Buckingham, then in Spain, of the 21st February, 1622-23, asks to be remembered to the Prince (Charles I.), "who, I hope ere long, will make me leave King Henry VIII. and set me on work in relation of his Highness's heroical adventures."

Now it should be remembered that about this date the first folio of Shakespeare's works must have been going through the press, or being prepared for it. And I think I shall be able to show strong reasons for believing that Bacon was not at this time writing the life of Henry VIII., as he led the world to believe, but was assisting Jonson to write the play of that name, as we find it in the folio. It is with this in view that it becomes necessary to watch such evidence as we have very closely. It appears that the Prince (Charles) took an interest in this life of Henry VIII. ; but we shall find, notwithstanding Bacon's desire to please him, that he makes excuses for not going on with the work, for in a letter to Mr. Toby Matthew, (26th June, 1623), he says—

Since you say the Prince hath not forgot his commandment touching my history of Henry VIII., I may not forget my duty. But I find Sir Collier who poured forth what he had in my other work somewhat dainty of his materials in this.

With this excuse he proceeds to say that—

"My labours are now most set to have those works which I had formerly published, as that of 'Advancement of Learning,' that of 'Henry VII.,' that of 'The Essays' being retractate and made more perfect, well translated into Latin by the help of some good pens which forsake me not."

This we know was done, and some consider that Ben Jonson's was one of the good pens that helped him.

And he afterwards writes to the Prince himself—

For Henry VIII., to deal truly with your Highness, I did so despair of my health this summer, I was glad to choose some such work as I might compass within days, so far was I from entering into a work of length.

That the Prince was undoubtedly interested in the proposed life of Henry VIII. is confirmed by Dr. Rawley's dedication of Bacon's "Sylva Sylvarum," after Bacon's death, to the Prince, now Charles I., wherein he says, if Bacon had lived—

"Your Majesty e'er long had been invoked to the protection of another History, whereof not nature's kingdom as in this, but those of your Majesty's (during the Time and *Raigne of King Henry the Eighth*), which since it died under the designation meerely, there is nothing left; but your Majesty's Princely goodnesse graciously to accept of the Undertaker's Heart and Intentions, who was willing to have parted for a while with his darling *Philosophie* that he might have attended your royal commandment in that other worke."

The facts, therefore, that stand upon record, are that Bacon gave out, as early as March, 1622, that he was about to write the life of Henry the Eighth, that some months afterwards, in July, 1623, he asked permission to have the documents in possession of Sir T. Wilson to use for this purpose. That notwithstanding Sir T. Wilson was authorized by James to give him these papers, and Charles had asked him to go on with this work, he only excuses himself; and after his death we have only a short commencement of the life which, Rawley says, was only one morning's work, which consists only of mere introductory matter which would hardly occupy a page of this book, and shows no sign of requiring any State papers.

Except this short note there is no reason to suppose that he ever put pen to paper on the subject of The Life of Henry the Eighth. In fact Dr. Rawley says so; he tells us on the one hand, that he "was trusted with his lordship's writings, even to the last," and on the other, that the life that Bacon was to write "died under the designation meerely." Whereas Bacon, writing to Buckingham 21 February, 1622-23, just when the Folio would be going through the press, speaks of being made to leave King Henry VIII., though when, apparently, the Folio was published he tells the Prince that the work was too long for him to attempt. There is one solution of these inconsistencies which I venture to suggest, and that is, Bacon may have originally contemplated writing the life of Henry VIII. But that he very early changed the idea, and only kept up the pretence that he was engaged on it, because he wanted a pretext for getting the State Documents from Sir T. Wilson, that he might help Jonson to re-write the old play of "Henry VIII.," so as to create sympathy for his own case.

CONCLUSION.

To sum up the facts which seem to point to Bacon as Shakespeare's assistant, I have already said that though there may not be that direct proof, which a jury requires to convict a prisoner of a crime, yet it does seem that, when the facts are ascertained, they do constitute a very strong chain of circumstantial evidence, which we may give effect to, as we are not seeking to convict Bacon of a crime, but bringing home to him an honour which he was foolish enough not to appreciate when alive. But, supposing it were a crime, say a murder, that was proved not to be a suicide; that suspicion pointed to a particular individual; that this individual was found preparing a poison or acquiring a weapon, which might have caused the death; that he was giving a false account of his movements, and that he was found loitering about the spot where and at the time there was reason to believe the crime was committed, no one would dispute that, even if the jury did not convict, there could be but little real doubt. Now, these circumstances are to be found in Bacon's case.

Somebody assisted Shakespeare, as he did not find the law himself.	It was not suicide, *i.e.*, somebody else did it.
The parallel passages and expressions which have been collected by Mr. Donnelly and others point to Bacon.	Suspicion is directed to a particular person, A. B.
Bacon is found to have prepared the "Promus," and to have asked for and obtained the papers relating to Henry VIII.	A. B. is found to have possessed the poison or weapons with which the crime may have been committed.
Bacon obtained the latter by pretending he wanted them for a history of Henry VIII.	A. B. gave a reason for procuring these, which upon investigation appears to be untrue.
As far as can be gathered, Bacon assisted in the production of the "Comedy of Errors" at Gray's Inn in 1594, and in the writing of "Henry VIII.," in 1623.	On more than one occasion the said A. B. was found at the place and time where the crime or crimes might have been committed.

It is, after all, a question of evidence. As I stated originally, I had no theory to support, but my object was to see if, amidst all the mystery that surrounded Shakespeare and his works, there was any real foundation for the Baconian theory. I have tried to ascertain the facts, and what I have ascertained, or thought I had, I have given to the reader. It is for him to challenge my facts if they are wrong, and my conclusions if he will not accept them.

In the supplementary chapter, I have inserted certain matters of interest connected with Shakespeare, Bacon, and Jonson, which I thought might interfere with the main argument if not kept apart from it.

SUPPLEMENTARY CHAPTERS.

I PROPOSE in these Chapters to deal with certain matters which illustrate and confirm, in my opinion, the view taken in the previous pages, *i.e.*, that whilst legal knowledge is found in some plays, legal ignorance is shown in others, so that the Poet must have been assisted in his law. In working out the evidence, it seemed better not to overload the body of the argument with extraneous matter, but to confine the reader's attention to the real issue; but, that being dealt with, a few words on what one might term matters of corroboration do not seem out of place.

CHAPTER I.

THE ACTOR-AUTHOR.

I HAVE dealt with the legal author and have shown there is good evidence that Shakespeare was the principal author.

This is, I think, confirmed by another discovery that an inquirer might make, from an examination of the plays of Shakespeare, which is that the legal knowledge including the familiarity with the habits and thoughts of lawyers, which I have so often referred to in the previous pages, is balanced, as it were, by a similar knowledge of the stage and the manners and customs of actors; that is to say, acquaintance with forensic life and with life behind the scenes seems to be equally present, or rather whilst the legal knowledge is wanting, as I have shown in some of the plays, knowledge of the theatre seems to be present in some form or other in all the plays I have read for the purposes of this study.

It has often been suggested that Shakespeare was a physician, a soldier, &c., and one ingenious writer has shown that he uses the technical language of a printer, which he suggests he must have acquired by himself being a printer. Be that as it may, we have neither in the passages that refer to the law, nor in those that refer to acting, mere solitary examples, but something that seems to be worked into the very fabric, and to be part of the material itself.

In dealing with this evidence which to my mind shows knowledge of stage life, I feel some diffidence, as I have not had the training of an actor, dramatist, or manager, nor have I ever experienced the difficulties of placing a play upon the stage; and as I do feel qualified to speak of the evidence of legal training, having some experience as a lawyer, so I hesitate to express an opinion on matters with which I have had no special knowledge. It is for this reason that I have left this part of the inquiry to be dealt with apart from the main argument.

This evidence may be considered under three heads.

First, the continual references made to acting and the illustration drawn from it, which in many ways resemble the legal allusions already referred to.

Secondly, the workmanlike way in which the movement and action of the actors on the stage is worked up with and into the dialogue.

Thirdly, the continual references to the women's parts being played by boys, and the difficulties arising therefrom, such as the boys growing too tall, their voices changing, &c., &c.

With regard to the first heading. Many of these references are so well known, such as the "Seven Ages of Man," it seems almost idle to refer to "All the world's a stage."

We have continual references to players and playing parts, and the stage, but our author does more—he describes particular actors and the effect they produce: as in Hamlet's advice to the players, wherein he speaks of the robustious periwig-pated fellow who tears his passion to rags, and the clown who delays the action of the piece to make barren spectators laugh ; again he tells us—

> In a theatre, the eyes of men,
> After a well graced[1] actor leaves the stage,
> Are idly bent on him that enters next.

Other references are perhaps not so well known, thus in "Troilus and Cressida" we have—

> And, like a strutting player,—whose conceit
> Lies in his hamstring, and doth think it rich

---

[1] Shakespeare was very fond of this word *grace*, by it he generally refers, I think, to the unspoken part of acting, sometimes called "business" or "action."

>   To hear the *wooden dialogue* and sound
>   'Twixt his stretched footing and scaffoldage.[1]
>
> *   *   *   *
>
>   Now play him[2] me, Patroclus,
>   Arming to answer in a night alarm,
>   And then, forsooth, the faint defects of age
>   Must be the scene of mirth; to cough and spit,
>   And with a palsey-fumbling on his gorget,
>   To shake in and out the rivet.

So in "Richard III." we have Gloster and Buckingham in the Tower—

> *Glo.* Come, cousin, cans't thou quake, and change thy
>   Murder thy breath in the middle of a word,— [colour?
>   And then again begin, and stop again,
>   As if thou wert distraught, and mad with terror?
> *Buck.* Tut, I can counterfeit the deep tragedian;
>   Speak, and look back, and pry on every side,
>   Tremble and start at wagging of a straw,
>   Intending[3] deep suspicion: ghastly looks
>   Are at my service, like enforced smiles;
>   And both are ready in their office,
>   At any time, to *grace* my stratagems.

There are other allusions to life on the stage and references to play-acting, to which I need not make more reference; but I think there can be no doubt that there is sufficient evidence to show that our author was a close observer of the actors of his day.

Secondly, we have the intimate connection between the dialogue and the action or business, which runs on with the spoken words. I think the mere poet, at least in those days, wrote principally for the effect he might produce by his verses, and in many cases the dialogue might almost be carried on by actors sitting in chairs. But in these

---

[1] This reference to the stamp and clatter of not the stage-struck but stage-striking tragedian is very happy. I suppose the strut upon the high wooden heels is the origin of our expression "stilted performance."

[2] Nestor.   [3] Pretending.

plays, although we have occasional set speeches, yet in general, a great deal of movement is going on. I think the peculiarity of Shakespeare's plays is that the action is often not only described but prescribed by the dialogue itself. We find the action suited to the word and the word to the action, as Hamlet says, not as the actor has to do when the words are written down for him, but during the composition of the plays themselves, which, I think, must have been in many places written or arranged upon the stage itself, when the author had the actual business of the play before his eyes.

It is astonishing what amount of incident is sometimes crowded into a scene, and how much is suggested in a few lines. This I believe to be a striking peculiarity of Shakespeare.

The example taken from "Measure for Measure," to which I have already referred, shows what I mean. The judge Escalus, being invited by Clown to look at Froth, at once acquits him of the charge of soliciting the constable's wife. As I have stated, there could be no wit or reason in this if the audience did not see why the judge so acquitted the man, and therefore I have ventured to suggest that the necessities of the piece require that Froth should be made up as a simpleton, and as good-looking as possible. I now propose to refer to some other examples to show how the actor's business is so necessary to give effect to the dialogue, that it becomes "unwritten law." And as some documents are partly printed and partly written, so many scenes lie partly in spoken word and partly in action. In nearly all plays the ability of the actor enables him to add to the piece and interpret it better to the audience by the "business" he adds. But in the plays there are situations and acting that are the author's and not the actor's, though they are not given as stage directions, but are to be gathered from the dialogue.

A very good example of this is the scene where Edgar leads his blind father, as the latter thinks, to the top of the high cliff near Dover. When there, Edgar, who has appeared in the character of a madman, is supposed to leave him. Gloster throws himself down, as he thinks, over the cliff. Edgar comes up to him as a sane person and persuades him he has fallen down the cliff without injury, and then ridicules the appearance he was supposed to have had when Gloster's companion on the top of the cliff; in reality Gloster has only fallen to the ground. This is a little difficult to convey to the audience, except for the dialogue that explains it. In the folio, there are no stage directions given; the extract is too long for insertion here. The same suggestive dialogue is to be found in "Hamlet." In the first scene, two sentinels appear—the one to relieve the other; though as an old soldier, I may point out a slip, inasmuch as a sentry can only be relieved by the officer or non-commissioned officer of the guard. So we should have had a third person introduced. But the challenge and the pass-word are given, and then Francisco, the one relieved, is dismissed by Barnardo, who remains and asks him if he meets

Horatio and Marcellus,
The rivals of my watch, bid them make haste.

(*Enter Horatio and Marcellus*)

is the only stage direction, yet Barnardo must have left the stage upon his beat, for Francisco is alone when he says to himself—

I think I hear them.   Stand! who's there?

a challenge he is hardly entitled to make being relieved. The newcomers answer—"Friends to this ground," &c., ask him who has relieved him, and then Francisco says, "Good night," and exit, probably to re-appear in some other part. Meanwhile, Barnardo has returned, for Marcellus says—

"*Hulla!* Barnardo!"

as if speaking to someone at a distance. Barnardo asks for Horatio, &c., and the conversation continues till the ghost enters. Now, it would make no sense of the dialogue unless

Barnardo was away on his beat when Francisco first greets Horatio and Marcellus.

In the ghost scene, we find the same absence of stage directions, though without the proper action being taken by the actor who plays the ghost, it would be difficult for the audience to appreciate the dialogue. The necessary information as to what that action should be is given in the play itself. On the re-entry of the ghost, Horatio addresses it. In the second quarto there is a stage direction, that during this speech it spreads his arms. This is, however, omitted in the folio; but we learn from the words of Barnardo, who says—

It was about to speake, when the cock crew.

Horatio, when he describes the scene to Hamlet, tells us more explicitly what the ghost has to do—

Ham. Did you not speake to it?
Hor. My lord, I did;
But answer made it none; yet once, methought,
It lifted up its head, and did addresse
Itselfe to motion, like as it would speake;
But, even then, the morning cock crew loud,
And at the sound it shrunk in haste away,
And vanish't from our sight.

Here we have clear directions how the ghost is to act in dumb show. The scene of the ghost's vanishing is thus told—

Hor. Stop it, Marcellus.
Mar. Shall I strike at it with my partizan?
Hor. Do, if it will not stand.
Mar. 'Tis here.
Hor. 'Tis here.
Mar. 'Tis gone. [*Exit* Ghost.

This requires the ghost to appear in different parts of the stage almost simultaneously. And as the conjuror with his three thimbles and one little pea has more peas than one, when he is apparently making it appear and disappear, so there should be behind the scenes more than one ghost, so that as he apparently disappears from one part of the stage, he may almost immediately reappear at another.

It is to be noticed that our author with a great knowledge of human nature, when he makes Horatio describe this scene to Hamlet, carefully causes him to omit all reference to the threats and blows bestowed on the ghost. Hamlet would probably have been offended at the indignity offered to his father's spirit: people like their relations to be respected even when dead.

Now, in this matter of the ghost there are one or two slips which we so constantly find in our author. For instance, Horatio is a fellow-student of Hamlet. He has come to Elsinore to attend the king's funeral. This has taken place some two months before the marriage with the uncle, and this was over and Horatio was such a friend that the sentries communicated to him the fact of the ghost appearing. Yet Hamlet does not know he is in Elsinore, nay, is not quite certain it is Horatio—

For at first Hamlet does not give him his name.
   Enter Horatio, Barnardo, and Marcellus.
Hor. Hail to your lordship!
Ham. I am glad to see you well,
   Horatio,—or I do forget myself.
Hor. The same, my lord, and your poor servant ever.
Ham. Sir, my good friend.

Then the first scene opens as we have seen with Barnardo on duty as a sentry, challenges, countersigns, &c., all of which is dwelt upon as being necessary in consequence of the meditated attack of young Fontinbras; and in the scene with Hamlet, he asks—

  Hold you the watch to-night?

Barnardo and Marcellus answer—
  We do, my lord.

In the second scene with the ghost there is no mention of watch or sentry; all this is forgotten, even Barnardo, the sentry, is absent. For Horatio, Hamlet, and Marcellus walk on together, and when Hamlet follows the ghost to a distant part of the castle Marcellus and Horatio follow him, and, in fact, desert their post, or rather Marcellus does.

There are many other examples in the plays showing how the business of the actors has been sometimes well and sometimes carelessly thought out, and directions given not by marginal notes, but in the dialogue itself, as, for example, the scene where the king is conscience-stricken by the mimic play. See how the action is told by the actors themselves:—

> *Oph.* The king rises!
> *Ham.* What! frightened with false fire?
> *Queen.* How fares my lord?
> *Pol.* Give o'er the play!
> *King.* Give me some light;—away!

Now Ben Jonson, who was, as we shall have occasion to point out, careful to give full directions to his actors, who were mostly amateurs—I mean in his Masques—would probably have given a long note, something like this:—

> [*The King becomes agitated—is unable to keep his seat. This attracts the notice of Ophelia, who calls the attention of the company to it. The Queen becomes anxious, and addresses the King. Hamlet is satirical, and Polonius, as chamberlain, orders the play to stop. The King staggers off the stage, &c.*]

So, in the fencing scene, we have a number of actors each carrying on their different business separately from the others; yet all is necessary to make the dialogue comprehensible. The full stage direction, apparently, would be whilst Hamlet and Laertes are fencing, the king drinks from the cup and then puts the poison in; he then directs an attendant to offer it to Hamlet, who, in the excitement of the contest, puts it on one side; the attendant returns with it to the king, and as he passes the queen she takes the cup and drinks from it; the king tries to warn her but is too late. Meanwhile Hamlet grows hot with his exertion (Burbage, who played the part of Hamlet, is said to have been fat); the queen sends him the cup also, which he again refuses, and then she calls him to her that she may wipe his face. Laertes takes advantage of this interruption to approach the king and tell him that he intends to hit Hamlet in the forthcoming bout. All this is contained in the following dialogue :—

King. Give him the cup.
[*Trumpet sounds and shot goes off.*]
Ham. I'll play this bout first; set by awhile.
Come! another hit; what say you?
Laer. A touch, a touch, I do confess.
King. Our son shall win.
Queen. He's fat and scant of breath.—
Here's a napkin, rub thy pores.
The queen carouses to thy fortune, Hamlet.
King. Gertrude, do not drink.
Queen. I will, my lord ;—
I pray you, pardon me.
King. It is the poisoned cup! It is too late.
Ham. I dare not drink yet, madam;
By and by.
Queen. Come, let me wipe thy face.
Laer. My lord, I'll hit him now.
King. I do not think it.
Laer. And yet, 'tis almost against my conscience.
Ham. Come, for the third.
Laertes, you but dally, &c.

Now, some musicians, it is said, compose at the desk, and others at their instrument. So I think a great part of the dialogue we find in the plays was not written by the author in his study, but was arranged and considered on the stage itself. Some modern play-writers have a small stage made to scale, and representations of the actors, so as to arrange the action of the scene; but it seems, from the ease and smoothness with which some of the dialogues are written, the author must have been in direct communication with the actors themselves, and have seen how the play required to be worked out by the dialogue, and in that way suited the dialogue to the business. Now, if we turn to the other writers of the period, we find little or no traces of this speciality. For the most part we have long speeches that require no action, and might almost be spoken by actors, as I have said, sitting in chairs; and I have come across nothing which strikes me, as the plays do—that some parts were written on the stage itself; no examples of the fitting of the dialogue to the movements of the actors. This view may be wrong. One would like the opinion of some stage manager or leading actor.

There is, however, other evidence of the connection between the author and life in the theatre, both behind and in front of the curtain, which is even stronger. It is Shakespeare's treatment of and references to the boys, who played the women's parts. I have had already to refer to the position of the stage at this period. At the risk of some repetition, I propose to show how the feeling against the stage was increased by the practice of having the female characters played by boys. In doing this, I have little to say that may not be gathered from the pages of Malone and other writers on the subject. But the facts should be brought here before the reader's notice in order that he may understand the point at issue.

The position of the stage in Queen Elizabeth's time was a very peculiar one, owing, perhaps, to the stormy times through which the nation had recently passed. On the one hand, the revival of letters by the dispersing over Europe of the stored-up education of Constantinople by the taking of that city by the Turks had attracted men's attention to the old plays of insolent Greece and haughty Rome, and the Reformation had, by taking away the sanctity of the old Passion Plays, given the intelligence of England a field for display. The world was at peace. Science was only struggling in the womb. Politics were a dangerous pursuit. The higher a man climbed the nearer he seemed to get to the scaffold. And it almost seemed as if the only intellectual pursuit was that of writing verses. On the other hand, the plays were the outcome of the hated Catholic Church, and the Puritans had a strong feeling against the stage and all connected with it. Both feelings seem to have survived to our times. There are those who look upon the stage as the home of immorality, &c. Such persons would allow their children to go to a village circus, but not to a play. There are others who have a tendency to elevate abnormally what after all is only one of the ways men and women choose for getting their living, and throw a glamour upon what, in the majority of cases, is a very hard, over-worked, and over-stocked profession. But in the time of good Queen Bess, feelings ran higher than this. On the one side the puritan party had interest enough to have all strolling players—and the law knew no others—made rogues and vagabonds, except that Leicester, I believe, said if they were the servants of a nobleman, who chose to keep them for his amusement, they should be exempt from the law, and it was so enacted. It followed from this that the two companies of actors who played in London put themselves under the protection of noblemen. Burbage's company, to which Shakespeare belonged, called theirs the Lord Chamberlain's servants. Henslowe's company, whose principal actor was Alleyne, his son-in-law, who left his wealth for founding Dulwich College, called themselves the servants of the *Lord High Admiral*. Elizabeth was too astute to take any active part and identify herself with the actors openly, though she no doubt attended plays and listened to fulsome compliments as in "The Judgment of Paris," by Peele. But James boldly identified himself with the stage. One company was called the King's Company, another the Queen's, and a third the Prince's (Charles). Every student of history knows that the dispute, which in Charles's reign broke out into open war and lost the king his head, had commenced in Elizabeth's reign by disputes about money, was simmering up all through James's, and over-boiled in Charles's time. If there had not been a strong republican element at work, a *modus vivendi* would have been found. But it was not to be, and bad blood was brewing, and one of the ostensible causes of this was the stage; the Puritans would have none of it; the Court party fostered it; and the actors grew rich and spoke of themselves, like army officers do in the present day, as being in the king's service, and perhaps founded the expression of "Her Majesty's Service," that is so commonly seen on the outside of official letters. Down to the present generation I believe, certain companies had the right to call themselves her Majesty's servants. Now, this bitter difference of opinion that existed led, I think, to political results that historians have recounted without, perhaps, knowing their cause.

One of the principal points of attack by the anti-theatrical party were the female characters. Public opinion would not allow them to be played by women, and many persons, no doubt with good cause, objected to their being played by boys, as was the custom in England. As this custom and its results are often mentioned in the plays, I think it is very material for the purposes of this inquiry to put on record such information as can be found as to these boys, their training, &c.

We have some information about these boys in certain papers which were discovered by Halliwell in the Lord Chamberlain's office. These papers related to a dispute between the actors and those who held shares in the theatre. The householders, as those owning these shares were called, took a considerable part of the profits, and the actors the remainder, out of which, as they allege, they had to find the expenses of the theatre, lights, clothes, &c., including authors, and they claimed, I suppose by custom, a right to purchase some of the shares, and at an established price. Now these shares were very valuable, producing a considerable income, and the householders, who had ceased to be actors, did not wish to part with them; they put in an answer to the petition justifying their position. A decree, however, was made that certain of the shares should be sold to the actors. These papers of 1635, as I shall term them, are interesting for the light they throw upon many subjects connected with the theatre in those days. For instance, John Shankes in his answer, says[1] that he—

"Hath still of his own purse supplied the company for the service of his Majesty, with boys, as Thos. Pollard, John Thompson, deceased (for whom he paid 40*l.*)"—

a large sum in those days, computed to be about 200*l.* to 400*l.* at the present value of money.

"Your suppliant having paid his part of 200*l.* (2,000*l.*) for other boys since his coming to the company, John Heniman, Thomas Holcombe, and divers others, and at this time maintains three more for the same service."

So that the boys, it appears, were educated and maintained at the expense of the players, probably in the nature of apprentices.

Another source from which these boys were obtained, or at least the ranks of the players were filled up, was the Queen's Chappell's boys, who were trained by one Evans at the Blackfriars Theatre. This theatre, which was built by Burbage, the father, in 1596, though Payne Collier insisted that "it was built long before and only enlarged in that year," and as it is now suggested, did not hesitate to bring evidence of a most suspicious character to enforce his opinion, was not allowed to be opened for stage plays by Burbage when it was built. A strong opposition was got up on the part of the inhabitants, and in the end it was let to Evans on lease, who had a training school for boys, to which reference will have to be made hereafter. Cuthbert Burbage in his answer, one of the papers of 1635, already referred to, says of this theatre—

Our father (the elder Burbage) purchased it at extreme rates, and made it into a playhouse with great charge and trouble, which after was leased out to one Evans that first set up the boys, commonly called the Queen Majesty's children of the Chappell, in process of time the boys growing up to be men, which were Underwood, Field, Ostler (mentioned

---

[1] Page 482.

among the actors in the First Folio), and were taken to strengthen the king's service (that is, became actors).

A good deal of reference will have to be made to this incident of Evans taking the theatre, for, as we shall see, these boys soon took to acting plays, and for some time became the fashion, much to the disgust of the old actors. Ben Jonson, we shall find in particular, when he had either quarrelled or re-quarrelled with Shakespeare's company, had his plays acted by Evans' boys.

It is, no doubt, not a very wholesome custom, as I have said, to dress and paint up a young lad to represent a beautiful woman, especially as there is some reason to believe that they wore their assumed garb in private life; at least Ben Jonson, as we shall see, gives us one example of this being done. And, as I have stated, one of the principal objections of the Puritan party to the stage was that women's parts were played by boys—not that they liked women to do so. It must, however, be remembered that the boys could only take these parts when comparatively young, and their voices remained unchanged. In the plays we shall see so many references to this fact of the boys growing too tall, their voices breaking—matters which would hardly concern a poet writing in his study—that I consider the plays must have been in some measure at least the work of an actor, or one intimately connected with the stage. To return, however, to the facts we know about these boys.

Malone, in his "History of the Stage," has given us some very curious information about these boy actors. He tells us that in 1591 Nashe, speaking in defence of the English stage, that as players in his time—

"Were not as the players beyond sea . . . . that have common courtezans to play women's parts";

he continues. What Nashe considered as an high eulogy on his country, Prynne has made one of his principal charges against the English stage, and quoted many hundred authorities to prove that—

"Those plays wherein any men act women's parts or wear woman's apparell must needs be sinful, yea, abominable unto Christians."

The grand base of his argument is a text from Scripture, viz., Deut. xxii. 5 :—

The woman shall not wear that which pertaineth unto man, neither shall a man put on a woman's garment.

In a note Malone gives the opinion not only of Martin Luther, but of the learned Jesuit Louvre on this text, the former saying :—

This did not prohibit a woman from carrying the weapons of a man, or a man wearing the clothes of a female to escape danger, to play a trick, or to deceive the enemy, but such things are not to be done seriously and as an accustomed habit, so that the dignity proper for either sex be preserved;

and the latter :—

The gay disguise of dress can be made without sin for the representation of a character in comedy or tragedy, or in a similar case.

Still, no one can say that the objection to boys playing women's parts was altogether without foundation. Ben Jonson, with his rough coarseness, discomfits the puritan Busey, when he objects to the custom. He makes his puppet say :[1]—

Busey. Yes, and my main argument against you is that you are an abomination; for the male among you putteth on the apparel of the female, and the female of the male.[2]
Dom. You lie; you lie; you lie abominably!
Copes. Good, by my troth; he has given him the lie there.
Dom. It is your old stale argument against the players; but it will not hold against the puppets, for we have neither male nor female amongst us, &c.

This attack on the puppets may remind some of us of an attack that was made of recent years upon a puppet show at the Aquarium.

Gifford tells us, in his note to Ben Jonson's plays, that this old stale argument had been urged with great bitterness by

---

[1] Bartholomew Fair, Act V. Sc. 3. [2] This last was not true.

Stubbs and other Puritans of Elizabeth's days, and it appeared from Hawkins that many difficulties were encountered at Cambridge, which then abounded in Puritans, in procuring proper persons to act the parts of Sinda, Rosabella, &c., solely from the unwillingness of the students to put on a female dress which they affirmed it was unlawful for a man to wear.

The Puritans had an equal objection to women acting at all, a practice which did not obtain at all in Shakespeare's time. It is out of the scope of this inquiry to do more than refer to the action of Charles's Queen in allowing herself and ladies to appear on the stage, as they often did in Jonson's "Masques." Malone tells us in a note, Prynne, in conformity with notions which have been stated in the text, inserted in his index these words—

Women actors—notorious w——s;

by which he so highly offended the King and Queen that he was tried in the Star Chamber, and sentenced to be imprisoned for life, expelled Lincoln's Inn, disbarred and disqualified to practise the law, degraded of his degree in the university, to be set in the pillory, his ears cut off, and his book burnt by the common hangman, which rigorous sentence, says Whitelocke, was as rigorously executed.

Prynne's time came, and the stage players, the Court and the courtiers fell together. There was, therefore, a good deal of ill-feeling existing about the stage, even in Shakespeare's time—and as I have said a good deal of bad blood brewing.

To those who are interested in the matter it may not be out of place to say that women did not appear in English theatres till after the Restoration, when some actress, according to tradition, Mrs. Sanderson, in 1663, played Desdemona, though apologies had to be made for the indecorum of women so playing in terms which are given by Mr. Malone, but are not worth repeating here. Men, it appears, also continued to act after the Restoration. Malone says Mr. Kynaston, even after women had assumed their proper rank on the stage, was not only endured but admired—

That, being then very young, he made a complete stage beauty, performing his parts so well (particularly Arthrope and Aglaura) that it has since been disputable among the profession whether any women that succeeded him touched the audience so sensibly as he.

Hitherto we have only considered the facts connected with these boys so far as the same have been preserved. We now have to take ourselves back in imagination to the days of Queen Elizabeth and realize, so far as we are able, the practical effects of boys playing women's parts.

It has already been pointed out that there was only a short period during which this could be done. As a boy grew to manhood his stature increased, his voice changed, and his beard began to grow. We must, for a moment, imagine a company with a skilled youth whose personation of female characters was, as Malone states was sometimes the case, far beyond what a woman could do. We can realize this best perhaps, if we consider a cathedral choir with a boy whose voice has a sweetness that is renowned. He is clever, good looking, and a master of his profession. But the time is coming when he must sing no more as a boy at least. He may in a short time find he has his voice back, but it is that of a man; or he may never again have a voice worth hearing, and he may become a singing master, or may write music, or may turn to something else. This is the story of nearly all the clever singing boys. The few either appear again as great singers, the majority become choir masters or write music, or turn their hand to something else. I think the same story might be told about the boys. It was the story of Field, of Underwood, and Ostler, who are already referred to as commencing their career as the Queen's Chappell boys, and became men actors and are so named in the Folio of 1623. With the rank and file of these boys there might be little interest shown; but at times some boy of exceptional character and aptitude for portraying female characters would be found in the ranks of the company, a boy hard to replace, one who helped to fill the house and could command applause by Juliette or his Viola. We can conceive how anxious the company would feel when the time approached and it became more and more difficult to keep up the illusion; he was growing tall, his voice was reedy, running from one octave to the other at its own sweet will. Now we can, I think, understand the actor appreciating all this, but I do not see why the poet should. The duty of the latter is to write his play, create his characters, the embodiment of his ideas and the carrying it out is not his province unless he were so intimate with the stage as to take an interest in these matters. But even then I do not think he would invite the attention of the audience to the fact that the women's parts were played by men, as we find continually was done in the plays.

Perhaps the best known of these references is made in Hamlet's welcome to the players. In this scene, it may be remembered, Hamlet addresses the head of the company first, but greets the boy who plays the woman's part second, putting him before all the other actors. Good-humouredly he calls attention to his growing height, necessarily a sore point, and hopes his voice is not cracked within the ring, &c. Mr. Knight says that in those days a cracked coin was not passable if the defect went beyond the outside ring or margin; but as a coin loses its ring if cracked, it is evident another interpretation may be put upon what was probably an old theatrical joke, like the old circuit jokes that are told to every newcomer. The scene is as follows:—

In Act II. scene 2, in the stage direction in the folio is—

"Enter four or five players."

This occurs in the middle of a speech in which Hamlet is talking mad nonsense to Polonius which he breaks off and gives the players welcome.

You are welcome, masters: welcome all:—I am glad to see

thee well :—welcome, good friends.—O, my old friend! Thy face is valiant[1] since I saw thee last. Comest thou to beard me in Denmark?

The next person he addresses is the boy who plays the female parts, passing over the other and older actors—

What! my young lady and mistress! By-'r-lady (but), your lady is (grown) nearer to heaven by the altitude of a chopine,[2] higher than (you were) than when I saw you last. Pray God (sir), your voice, like a piece of uncurrent gold, be not cracked within the ring.

He then addresses the rest. In the first quarto, the words are—

"Come on, masters, we'll to't like French falconers, fly at anything we see: come, a taste of your quality; a speech, a passionate speech."

This differs very little from the folio. The sly hit at the French sportsman, which might be written to-day, is preserved. It is to be noticed that the word "vallanced" (in the second quarto "vallanct") is altered wrongly to "valiant" in the folio. But the material point is that the boy is brought forward as the second person, and though one time addressed as "lady," is in the first quarto called "Sir."

In this speech we have a direct reference to the fact that the women's parts were played by boys. We have many others, both directly and indirectly, referring to this secret of the craft.

Thus, in "Midsummer Night's Dream,"[3] we have Flute objecting to playing a woman's part, as he has a beard growing, but Quince replies—

"That's all one. You shall play it in a mask: and you may speak as small as you will."

Julia, in the "Two Gentlemen of Verona," when, as Sebastian, she wins back her lover, makes allusion to this

---

[1] "Vallanced" in the first Quarto, this, Malone explains, is fringed with a beard, and thus gives the cue to the next sentence.

[2] A high heel.   [3] Act I. Scene 2.

practice; she is explaining to Silvia what she, as Julia, is like—

Silvia. How tall was she?
Julia. About my stature; for, at Pentecost,
When all our pageants of delight were played,
Our youth got me to play the woman's part,
And I was trimmed in Madame Julia's gown:
Which served me as a fit, in all men's judgment,
As if the garment had been made for me.

Here, it must be remembered, she is representing that it was as the boy Sebastian she played a woman's part, for as stated before, as Julia, she could not have done so with propriety.

Our author is not content with referring to this custom and calling the audience's attention to it, and thereby running the risk of destroying the illusion with regard to the very female characters in the piece being played. But he delights in grappling with a very complicated position, namely, that of making these boys, acting as women, put on boys' clothes. It would almost seem as if he took a delight in relieving them from their female disguise, and bringing them before the world in their true characters, though, as we shall see, he took some pains to still keep up the belief that the apparent boys were women disguised.

This peculiarity of Shakespeare's of making his female characters masquerade as boys must, as the characters were played by boys, have led to some curious complications. We are accustomed in the present day to see boys' parts played by actresses, and we have little difficulty in knowing that they are women, and as long as the boys in Elizabeth's time were disguised in women's clothes, their sex might be well concealed; but when on the stage they quitted female dresses and appeared as boys, it must have been difficult to keep up illusion. The growing stature, the man-like walk, not to speak of the difference of figure, must have rendered it almost impossible to prevent the audience seeing that it was no woman in a boy's garb, but a lean loined, lanky lout, appearing as he was. I think one result of the absence of women from the stage was the coarseness which we find in the old plays. There are some expressions which are permitted at one time and not at another, and sometimes more licence is given, especially where the idea is to be amusing. The broad joke is to be found in Fielding and even in Marriott—writers, if allowed in other times, who would not be permitted now. But I believe the difference between an indecent joke and one that was not, was always well understood, and I believe there is a good deal in even the plays which would not be there had there been women on the stage. I remember seeing Mrs. Kean play the last act of the "Merchant of Venice," and she toned down the words without destroying the fun, at least so the audience seemed to think. The fun lay in the jealousy excited in the husband, and this could be made as extravagant as was wanted without the *equivoque*. So when in the "Merchant of Venice," we have Gratiano explaining that he gave his wife's ring to a little scrubby boy. A modern audience, who sees a beautiful woman playing the double part, laughs at him, Gratiano, giving himself away; but Shakespeare's audience, no doubt, saw only a true description of the youth who played Nerissa, who, however fascinating a female he made, was in real life a little scrubby boy. This very difficulty Shakespeare appeared to delight in. He, as I have said, seeks many occasions of making the change, though he is artist enough to prepare the audience for the different appearance of the boy *in propriâ personâ* from the woman he is playing, and forewarn them of the saucy strut, the swinging stride, and even descends to details of dress, that cannot well be referred to here, so that the audience may be led to believe that these details are not because the boy was a boy, but because the female character had adopted them to carry out the illusion more completely. All this, to my mind, points to a familiarity with the life behind the scenes, and the desire of the growing boy to emancipate himself from a woman's part, which a manly boy may have despised. All this seems to support the possibility of Shakespeare having gone through the mill himself.

One of the principal uses of dress is to conceal as well as clothe. But at one period the male costume hardly fulfilled this purpose. And we find in the plays reference to this fact, not, as I conceive, Rabelais and writers of that class would refer to it as a basis for some rude joke, but because there was a serious difficulty in supporting the illusion, that the boys were not what they were in fact, but women masquerading.

It is for this reason I conceive the details of such costumes were discussed, as in other cases the manly stride was spoken of. So that when the audience had the boys before them they might still believe them females.

The more one studies the plays the more one is surprised how often we find in the comedies a female character, played as we know by a boy, putting on male attire. We see how skilfully the author works up the situation so that the illusion that it is a woman representing a boy may not be destroyed, and how he, as it were, forestalls any observations that might arise by making the apparent woman discuss, and apparently assume, beforehand those traits and appearances which would betray the true sex of the performer. Thus, we shall see Portia says what she is going to do when she represents a boy. When, in the present day, we have some graceful actress making the speech, the audience is amused at her attempted mimicry. In Shakespeare's time the audience had to be persuaded that what was natural to the boy was going to be assumed.

Portia, in the "Merchant of Venice," thus describes to Nerissa what they will do as boys.[1]

> I'll hold thee any wager,
> When we are both accoutred like young men,
> I'll prove the prettier fellow of the two,
> And wear my dagger with the braver grace,
> And speak, between the change of man and boy

---

[1] Act III. Scene 4.

> With a reed voice; and turn two mincing steps
> Into a manly stride; and speak of frays,
> Like a fine bragging youth; and tell quaint lies
> How honourable ladies sought my love,
> Which I denying, they fell sick and died;
> I could not do with all;—then I'll repent,
> And wish for all that, that I had not killed them.
> And twenty of these puny lies I'll tell,
> That men shall swear I have discontinued school
> Above a twelvemonth. I have within my mind
> A thousand raw tricks of these bragging Jacks,
> Which I will practise.

When the dispute arises between Gratiano and Nerissa about the ring, Nerissa says:—

>   Gave it to a judge's clerk!—but well I know
>   The clerk will ne'er wear hair on's face that had it.
> *Gratiano.* He will, and if he live to be a man.
> *Nerissa.* If a woman live to be a man.
> *Gratiano.* Now, by this hand, I gave it to a youth,—
>   A kind of boy; a little scrubbed boy,
>   No higher than thyself, the judge's clerk;
>   A prating boy, that begged it as a fee.

In "As You Like It," there is the same double play; in fact, here it is threefold, for we have a boy playing Rosalind, who dresses up as a boy to deceive her lover—

"I will speak to him like a saucy lacquey, and under that habit play the knave with him;"

and then tries to induce her lover to make love to her as if she were a woman, and says if he does she will cure him of his love.

Orl. Did you ever cure any so?
Ros. Yes, one; and in this manner. He was to imagine me his love, his mistress; and I set him every day to woo me: At which time would I, being but a moonish youth, grieve, be effeminate, changeable, longing, and liking; proud, fantastical, apish, shallow, inconstant, full of tears, full of smiles; for every passion something, and for no passion truly any thing, as boys and women are for the most part cattle of this colour; would now like him, now loathe him; then entertain him, then forswear him; now weep for him, then spit at him; that I drave my suitor from his mad humour of love, to a living humour of madness.

THE ACTOR-AUTHOR.

Now this is very complicated; there is the actual boy who plays the part, Rosalind, as a woman, and Master Ganymede, the boy she pretends to be. And the fictitious description she gives of herself is, an effeminate youth, neither boy nor woman. The first of these, the actual boy, is supposed not to be before the audience, his personality is suppressed; but we shall see Shakespeare also makes reference to the fact that boys had to play the women's parts.

In "Twelfth Night" we have a description of the boy playing a woman's part, in which she or he masquerades as a boy. Viola, as a boy, insists upon seeing Olivia, and she inquires:—

Of what personage, and years is he?

Malvolio. Not yet old enough for a man, nor young enough for a boy; as a squash is before 'tis a peas-cod, or a codling when 'tis almost an apple; 'tis with him in standing water, between boy and man. He is very well favoured, and he speaks very shrewishly; one would think his mother's milk were scarce out of him.

These are the principal references that I have noticed. In "Richard II.,"[1] I find the expression, "And boys with women's voices"; but I think there is sufficient to show that our author alone of all his contemporaries, as far as I know, except Ben Jonson, has drawn the characters of young boys: has noticed their bragging propensities, their change of voice, their increasing stature, and made frequent reference directly and indirectly to their playing women's parts.

Ben Jonson, it is true, makes reference to this custom in an amusing way, at least, no doubt it was so, when it was more of a novelty than it is now to make reference on the stage to the private individuality of the actor. But it must be remembered that Jonson had the example of Shakespeare before him. And, as I have shown, there is reason to believe that the introduction of the players on the stage in "Hamlet" was an incident that was very likely to have been brought very prominently to Jonson's notice.

---

[1] Act III. Scene 2.

"The Devil is an Ass," a play which is said not to have been acted till 1616, the year of Shakespeare's death, contains some amusing references. One Meerecraft is introduced and made fun of as the author of absurd and ridiculous projects, all of which were to make enormous fortunes, the curious part being that the examples, given as utterly foolish and impracticable, have all become successes, and have no doubt made large fortunes. The first is "the recovery of drowned lands," referring to the draining of the fens, "making gloves out of dog skins," "bottling ale," and "making wine out of raisins." But the play bears upon the present inquiry in the fact that reference is made to a lad, Dick Robinson, who generally played women's parts, but then was, it appears, growing too tall, and was in the piece playing the part of one Wittipol, a man's part. In the course of the play, it was proposed to dress up some man as a woman to carry on an intrigue. One character proposes that Wittipol should do this, but another, separating the actor from his part, wants to have Dick Robinson, and reference is made to Wittipol's being too tall. There is a description given of Dick Robinson, which no doubt is drawn from life; but if Shakespeare's descriptions as given by Portia and others might be compared to a picture by Watteau, Jonson's description resembles one of Hogarth's engravings. *Meerecraft*, after discussing the scheme, says—

<pre>
              Why, this
     Is well, the clothes we have now; but where's this
     If we could get a witty boy, now, Engine,   [lady?
     That were an excellent crack, I could instruct him
     To the true height, for anything takes this Dottrel.
Eng. Why, sir, your best will be one of the players.
Meer. No, there's no trusting them; they will talk of it
     And tell their poets.
Eng.   What if they do; the jest
     Will brook the stage. But there be some of them
     Are very honest lads. There is Dick Robinson,
     A very pretty fellow, and comes often
     To a gentleman's chamber, a friend of mine. We had
     The merriest supper of it there one night.
     The gentleman's landlady invited him   [Robinson,
     To a gossips' feast. Now, he, sir, brought Dick
</pre>

        Drest like a lawyer's wife, amongst them all.
        I lent him clothes: but to see him behave it
        And lay the law, and carve and drink unto them,
        And then talk ———— and send frolics.[1] O,
        It would have burst your buttons or not left you a
Meer. They say he is an ingenious youth.   [seam.
Eng. O! sir, and dresses himself the best
        Beyond forty of your ladies. Did you never see him?
Meer. No, I do seldom see those toys.
        But think you that we may have him?
Eng.   Sir, the young gentleman[2]
        I tell you of can command him. Shall I attempt it?
Meer. Yes, do it.

But Engine, instead of bringing on Dick Robinson *in propriâ personâ*, gets Wittipol to dress up as the woman, and the scene runs as follows:—

        [*Enter* Engine *followed by* Wittipol.]
Meer.   Engine, welcome.
        How goes the cry?
Eng. Excellent well.
Meer. Will it do?
        Where's Robinson?
Eng. Here is the gentleman, sir,
        Will undertake it himself. I have acquainted him.
Meer. Why did you so?
Eng. Why, Robinson would have told him, you know.
        And he's a pleasant wit, will hurt
        Nothing you purpose. Then he's of opinion
        That Robinson might want audacity,
        She being such a gallant. Now, he has been
        In Spain, and knows the fashions there, and can
        Discourse, and being but mirth, he says, leave much
        To his care.
Meer. But he's too tall.
Eng.   For that
        He has the bravest device (you'll love him for it)
        To say he wears cioppinos,[3] and they do so
        In Spain; and Robinson as tall as he.

---

  [1] Doubtful mottoes wrapped round sweetmeats, apparently like Christmas crackers.

  [2] Apparently Wittipol in the play.

  [3] The reader may remember Hamlet's reference to the "altitude of a chopine."

Meer. Is he so?
Eng. Every jot.
Meer. Nay, I had rather
To trust a gentleman with it of the two.

I have given the principal contemporaneous references I have come across outside Shakespeare to this custom, and, as stated, Jonson followed Shakespeare, and the extracts given, I think, show a very considerable difference. The drawing by Jonson is from nature in all its crudeness, but the wit is poor, and there is an entire absence of that poetical fancy, which lightly and delicately touches what it describes, which is the great charm of Shakespeare.

There is in Ben Jonson's work another allusion.

In the "New Inn" which is a lamentable piece of stuff, Ben Jonson has taken Shakespeare's notion of making a boy represent a woman, who assumes to be a boy, &c. The "New Inn" was played, or partly played, on 19th January, 1629. But the audience would not allow it to finish. There was a girl's part, one Lætitia, brought up and educated by her father, thinking that she is a boy. He calls her Frank. The absurdity that a child could be brought up and its sex not discovered is self-evident. When Shakespeare makes the masquerade, the young ladies wear boys' attire for a short time only. But Lætitia is supposed to have been educated as Frank for years. Then comes further complications. The host thinks it a good jest to dress up the supposed boy, Frank, as a girl, and allow her to be married to a certain Lord Beaufort, with the result that when her sex is discovered, she is really married. Here we have rather more complications than in the case of Rosalind. A boy acts a girl's part, who dresses as a boy, and then intrigues as a woman. But what a difference there is! Rosalind is the centre of the play, Frank or Lætitia a mere by-character. It is not my intention to make comparisons between Jonson and Shakespeare, but to show that the former copied the latter in this particular incident.

Shakespeare and Greene.—I have at page 165 stated that in my opinion there seems strong reasons for believing that Shakespeare and Greene may have stood in the relation of pupil and tutor to one another. We have not sufficient data to determine this as a fact; but I have pointed out how Shakespeare used Greene's works for his plays, and that many of Greene's words, such as "Doom," were adopted by Shakespeare. I think this suggestion acquires some confirmation when we consider the peculiar way Greene refers to Shakespeare in his "Groat's Worth of Wit." He speaks of him as having a special knowledge of his ambition, &c., he calls him "upstart crow," &c., "beautified with our feathers," &c.; but while he speaks thus bitterly of him he does not mention his name, to which he only refers by the veiled allusion of *Shake-Scene*. Now we who know the great reputation of Shakespeare's name, have no doubt but that it was to him that Greene alluded; but unless Shakespeare's efforts were an open secret in 1592, I think we have no reason to believe that Greene intended the world to know whom it was he meant. He wished the upstart crow to feel the sting of his words, but not to expose him. We find, curiously enough, Shakespeare treating Greene in a somewhat similar manner.[1] I have shown that the play of "George-à-Greene," the Pinner of Wakefield, is attributed to Greene because of a note, which says that Shakespeare said the play was written by a minister, who played the part of the Pinner himself. This has been explained as meaning Robert Greene. This reference to Shakespeare is one of the few occasions when we find contemporaneous persons speaking of him personally, that is, apart from his works or his acting. There are, I think, only two or three events in all which show that Shakespeare was, apart from his writings, a real individual and not a myth. Here we find Shakespeare referring to Greene as a minister, and not giving his name. So that we have both Shakespeare and Greene showing an intimate know-

---

[1] Page 158.

ledge of the life of the other, a knowledge which is unknown to the world in general.

Besides this, we have in one of Greene's plays, a character introduced which seems very Shakesperian. In the "Looking Glass for London and England" we have an almost religious play where the prophet Oseas is brought to Nineveh by an angel to note all the sins of that rich and pampered city—

And see the wrath of God that pays revenge.

As soon as the solemn scene is finished and Oseas accepts the duty, we have a crew of "ruffians" bursting on the stage, very much as Elbow and his party come on to the stage after the solemn scene where Claudio is condemned to death in "Measure for Measure." Amidst this noisy band is Adam, an English smith fresh from his master's forge, with all the impudence of the clown, Jack Cade, and other well-known Shakespearian characters. It is not "impertinence" nor "insolence" which is the peculiar trait of these clowns, but impudence, that is, without shame. The clown in the trial scene I have already given at p. 43, shows this quality in its fullest sense, but even he can be moved. It may be remembered that Escalus, with a masterly touch, is made to speak kindly to him, and says—

Come, tell me true; it shall be better for you.

For a moment we can see him ashamed, and he replies—

Truly, sir, I am a poor fellow, that would live.

The effect is only temporary; his effrontery soon comes back. Adam is one of the same sort. There has been a solemn fast ordered by the repentant king of Nineveh to propitiate the wrath of Heaven; and to see that the fast is properly kept, searchers are appointed. The following extract shows how Adam's impudence equals that of the clown before Escalus:—

The two searchers interrupt Adam, who is enjoying a piece of beef and a bottle of beer, which he hides in his slops—

2nd Sear. Here sits one, methinks, at his prayers; let us see who it is.

1st Sear. 'Tis Adam, the smith's man; how now, Adam?

Adam. Trouble me not. "Thou shal't take no manner of food, but fast and pray."

1st Sear. How devoutly he sits at his orisons; but stay, methinks I feel a smell of some meat or bread about him.

2nd Sear. So thinks me too. You, sirrah, what victuals have you about you?

Adam. Victuals! Oh, horrible blasphemy! Hinder me not of my prayer, nor drive me not into a choler. Victuals! why, heardest thou not the sentence, "Thou shal't take no food, but fast and pray."

2nd Sear. Truth, so it should be; but methinks I smell meat about thee.

Adam. About me, my friends? *These words are actions in the case.* About me? no, no; hang those gluttons that cannot fast and pray.

1st. Sear. Well, for all your words, we must search you.

Adam. Search me? take heed what you do. *My hose*[1] *are my castles.* 'Tis burglary, if you break open a slop. No officer must lift up an iron hatch; take heed, my slops are iron. [*They search Adam.*]

2nd Sear. Oh, villain! see how he hath gotten victuals, bread, beef and beer, where the king commanded, upon pain of death, none should eat for so many days, no, not the sucking infant.

Adam. Alas, sir, this is nothing but a *modicum non nocet ut medicus daret;*[2] why, sir, a bit to comfort my stomach.

1st Sear. Villain, thou shalt be hanged for it!

Adam. These are your words, "I shall be hanged for it"; but first answer me to this question, how many days have we to fast still?

2nd Sear. Five days.

Adam. Five days, a long time; then I must be hanged.

1st Sear. Ay, marry, must thou.

Adam. I am your man. I am for you, sir; for I had rather be hanged than abide so long a fast. What, five days? Come, I'll untruss. Is your halter and the gallows, the ladder and all such furniture, in readiness?

1st Sear. I warrant thee shalt want none of these.

---

[1] A play upon the proverb, I suppose, "An Englishman's house is his castle."

[2] Referring to the relief from fasting allowed in case of sickness by the Romish Church.

Adam. But hear you, must I be hanged?
1*st Sear.* Ay, marry.
Adam. And for eating of meat. Then, friends, *know ye by these presents*, I will eat up all my meat, and drink up all my drink, for it shall never be said I was hanged with an empty stomach.

Which he at once proceeds to do.

In my view, these Shakespearian clowns are Bacon's work rather than Shakespeare's. As I have said, Bacon was fond of these studies of low life, perhaps as a contrast to his more serious works. I do not remember to have found these "impudent varlets" in the non-legal plays. And if I am right in giving the trial scene in "Measure for Measure," that is, the part not in blank verse, to Bacon, and "Macbeth" to Shakespeare, then, I think, we have some test of their respective styles. If this be so, the creation of Adam may be Bacon's and not Shakespeare's, especially as he quotes English law[1] in Nineveh, and thus follows the peculiarity of the law in the legal plays. It is possible that it was through Greene that Bacon and Shakespeare met. This is, no doubt, only conjecture. But I do not remember in Greene's other plays an impudent character like Adam, yet he is clearly one of the type we find so commonly in Shakespeare's plays.

The Three Parts of "Henry VI."

There is, I think, another connection between Shakespeare and Greene to be found when we come to consider the three parts of "Henry VI." A great deal has been written as to whether Shakespeare was or was not the author of all or any of these parts. But it seems to me there is no difficulty in getting at the truth if we take the simple facts as they have come down to us.

I think all the confusion has arisen because the three parts are written in "reverse order." Usually, if a work appears in three parts the presumption, as lawyers say, is that Part I. was written first, then Part II., and then Part III. But, in

---

[1] And drinks English beer.

this case, exactly the opposite took place, and we shall find that Part III. was the first of the plays and is not the work of Shakespeare: that Shakespeare produced Part II. as a separate play to rival the existing play Part III.; and some time after Part I. was written by Shakespeare. It is the discoveries made by Halliwell in modern times which enable us to trace this out. But with Malone and writers of his time there is considerable excuse for the confusion they got into over these three parts of "Henry VI.," because they had not the advantage of seeing the earlier copies of the second and third parts published by Millington in 1594 and 1595 respectively, which Mr. Halliwell reproduced in the Shakespeare Society's papers in 1843. All Malone knew was that there was published in London (no date), but supposed to be in 1619, what purported to be—

THE WHOLE CONTENTION
BETWEEN THE TWO FAMOUS HOUSES
LANCASTER AND YORKE.

WITH THE TRAGICALL ENDS OF THE GOOD DUKE *HUMFRY*, *RICHARD* DUKE OF *YORKE*, AND KING *HENRY* THE SIXT.

Divided into Two Parts and newly corrected and enlarged.

Written by William Shakespeare, Gent.

Printed at London for T. P.[1]

Now this, undoubtedly, attributes these two parts of the Contention to William Shakespeare, and as in the second part we find the line—

Oh, tiger's heart, wrapped in a woman's hyde.

---

[1] Thomas Prince.

And as Greene used the line in his "Groat's Worth of Wit," in 1592—

O tiger's heart, wrapped in a player's hide,

it is generally supposed he was quoting from Shakespeare's play, and therefore Shakespeare must have written it by that date. But Greene was complaining of the upstart crow (Shakespeare), who thought himself able to bombast blank verse as well as any, and would hardly have quoted from his rival's lines; and I think we shall see this is so, when we come to Halliwell's reproduction, and that the whole order and history of these plays is very clear. Halliwell seems to have been near the fact, but he does not seem to be so skilful in using what he discovers as in discovering it. By his reprints we find the two plays were published originally as follows :—

The original play on which Part II. of "Henry VI." was founded was printed—

THE
FIRST PART OF THE CONTENTION
BETWIXT THE TWO FAMOUS HOUSES
OF YORKE AND LANCASTER, WITH
THE DEATH OF THE GOOD
DUKE HUMPHREY,
&c.,   &c.
1594.

The play on which Part III. of "Henry VI." was founded was published as—

THE
TRUE TRAGEDIE OF RICHARD
DUKE OF YORKE, AND THE DEATH OF
GOOD KING HENRY THE SIXT.
with the whole contention betweene
&c.,   &c.
1595.

THE ACTOR-AUTHOR.

Now, if we compare these two titles we are, I think, at once reminded of a new shop being opened next to an old-established one in the same line of business, when the older shopkeeper, disgusted at the presence of the new comer, puts up a notice that "there is no connection with next door."

It is evident if the play of 1594 is the First Part of the Contention play No. 2 cannot be the *Whole* of the Contention. Now, when we find play No. 2 was performed by Lord Pembroke's servants, who, Halliwell tells us, never performed Shakespeare's plays, it seems to me clear the "Tragedy of Richard, Duke of York," was the original play, probably written by Greene, who uses one of his own lines when he speaks of the tiger's heart, &c., and this play, as a second title, was known as the Contention between the famous Houses of Yorke and Lancaster, which is a fair description of it, as the contention or actual struggle begins and ends in the play. Then it seems that Shakespeare's company, needing a play to rival the other, commissioned Shakespeare to write one like it, and he, with the assistance of his legal friend, wrote his play, which deals with the causes that led to Yorke raising the banner of rebellion, the murder of the Duke Humphrey, Jack Cade's outbreak, which is supposed to have been the work of Richard of Yorke, &c., and called it the First Part of the Contention, by which, I think, it was intended to say not the first part of one play, but the *commencement* of the struggle. This, I think, led to the publication of Greene's play, "The *Whole* Contention," meaning that the other play had no right to call itself the First Part of the Contention. The word *whole* would not be used unless there was another Richmond in the field. Now Millington in some way became possessed of the right to publish Shakespeare's play, and did so in 1594; and Greene being dead in 1595, he published his work; not attributing either to Shakespeare. Then comes the undated publication, when the two are attributed to William Shakespeare. In addition to these plays, it appears that Shakespeare and his legal friend, finding there was a large part of Henry VI.'s reign not dramatized, viz., the period of the king's infancy, when France was lost to England and Talbot killed, wrote a third play, of which we have no copy earlier than the Folio, wherein it appears as "Part No. 1 of Henry VI." (There is evidence that this first part was written and played before the play of "Henry V.," as it is referred to in one of the choruses of that play.) Part No. 2 was the First Part of the Contention, and the work of Shakespeare and his legal friend, and Part No. 3, the oldest and original play, the work of Greene or some other author, not Shakespeare, as it contains no legalisms, and is altogether written in a different style, without interest or incident, with long speeches, &c.

Bacon's Secret Compositions.

Bacon somewhere says he is "a concealed poet," and Jonson said that he had "filled up all numbers." A great deal has been made of this by the Baconians, but Jonson does not say that he wrote numbers or verses, but that he "filled them," whatever that may mean. We have no evidence that Bacon ever wrote poetry that was worthy of that name. We have, however, the strongest evidence that Bacon was very fond of the theatre, he was continually getting up masques and similar entertainments which he, for the most part, wrote himself in prose though there is reason, in one case at least, to believe that his prose was put into blank verse, so that, although we cannot bring home to him by direct evidence that he ever wrote or arranged the matter for any of Shakespeare's plays, yet I think there is very good reason to believe that on more than one occasion he wrote or helped to write masques which were afterwards put into blank verse.

In November of the year 1595 Essex produced a device or masque, which was admittedly written by Bacon. Spedding gives an extract from a contemporary report to which I shall refer directly; of it he says,[1]—

"It is not much that one can gather from this report (which appears, moreover, to have suffered from the errors of the transcriber) as to the character of the entertainment, but it serves to identify, as belonging to it, a paper without heading, docket, or date, found in the Lambeth collection; which paper is further proved by some notes and portions of the rough draft still extant in Bacon's handwriting to be of his own composition."

Now it appears that the papers in the bundle, which is in Bacon's handwriting, consist of certain speeches, as that of the hermit or philosopher, the squire's speech in the tiltyard, the hermit's speech in the presence, the soldier's speech, the statesman's speech, and the reply of the squire.

Of these Mr. Spedding says—"there can be no reasonable doubt that the foregoing speeches were written by Bacon,"[2] though he points out that it is only by accident that they pass for his, for by contemporary writers they were thought to be Essex's writings. But Mr. Spedding has no doubt, for he says,[3]—

"If it could be quite certain that it" (the masque) "was the earl's own composition, his style in things of this kind must have been so like Bacon's that I, for my part, should despair of distinguishing their several works by examination of the workmanship."

The view taken by Mr. Spedding receives a remarkable confirmation, if it were necessary, from a document that was discovered after Mr. Spedding had written his book. It is usually known as the "Northumberland Manuscript." Its peculiarity is that the outside leaf, which forms its cover, contains a list of the pieces which were to be found inside. Mr. Spedding has, by leave of the Duke, published a short

---

[1] Vol. 1, p. 375.
[2] *Ibid.* p. 386.
[3] Page 391.

account of it, in which a *fac simile* is given of this front or title page. Originally it was as follows:—

> Mr. Frauncis Bacon
> on tribute or giuing what is dew.
> The praise of the worthiest vertue.
> The praise of the worthiest affection.
> The praise of the worthiest power.
> The praise of the worthiest person.

Some one subsequently has added the following titles, which I do not quite read as Mr. Spedding does. As I read them, they run as follows:—

> Earle of Arundell's letter to the Queen.
> Speaches for my lord of Essex at the tilt.
> A speach for my lord of Sussex tilt.
> Leycester's commonwealth. Incerto auth[ore].
> Orations at Graie's Inne revells.
> By Mr. Frauncis Bacon.
> Essaies by the same author.
> Richard the second.
> Richard the third.

I think this closes the second list. There are, in addition, a considerable amount of scribblings over the whole sheet, which are not material to the present inquiry.

Amongst these scribblings are to be found repetitions of the titles given. Thus, "Earl of Leicester's Letter to the Queen" is to be found, and curiously enough, William Shakespeare's name is written, both in full and partly, very many times. Mr. Spedding thinks this shows no connection between Bacon and Shakespeare, but it is the idle caprice of the penman, who spoils paper by writing down the name several times of a favourite actor. As if a copyist of Tennyson's

BACON'S SECRET COMPOSITIONS. 321

Poems were to write Mr. Irving's name several times on the front sheet. This explanation does not seem very satisfactory. It is impossible to say at this date under what circumstances William Shakespeare's name was written over the covering page of a bundle of Bacon's works. But it is an interesting fact that some one at the end of the sixteenth century found some reason for bringing the two names together.

Speaking of these titles, so far as they are material to the present inquiry, Mr. Spedding says in his Introduction,[1] "The *Speaches for my lord of Essex at the tilt* are evidently the speeches of the hermit, the soldier, the secretary, and the squire." And "The *Orations at Graie's Inne Revells*," he says, "are the speeches of the six councillors to the Prince of Purpoole at the Gray's Inn revels in 1594." To these I have already referred.[2]

The peculiarity of the Essex Device (and as I think of the Gray's Inn Masque) is that Bacon did not give his speeches to his principal personages, but employed either professional actors or some friend, like Toby Matthew, the reason being, I suppose, that people like my Lord Essex and others did not care to undertake the task of uttering Bacon's didactic and somewhat pompous essays, for they are no more. And we learn that this was so from the contemporary account quoted by Spedding already referred to. In it we are told [3]—

"The old man" (the hermit) "was he that in Cambridge played Giraldy, Morley played the Secretary, and he that played Pedantiq was the soldier, and Toby Matthew acted the Squire's part."

We are also told that this was not known generally, for the account continues—

"The world makes many untrue constructions of these speeches, comparing the Hermit and the Secretary to two of the lords, and the Soldier to Sir Roger Williams."

---

[1] "A Conference of Pleasure," xxi.
[2] *Ante*, p. 223.
[3] Spedding, Vol. I, p. 375.

The reporter also adds, showing that the Queen was still angry with Essex, or that Bacon's fulsome flattery bored her—

"The Queen said that if she had thought there had been so much said of her, she would not have been there that night —*and so went to bed.*"

Now when we come to the masque that was given by the Prince of Purpoole, we shall see that her Majesty was in better humour, but we shall also find exactly the same construction and arrangement of the speeches as we have in Essex's Device. In the former, we have Mr. Helmes, who was the Prince of Purpoole, confining himself to dancing, whilst the principal speeches are made by the squire, who may have been Toby Matthew, or "He that in Cambridge played Giraldy." And though the speeches are put into blank verse, they are in Bacon's too well-known style of didactic sententiousness; and in each case the squire lauds his master and flatters and compliments the Queen. I do not propose to give any lengthened extracts from this Device; it is to be found in Nicol's "Progresses of Queen Elizabeth"; but I think if the one masque was Bacon's, the other was; although one was in prose, the other in blank verse.

A few short extracts from the Gray's Inn Masque will serve to show that it is really Bacon's prose put into blank verse. But before doing so, it may be pointed out that amongst other titles mentioned on the outside of the Northumberland MS. is a speech, "For the Earl of Sussex at ye tilt an 96," and is one of the many examples of the *cacoethes scribendi* of Bacon and his desire to write speeches, &c. (and if so, why not plays), for others to use and get the credit for.

Mr. Spedding unfortunately does not give this speech, but he thus describes it :—

"This is a speech made to be spoken at one of these court triumphs, and is written in the artificial style which it was the fashion to affect in them, which makes it the more difficult to supply the lost words; but it is addressed to the Queen, and meant apparently to convey an apology for the absence of the

Earl of Essex, who was very likely keeping aloof in one of his fits of discontent."[1]

We have no means of knowing whether this was ever used or even left in Bacon's desk, and thus shared the fate, as I believe, of many of his compositions. For I cannot help looking at Bacon as resembling that character in Dickens who was always writing notes to himself and then destroying them, only Bacon wrote for others; but I by no means think that all that he wrote saw the light of day, except those documents that remained after his death.

The Gray's Inn Masque commences with a hymn in the praise of Neptune, which is attributed in Davidson's "Rhapsody"[2] to *Thomas Campion*. And Mr. Nicolas, in Mr. Pickering's edition, attributes the rest of the masque to Davidson himself, because he sent a copy of it to a lady. The sonnet which accompanied it is given at p. 110; it concludes as follows :—

> Or who of Proteus' sundry transformations
> May better send you the new feigned story
> Than I, whose love unfeigned felt no mutations,
> Since to be yours I first received the glory,
> *Accept then of these lines, though meanly penned,*
> *So fit for you to take and me to send.*

It is to be observed that Davidson does not say that he was the author, but only that he penned them: that is, he may have made a copy for the lady if she wanted one; and, as Mr. Nicolas says, there is "a transcript very beautifully written in the author's [that is, Davidson's] own hand in Harl. MS. 541, f. 138," this may be the copy Davidson sent, and therefore, with a lover's desire to be complimented, he calls it "meanly penned." It may be Davidson who put the matter into blank verse, though he does not appear to have written anything else in this form, nor to have inserted this masque

---

[1] "A Conference of Pleasure," xvii.
[2] Vol. 1, p. 106.

amongst his collection. But whoever did the versification, I think the reader will be convinced that Bacon composed the substance of the masque.

The first verse of the opening hymn, said to be **Campion's**, is—

> Of Neptune's empire let us sing,
>   At whose commands the waves obey,
>   To whom rivers tribute pay,
> Down the high mountains sliding;
>   To whom the scaly nation yields
>   Homage for their chrystal fields,
>   Wherein they dwell.
>   And every sea-god praise again,
>   Yearly out of his watery cell,
>   To deck great Neptune's diadem.

After two verses had been sung of this not over-poetical poetry, a character called "Esquire" comes on to the scene and commences a dialogue with Proteus in blank verse.

The following are the first two speeches—

Esquire Proteus, it seems you lead a merry life;
  Your music follows you where-e'er you go.
  I thought you sea-gods, as in your abode,
  So in your nature, had not been unlike
  To fishes; *the which, as say philosophers,*
  Have so small sense of music's delight,
  As 'tis a doubt not fully yet resolv'd,
  Whether of hearing they have sense or no.

Proteus 'Twas great discourse of reason, to regard
  The dreaming guess of a philosopher,
  That never held his idle buzzing head
  Under the water half an hour's space,
  More than that famous old received history
  Of good Arion, by a dolphin saved.

As soon, however, as we have had this preliminary inquiry in natural history, *i.e.*, whether fish can hear, the Esquire turns to the subject of the masque, saying,—

> Well, let that pass; and to the purpose now,
>   I thought, &c.

The purpose is to describe a very affected wager between the Prince and Proteus. It appeared that Proteus possessed

BACON'S SECRET COMPOSITIONS.   325

an adamantine rock that attracted all iron, but the Prince, Esquire's master, said he possessed something—

> Which in attractive power should surpass
> The woundrous virtue of his iron-drawing rocks.

This is, of course, poor old Queen Elizabeth, whom Esquire thus addresses,—

> Excellent Queen, true adamant of hearts;
> Out of that sacred garland ever grew
> Garlands of virtues, beauties, and perfections,
> That crowns your crown, and dims your fortune's beams,
> Vouchsafe some branch, some precious flower, or leaf,
> Which, though it wither in my barren verse,
> May yet suffice to over-shade and drown
> The rocks admired of this demy-god.
> Proteus, stout iron-homager to your rock,
> In praise of force, and instruments of wars,
> Hath praise ended; yet place your praises right;
> For force to will, and wars to peace do yield.
> But that I'll give you. This I would fain know,
> What can your iron do without arms of men?
> And arms of men from hearts of men do move:
> That hearts of men hath it, their motion springs.
> Lo, Proteus, then, the attractive rock of hearts:
> Hearts, which once truly touched with her beams,
> Inspiring purest zeal and reverence
> As well unto the person, as the power,
> Do streight put off all temper that is false,
> All hollow fear, and schooled flattery,
> Turn fortune's wheel, they ever keep their point,
> And stand direct upon the loyal line.
> Your rock claims kindred of the polar star,
> Because it draws the needle to the north;
> Yet even that star gives place to Cynthia's rays,
> Whose drawing virtues govern and direct
> The flots and re-flots of the ocean,
>   &c.,   &c.

But previous to this lengthy compliment, we have a dissertation by Proteus upon the respective qualities of iron and gold in the following lines :—

> *Proteus.* What needeth words, when great effects proclaim
>   Th' attractive virtue of th' adamantine rocks,
>   Which forceth iron, which all things else com-
>   Iron, of metals prince by ancient right; [mands.

> Though factious men in vain conspire to seat
> Rebellious gold in his usurped throne.
> This, sundry metals, of such strength and use
> (Disjoin'd by distance o' th' whole hemisphere)
> Continually, with trembling aspect,
> True subject-like, eyes his dread sovereign.
> Thus hath this load-stone, by his powerful touch,
> Made the iron needle, load-star of the world,
> A Mercury, to paint the gainest way
> In watery wilderness, and desert sands;
> In confidence whereof, the assured mariner
> Doth not importune Jove, sun, or star.
> By his attractive force, was drawn to light,
> From depth of ignorance, that new found world,
> Whose golden mines iron found out and conquer'd,
> These be the virtues, and extend so far,
> Which you do undertake to counterpraise.

After the delivery of these speeches Proteus strikes the rock, and the Prince of Purpoole (W. Helmes) and seven knights—

"issued forth the rock, in a very stately march, very richly attired, and gallantly provided of all things meet for the performance of so great an enterprize. They came forth of the rock in couples, and before every couple came two pigmies with torches. At their first coming on the stage they danced a new devised measure, &c., after which they took unto them ladies, and with them they danced their galliards, courants, &c.,"[1]

and finally, they all went back into the rock and sang another new hymn within the rock.

I have already, on page 213, given the extravagant compliment with which the report of these revels concludes.

The peculiarity of these lines seems to be extravagant compliments to Elizabeth, and a somewhat childish and pedantic display of commonplace knowledge; and the fact that the principals only act in pantomime, the esquire delivering the greater part of the speeches: these are all peculiarities of Bacon, and we shall, I think, admit this to be so, when we read the following extracts from Essex's Device, which is undoubtedly Bacon's.

---

[1] Nicol's "Progresses of Queen Elizabeth," p. 48.

"*Essex's Device.*"—This is the name it is known by, and it is useful to keep to it, as it distinguishes it from the Gray's Inn Masque, though, as I have said, it is really Bacon's. It is to be found in Spedding's "Letters of Bacon," Vol. I., p. 376. That author tells us that there is a page in Bacon's most careless hand which seems to be a discarded beginning (but) explains the design; from this we find the character of the esquire playing the principal part, as in the Gray's Inn Masque.

"The persons to be three—one dressed like an *heremite or philosopher*, representing contemplation; the second like a *captain*, representing fame; and the third like a *counsellor of state*, representing experience; the third to be given to the squire as being the master of the best behaviour or compliment, though he speak last."

In the speeches, which are prosy and pedantic, we have the same commonplace references to natural phenomena, thus:—

"Remember, what time your opposition against the force of her arguments was like the opposition of the rainbow against the sun, pretty colours but easily scattered."

The squire says:[1]—

"Give ear now to the comparison of my master's condition, and acknowledge such a difference as is betwixt the melting hail-stone and the solid pearl. Indeed, it seemeth to depend, as the globe of the earth seemeth to hang in the air; but yet it is firm and stable in itself. It is like a cube or die form, which toss it or throw it any way, it ever lighteth upon a square.[2]"

* * * * * *

"His clouds are like the clouds of harvest, which make the sun break forth with greater force; his wanes and changes are like the moon, whose globe is all light towards the sun when it is all dark towards the world."

---

[1] Spedding's "Letters of Bacon," p. 384.
[2] This is, as many of Bacon's statements are, not true; a die or cube may fall upon an edge or a point, and there it would remain if the centre of gravity were over the part in contact.

If, therefore, we come to the conclusion that the Gray's Inn Masque is the composition of the same author as Essex's Device, viz., Bacon,—and I think no one could read the two together without coming to this conclusion,—we have Bacon's ideas put into blank verse either by himself or by someone else. And even if this be not admitted, we have this fact, which cannot be disputed, that in Essex's Device we have an example of Bacon's habit of writing out matter for others to represent as their own, which proves him to be a concealed author if not a poet.

There are other masques in the production of which Bacon took the principal part. Mr. Douthwaite, in his "History of Gray's Inn," tells us—

"On the occasion of the marriage of the Count Palatine with the Princess Elizabeth, Francis Beaumont prepared a masque which was performed before the King and the royal family in the Banqueting House, Whitehall, on the 20th February, 1612-13. The cost was considerable, and to meet this charge the Readers of Gray's Inn were assessed each man at £4, the Ancients,[1] and such as at that time were to be called Ancients, at £2 10s. a-piece, the barristers at £2 a man, and the Students at 20s. (*Orig. Jurid.* 286). The Solicitor-general (Sir Francis Bacon) is said to have 'spared no time in the setting forth, ordering, and furnishing' of it."

This was a heavy contribution, as money was then about eight times its present value.

Again, the same author tells us that on the occasion of the marriage of the Earl of Somerset—

"In 1613-14, *The Maske of Flowers* was *presented by the gentlemen of Graies Inn, at the Court of Whitehall*, in the Banquetting House, upon Twelfe Night."

It was dedicated to Bacon, then Attorney-General, by three persons, I. G., W. D., T. B. It appears[2] from a "letter from Chamberlain, 23 Dec., 1613," that—

"Sir Francis Bacon prepares a masque to honour this marriage which will stand him in above £2,000 [£16,000,] and

---

[1] Bacon was an Ancient.   [2] History of Gray's Inn, p. 234.

although he have been offered some help by the House, and specially by Mr. Solicitor Sir Henry Yelverton, who would have sent him £500, yet he would not accept it, but offers them the whole charge with the honour."

Mr. Spedding tells us[1] that Jonson produced a masque for Bacon in 1618.

"On Thursday night," says Chamberlain, "the gentlemen of Gray's Inn came to the court with their show, for I cannot call it a masque, seeing they were not disguised, nor had vizards. For the rest, their fashion and device were well approved, though it were thought to be somewhat out of season to revel in Lent."

It appears from a letter, an extract from which Mr. Spedding gives us in a note, that this masque had been previously acted with little applause :—

"The masque on Twelfth Night is not commended of any. The poet is grown so dull that his device is not worth the relating much less the copying out. Divers think fit he *should return to his old trade of bricklaying again.* Nathaniel Brent to Sir D. Carleton, 10th Jan., 1617 (1618)."

I do not think at this time Jonson had shown any symptoms of want-of power. We have other masques of his written at and after 1618, which show no signs of falling off. And we are told that he was generally employed at this time writing masques for the court and the nobility. Perhaps the solution of his dullness was that Bacon had written out one of his wearisome devices, which poor Jonson had to dramatize and the gentlemen of Gray's Inn had to perform, and that was the reason his work was not up to the standard of the "Masque of Lethe," and many other masques which we find in his pages.

The Masque of Mountebankes.

In the Gray's Inn Library there is a manuscript of a masque which, at first, I believed to be in Bacon's handwriting or in that of his servant Meauty's, which, though

---

[1] Vol. 6, p. 298.

distinguishable, very much resembles Bacon's. It is very often found that where two people see a great deal of each other's writing, they unconsciously copy one another. But after having the MS. submitted to an expert, he was satisfied that it is not the handwriting of either, but of some one whose writing has many of the peculiarities of both Bacon and Meauty, though it has, at the same time, peculiarities of its own. It may be one of the "other pens" which assisted Bacon. It appears from the manuscript, this masque was given by the members of Gray's Inn, apparently to Bacon, at the Hall of the Inn, as there is a song sung on the entrance of Bacon and other lords, and he might have had a copy made for himself. It also appears it was afterwards played before James. I think there is some reason to suppose that Bacon himself was the author of the Antemasque; if so, we have a curious illustration of Bacon's love of secret composition, for we have him composing something to be presented to himself, like one who subscribes to his own testimonial.

My reasons for thinking that Bacon composed part of this masque are these—

First, the strong similarity between the writing of Bacon's and Meauty's, which it resembles as Meauty's does Bacon's. And this becomes more important, if I am right in the view I take, that the MS. in Gray's Inn is the original and not a copy.

Secondly, because the part I attribute to Bacon is a collection of sentences, written very much in Bacon's style, as we find it in the Apothegms, &c., which are admittedly his.

Thirdly, there are at the end of the MS. two songs, which were sung the one at the entrance of Bacon and his friends and the other to Bacon alone during dinner, which are so wanting in the customary adulation of those times which one would expect a Lord Chancellor to receive from Members of his Inn, that I fancy Bacon must have written them himself.

The Gray's Inn Manuscript.—The "Masque of Mountebankes" is printed in Nicol's "Progresses of Queen Elizabeth," as part of the proceedings of the *Gesta Grayorum* on the second occasion, the date of which is not fixed. In a note we are told that Henry the Second, Prince of Graya and Purpulia, occurs in the list of subscribers to Minshew's Dictionary, 1617.

It appears from Mr. Douthwaite's "History of Gray's Inn," that this masque attracted considerable attention. Brent, writing to Carleton, says—

"On Thursday night, the maske of Grayes Inne pleased tolerably wel, for divers of the 18 maskers danced gracefully enough, and there was in it som wittie ribalderie that made the companie merrie.
"London Feb. 21, 1617.
  stilo vet."

Sir Gerrard Herbert, writing to Carleton, says—

"Grayes Inn maske was the thursday night after, which was well liked, and the dances well performed of the gentlemen: the ayres and dances well devised. Some of the dances danct by the voices of boyes (insteed of musick) which songe excellent well, and which gave more content then musickes. The speeches weare acted by some of there owne gentlemen: one, called Paradox, who spake most, and pleasinge in many thinges, was much comended, &c.
"London 22 of
  Febr: 1618 veteri."

This date should be 1617 or the other 1618, as they evidently both refer to the same occasion. But whether this masque was performed in 1617 or 1618 is not very material. Bacon was in both years filling the chancellorship, and the only question we have to consider is whether he wrote at least part of it.

First.—Bacon's Writing.—Bacon wrote in very many different styles. The usual writing of the period was very much like modern German writing. Shakespeare's well-known signature begins with a German capital $\mathfrak{S}$. Besides this there was the Court hand, stiff and formal, and the Italian hand, which is our modern form of writing small round hand. Bacon could write all these, and could write them very well and very badly, so that his writing was capable of many variations.

The reader may remember how Hamlet says, he—

> Devised a new commission; wrote it fair;
> I once did hold it, as our statists do,
> A baseness to write fair, and laboured much
> How to forget that learning; but, sir, now
> It did me yeoman service.

We do not know whether Shakespeare had many modes of writing. But Bacon had—some of them are neat as copper plate; others almost as bad as mine. Spedding often speaks of Bacon's "most careless style." But, however he wrote, he had, as far as I have seen his writing, this peculiarity: he had more than one form for the same letter, particularly the letter e, which he wrote in four different ways *in as many words*. Most of us have the small Italian *e*, and we use the $\mathcal{E}$ as a capital. But Bacon had four small e's: the ordinary Italian one *e*, and a small Greek ε, an e written backwards like a ϑ, and a modification of the last, *i.e.* written backwards, but with the tail brought up to the loop, so that it looks like a small *θ*. Another peculiarity of his was in the way he made his numbers: 1 he often wrote like a 2, so that in many of his letters dated 1616, the figures look like 2626. Now all these peculiarities are to be found in the *fac simile* of a page of the manuscript of the "Masque of Mountebanks," which is in the Gray's Inn Library, which shows how the author has started writing his so-called Masculine Paradoxes in the same semi-Italian hand that the rest of the Antemasque is written in. This continues to and includes No. 11. After that the writing is in different ink, and in many ways resembles Bacon's or Meauty's writing. We see the peculiar shape of 1 which makes it look like 2. This is more particularly seen in 19, which I think any one would take for 29; but when we look at No. 12 we see the careful way the 2 is made. The other figures are very like those to be seen on Bacon's and Meauty's admitted letters at Lambeth Palace.

We have also the examples of Bacon's four different e's. In No. 12 we see it has had A C put to it in different ink, but it reads:—

A Caniball is the lovingest man to his enymy, for willingly no man eates that he loves not.

Compare the e's in—the, enymy, eates.

In No. 3 we have the ordinary Italian *e* used; and so it is in No. 4, except in the last word, where we find the Greek ε; in No. 5 we have the Italian *e*, except in the word constable, where we find the e made backwards like a ϑ; but in the next line, in the words the stokes (stocks), we have the e made round like a θ. There is not much difference between the last two e's, except the one like a ϑ is done with a small loop, which, in the one like θ, is half the whole letter.

The Gray's Inn Manuscript differs very materially from the masque as it is printed by Nicol, and apparently the former is the original document, and the latter is taken from an altered copy. My reason for saying this is, that the Gray's Inn MS. shows the corrections that have been made, and more particularly shows that the author had arranged certain "paradoxes" into masculine, feminine and neuter, and commenced the three descriptions in different places in the manuscript; and then having written more than he originally thought of doing, found in some cases difficulty in getting the matter into the space reserved for it, and in others there is more room than is required. This crowding of the matter into a small space would not have occurred, it is needless to say, if the MS. had been a copy, which, going on from sentence to sentence, would have given sufficient space to each line.

REDUCED FACSIMILE.

Translation.

3. A drunkard is a good philosopher for he thinks aright that the world goes round.
4. The devil cannot take tobacco through his nose for St. Dunstan seared up that with his tongs.
5. A shoemaker is the fittest man for a Constable for he *virtute officii* may put any man in the stocks [stokes] and inlarge him at the last.
6. A prisoner is the best fencer for he ever lies at a close ward.
7. An elder Brother may be a wise man for he hath wherewithal to buy wisdom at any rate.
8. A nimble page is more useful for a lady than a long gentleman usher for a sparrow is more active than a bauld Buzzard.
9. Burgomasters ought not to wear their fur gowns at midsummer for so they may bring on the sweating sickness again.
10. It is better to be a coward than a captain for a goos[e lives longer than a cock of the game.
11. A cutpurse is the surest trade for his work is no soone[r done but he hath his money in his hand.
12. A cannibal is the lovingest man to his enemy for willingly no m[an eats that he loves not.
13. A musician will never make a good vintner for he deals too mu[ch with flats and sharps.
14. A man should do in the choice of a wife as he does in the choi[ce of a piece of satin feel and see and turn up both ends for he may find a breach in the fagge end.
15. A bankrupt is a good house-keeper for he seldom flits from [home.
16. He cannot be a brave gentleman that is not in debt for he must follow the fashion though it grew to a disease.
17. A city heir cannot be a prodigal for: *est in juvencis pa[trum virtus.*
18. Of all men a scholar makes the nimblest warrior for: *pru[dentia est magister virtus.*
19. A fool is the happiest of men for he hath often entrance wh[ile his betters are kept out.

As an example of the corrections that have taken place, I may mention we find the opening as follows:—

of
The Ante Maske Mountebankes of
^
English Italian Ducth Russian
Frenche Spanish Egiptian Jewe.

The mountebankes speech.

The greate m̅ͬ: Medecine Esculapius preserve and prolong the sanity of these royall and princely spectators.

As printed in Nicol, it is:—

The first antemask of mountebanks.

Mountebank's speech.

The greatest master of medicine Æsculapius preserve and prolonge the saivty of the royall and princely spectators.

There are other corrections to be found in the Gray's Inn MS.

Secondly.—The MS. contains an antemasque besides the masque itself, called in the MS. the Maine Masque. The antemasque, which I believe to be principally Bacon's composition, consists chiefly of a number of Paradoxes, really very silly jests, more worthy of a schoolboy than a Lord Chancellor approaching sixty. That Bacon was fond of this kind of wit anyone may see who chooses to read his collection of Apothegms which is to be found in his published works. Besides the Apothegms, many of which have the same broad wit that we find in these Paradoxes, Bacon has left us a collection of antithetical ideas relating to religion which he terms "The Characters of a Believing Christian, or Paradoxes and seeming Contradictions," of which I give an example or two:—

1. A Christian is one that believes things his reason cannot comprehend; he hopes for things which neither he nor any man alive ever saw, &c.

2. He believes three to be one, and one to be three; a father not to be elder than his son; a son to be equal with his father, &c.

In Nicol's "Progresses of Queen Elizabeth," the Paradoxes in the "Ante-Masque of Mountebanks" show signs of having been altered from those in the Gray's Inn copy. Some are to be found in one and not the other, and the order has been altered. Whether these Paradoxes are, or are not, Bacon's composition, or rather collected by him, must, of course, without further evidence, be a matter of conjecture. But the reader must judge for himself by comparing the extract here given with Bacon's admitted works, the Apothegms, &c.

Something must be allowed for the manners of the time, and that this sort of low wit—I was going to say low comedy wit, but it seems lower than that—pleased some people is to be gathered from the letters already given.[1]

The difference between the antemasque and the masque is very marked. The antemasque is, as I have pointed out, full of small and not always decent wit. The masque has nothing to offend, and is in verse of some poetical merit. Take the following in praise of music and dancing:—

> Musicke is the soule of measure
> Mixing both in equall grace,
> Twins are the [they] begot of pleasure,
> When she wisely numbred space.
> Nothing is more ould or newer
> Then number all advancing,
> And noe number can be truer
> Then musicke *joynd* with daunting.

"Mixing" is altered to "speeding," and "music joined" in the last line is printed in Nicol as "musick-wynd," which seems to be a misprint.

Thirdly.—There is an addition to this masque on the last leaf of the MS. This does not appear to have been published.

---

[1] *Ante*, p. 331.

338   SHAKESPEARE: A STUDY.

The welcome which a Lord Chancellor would receive from the members of his Inn in those days of elaborate flattery, one would expect to be a warm one. But this seems so cold that I believe Bacon wrote it himself—

Reduced Facsimile.

> The Songe for entertainement of the
> Lord Chancellor at grais Ine on
> Candlemas day and of other Lords
>
> Chorus welcome grandees to you all
>   all our best of wishes fall
>   On you now as still they shall
>
> *This song was songe*
> *by 4 voices to 6*
> *lutes at the Lords*
> *first comming*
>
>   Would we knew great lords the way
>   Best to welcome you this day
>   You deserve our best who thus
>   Come and seeke to honor us
>   But as men with too much light
>   Dazzled, yf not blinded quite
>   Or as men haste past theire hope
>   Forride beyonde theire wish we grope
>   And at somwhat cacthe and say
>   What we wot not that you may
>   Seeby that our hartes be filled
>   That as yf we were distilled
>   Into wonder we give ore
>   Crieing welcom and no more
>
> In midle of dinner this Song to my lord Chancellor
>   you are the first in this great common wele
>   Whose selfe and sire weere Peeres of the seale
>   Sprunge from that gouldon stem of over the row
>   Who or his wife dome luyes admired yet
>   And wheras other families decline
>   In honor you yow Ancetors outshine
>   Hence Sprunge your roote and you still cald for
>   Both growe the goodliest trees on Libanus
>   O that your fate might with out wish agre
>   You should be then as fertile as he
>   And put forth Branches ere you leave this

TRANSLATION.]
The Songe for entertainement of the Lord Chancellor at Grais Ine on Candlemas Day and of other Lords.

Chorus.—Welcome grandees to you all
          All our best of wishes fall
          On you now as still they shall.

This song was songe by fives voices to six flutes at the lords first comming.
Would we knew great lords the way
Best to welcome you this day
You deserve our best who thus
Come and seeke to honour us.
But as men with too much light
Dazzled if not blinded quite
Or as men haste past theire hope
Joynde beyonde theire wish we grope
And at somwhat cacthe [catch] and say
What we wot not that you may.
     See by that our hearts be filled
     That as if we were distilled
     Into wonder we give ore
     Criing welcom and no more.

In midle of Diner This Song to my Lord Chancellor.

You are the first in this great commonwe[1] | al
Whose selfe and sire weere kepers of the seale
Sprunge from that goulden home of worthe[1] | iest
Who for his wisdome lives admired yet
And whereas other families decline
In honnor you your ancestors outshine ⸢us
Hence springe your roote and you till cald fro[1] | m
Both grewe the goodliest trees in Libanus.
O that your fate might with our wish ag[1] | ree
You should be then as fertile as was he
And put forth branches ere you lefte this[1] | ——.

Opinions no doubt will differ also as to whether this masque, or rather the antemasque, was or was not the work of Bacon. But looking at the whole circumstances, and the nature of these semi-legal jests, which are called Paradoxes, and the unusually modest song of welcome, I look upon this as another example of Bacon's love for secret composition, though I hesitate to express any strong opinion.[2]

---

[1] The rest has been cut off.
[2] See also p. 208, for examples of Bacon's love of secret prose composition.

CHAPTER II.

COLLABORATION.

THERE are several other matters that are, to a certain extent, confirmatory of the suggestion that Bacon helped Shakespeare. These I propose to refer to, but very shortly, as the view taken of them must depend on the view one takes of the main question. If what has been set out in these pages does not prove that Bacon acted with Shakespeare, the circumstances, to which I am about to refer, will not prove it. But if this fact be considered as proved, they will confirm and strengthen it.

The first matter is, supposing Bacon helped Shakespeare, can we distinguish their work? If we suppose "Hamlet" and "Measure for Measure" to be specimens of the joint work, and "Macbeth" and "Othello," not to mention "Titus Andronicus," to be Shakespeare's unaided work, then if we subtract what we find common to both sets of plays, we have some idea of Shakespeare's and Bacon's respective productions. Bacon's, by this process, seems "law," "learning," and "low comedy," Shakespeare's "great poetical beauty," "magnificent language," sometimes becoming exaggerated in the sentiment, as we see in Lady Macbeth's soliloquy,—

> Come, come, you spirits
> That tend on mortal thoughts, unsex me here, &c., &c.

This view of their respective labours is, I think, confirmed when we come to consider Bacon and Shakespeare as far as we know them. Bacon was fond of collecting stories, sometimes doubtful, as his "Apothegms" show. He was beloved by his servants, with whom he associated rather than with his equals. We have only to turn to the accounts published by Spedding to see how extravagantly he tipped those who brought him presents, &c., and his wasteful way of living and the enormous household he kept. Besides this he dabbled in science, and though he had no real knowledge, he *thought* a good deal, and in his " Sylva Sylvarum : or a Natural History," we find him hazarding the wildest explanations of natural phenomena. Shakespeare on the other hand was, as far as we know, a person who was ambitious of social distinction, seeking a grant of arms for his father, one who, I think, would rather affect gentility.

I think we may next consider if Bacon assisted Shakespeare; how was it done? Collaboration was known to the ancients, and was a common practice in Shakespeare's time. It might be carried out, by one writing one part, the other the rest, as I conceive was the case in the "Antemasque and Main Masque of the Mountebanks,"[1] or Bacon may have written out the prose story which Shakespeare may have dramatized. I have given an example where I think this was done in the masque given during the Gesta Grayorum. It is possible that the "History of Henry VII." was originally written by Bacon for this purpose ; but Shakespeare refused to, or did not dramatize it. It is clearly not a work of a single vacation, as Spedding describes it, nor written *currente calamo* by Bacon after his fall. The body of the work is written consecutively and without unnecessary repetition ; but this part had evidently been lying for a long period in Bacon's desk, and he had from time to time written commencements to it, which were all put together by some one else, as anyone can see by referring to the work, where in the first pages numerous repetitions will be found clumsily put together, and where facts are told more than once. We have them on each

---

[1] *Ante*, p. 331.

occasion given as if not mentioned before, as if from time to time additions had been made covering ground already written about, whilst the person who undertook to prepare the work for publication seems to have hesitated about striking out anything, but has put in a few words to make the narrative appear to run consecutively.

It is difficult to show this patchwork without having the work before the reader; but it may be mentioned that the history, as we now have it, commences with, that on the death of Richard, the Earl of Richmond succeeded to the kingdom, and in a kind of military election, in the presence of the whole army, was saluted king. It is with this incident, it may be remembered, that the play of "Richard III." ends. The story then goes back to the character of Richard III., &c., and then the narrative returns to Henry—"*But* king Henry, at the very entrance of his reign," &c., as if there was some antithesis between the difficulty Henry felt in determining whether he should rely on the title of his wife that was to be, his own title as of the house of Lancaster, or his title as Conqueror; and in dealing with the latter, the fact is repeated as given in "Richard III.," that he was crowned on the field of battle, which was already mentioned on the first page.

On page 20 is commenced the story of Lambert Simnell in these words:—

"There was a subtile Priest called Richard Simon, that lived in Oxford, and had to his pupill a baker's sonne named Lambert Simnell, of the age of some fifteene yeares; a comely youth, and well favoured, not without some extraordinarie dignitie, and grace of aspect," &c.;[1]

and the story goes on that this priest first fancied to make his pupil personate the second of the young princes, who were supposed to be, as we now know they were, murdered in the Tower, but who changed his intention and substituted Edward Plantagenet, the son of Clarence, whom Henry had confined in the Tower; and Bacon suggests that the instigator

---

[1] Page 20.

of the plot was the Dowager Queen, Edward the Fourth's widow, as it is put—

"Thinking her daughter (as the king handled the matter) not advanced, but depressed: and *none could hold the booke so well to prompt and instruct this stage play, as she could.*"[1]

And then the story goes on to tell for the *first* time:—

"It was one of the king's first acts to cloister the Queene Dowager in the Nunnery of Bermondsey, and to take away all her lands and estate; and this by a close counsell without any legall proceeding, upon farre-fetch pretences: *That shee had delivered her two daughters out of sanctuarie to king Richard, contrarie to promise.*"[2]

Now, this fact, which is told once as other facts are in both Hall and Hollinshed as one of the events of this reign, seems to have excited Bacon's interest, and he seems to have considered whether the real reason for her treatment was that she was mixed up in Simon's conspiracy, and the taking her daughters out of sanctuary at Richard's request was only an excuse. He tells the story four times, and sometimes makes this suggestion, and sometimes does not mention it; but in each of the four times he tells it, he tells it each time as something not told before. The paragraph on p. 22 closes with further reflections upon the secret connected with this conspiracy. But the next paragraph commences with the words:

"But to returne to the narration itselfe,"

and we are then informed for the second time that—

Simon did first instruct his scholler for the part of Richard, Duke of Yorke, second sonne to King Edward the Fourth;

but that on a rumour that Plantagenet had escaped—

The cunning priest changed his copie and chose now Plantagenet to be the subject his pupill should personate, &c.,

of which fact we have been informed before.

---

[1] Page 21. This and other theatrical allusions make me think it possible that Jonson helped Bacon to put this work through the press.
[2] Page 22.

We *are then* told for the *second* time, by a decree of the Council—

That the Queene Dowager, for that shee, contrarie to her pact, and agreement with those that had concluded with her concerning the mariage of her daughter Elizabeth with King Henry, had neverthelesse delivered her daughters out of sanctuarie into King Richard's hands; should be cloistered in the Nunnerie of Bermondsey, and forfeit all her lands and goods.[1]

We are then told on the next page that the decrees of the Council were put into execution.

And first, the Queene Dowager was put into the Monasterie of Bermondsey, and all her estate seized into the King's hands, whereat there was much wondering; That a weake woman, for the yeelding to the menaces and promises of a Tyrant, after such a distance of time (wherein the King had shewed no displeasure nor alteration), but much more after so happie a mariage, betweene the King and her daughter, blessed with issue male, should upon a sodaine mutabilitie or disclosure of the King's mind, be so severely handled.[2]

Bacon then goes on to describe her chequered career, having, after being Edward's Queen, "lived to see her brother beheaded, her two sons deposed from the Crown, bastarded in their blood," and cruelly murdered, and "through all this while" she enjoyed her liberty, state, and fortune.

But afterwards againe, upon the rise of the wheele, when she had a king to her sonne-in-law, and was made grandmother to a grandchild of the best sexe; yet was she (upon darke and unknowne reasons, and no lesse strange pretences) precipitated and banished the world, into a nunnerie.[3]

It seems to me that if Bacon had written his story consecutively from day to day, as he would have had to write it if he had begun and produced it, as Mr. Spedding supposes, in a single vacation, he would hardly have told this story of the Queen-Dowager being sent to a monastery four times, and would not have forgotten, when he speaks of this on the third occasion, as being due to a sudden mutability or dis-

---

[1] Page 25.   [2] Page 26.   [3] Page 27.

closure of the King's mind; on the last as caused by the dark and unknown reasons, that he had carefully suggested on the first and second occasion that it was due to her being suspected of complicity in Simon's plot to bring forward Lambert Simnel as Edward Plantagenet, and that he would have so arranged his facts as to make the statement once. It seems, therefore, it is not unreasonable to conclude that this incident of the widow of Edward, who was the principal instrument of Henry VII.'s success in England, being sent by him to a nunnery was one of those illustrations of the change of human fortunes, which would strike a mind like Bacon's, and he might have, from time to time, put this fact down upon paper and made his reflection upon it, which is the reason why the person who assisted him put the different incidents together as best he could; whereas, if Bacon had himself revised the manuscript before it went to press he would have told the story once and only once.

If it was the fact that the "History of Henry the Seventh" was originally written for Shakespeare to dramatize, it may be that the Northumberland MS. which, according to the list given before[1] as containing "Richard the Second" and "Richard the Third," may not be the plays of Shakespeare as Spedding supposes, but the essays or histories of those kings written by Bacon. It may be noticed that if we consider the order in which, as far as we know, the historical plays were written, first the third part of "Henry VI.," perhaps by Greene,[2] then the second part by Shakespeare followed by the first part; then "Henry V." and next the two parts of "Henry IV."; the plays of "Richard II." and "Richard III." would be the two next plays to be added to the series, so that they might be written about the same time; then would come "Henry VII." after "Richard III.," and finally, "Henry VIII.," a play which I have given reasons for believing was written in its present form by Bacon and Jonson for the Folio of 1623.[3]

---

[1] *Ante*, p. 320.   [2] *Ante*, p. 314.   [3] *Ante*, p. 230.

Another matter to be considered is whether there is not evidence that Bacon, finding that Jonson had discovered he was helping Shakespeare, did not patch up a peace between the two, and whether both Bacon and Shakespeare did not help Jonson with his "Sejanus." It may be remembered that in "Cynthia's Revels" Jonson objects[1]—

That they (your poets) would not so penuriously glean wit from every laundress or hackney man, or derive their best grace with servile imitations from common stages *or observation of the company they converse with*, as if their invention lived wholly upon another man's trencher.

If I am right in considering that it was Bacon and not Shakespeare who delighted in this low life, it is evident, I think, that Jonson did not at the time know of the collaboration between the two. But in his next play, the "Poetaster," there are allusions which I think show that Jonson had discovered the secret. In this play we have the character of young Ovid, who neglects his business as a lawyer and writes plays. His father attacks him for doing this, he defends himself upon the ground that he does not do so publicly.

> They wrong me, sir, and do abuse you more,
> That blow your ears with these untrue reports;
> I am not known unto the open stage,
> Nor do I traffic in their theatres.
> Indeed I do acknowledge, at request
> Of some near friends, and honorable Romans,
> I have begun a poem of that nature, &c.

This may refer to Bacon, and probably did, if, as I have so often said, Bacon did assist Shakespeare; at all events, shortly after, a truce was proclaimed between Shakespeare and Jonson, and the former admittedly helped Jonson to produce "Sejanus." This play is written in a very different style from anything that Jonson had produced before. It is true it is taken from history, but it is written with a dignity

---

[1] *Ante*, p. 181.

and refinement we do not find in any of Jonson's previous plays. But the quarrel broke out again and Jonson took out, or believed he took out, all Shakespeare had written. He says,—

This book in all its numbers is not the same which was acted on the public stage, wherein a second pen had a great share, in place of which I have chosen to put weaker, and no doubt less pleasing lines of my own than to defraud so happy a genius of his right by my loathed usurpation.

Now it is to be observed if Bacon were the sole author of Shakespeare's plays, then the presumption is that it was Bacon and not Shakespeare who assisted Jonson; now Jonson looked up to Bacon as Virgil did to Mæcenas, and Jonson would never have written thus of him. But in the trial scene of Silius, I think we find the same legal mind which is so prominent a factor in some of Shakespeare's plays. If in " Measure for Measure " we have a picture of the judge on circuit, in " Henry VIII." a sketch from life of an English Lord Chancellor, in " Sejanus " we have a picture of an English state trial as it was conducted under the Tudors. The scene is closely taken from Tacitus, but it is drawn by one who was at home in Westminster Hall. The peculiarity of the state trials under the Tudors was that they were not the real trials. A prisoner had been examined by the council and generally had been condemned by that tribunal before he was sent into court. And the government having satisfied themselves that he was guilty, sent him not so much to be tried as to be convicted. There are both advantages and objections to this form of proceeding, the principal objection being, that the escape of a prisoner was a reflection on the government. This might strike the reflective mind of Bacon, and, though he would hesitate to express his view about his own Courts, he might have used the scene when Silius is brought before the senate, to give expression to his thoughts, when such things could be said without giving offence to the powers that be.

Sejanus having interfered in favour of the accusers, who had received their briefs, before Silius enters unwarned and unprepared, Silius says :

> Ay, take part.   Reveal yourselves ;
> Alas ! I scent not your confederacies,
> Your plots and combinations, I not know.
> Minion Sejanus hates me ; and that all
> *This boast of law and law is but a form—*
> *A net of Vulcan's filing—a mere engine*
> To take that life by a pretext of justice
> Which you pursue in malice.   I want brain
> Or nostril to persuade me, that your ends
> And purposes are made to what they are
> Before my answer, &c.

Afterwards he says—

> Come, do not hunt
> And labour so about for circumstance
> To make him guilty whom you have fore-doomed, &c.

Finally he kills himself. Of course it is impossible to speak with anything like absolute certainty, but all this savours, to my mind, of the ideas of a learned lawyer who alone would appreciate the evils of the then existing systems.

This three-sided arrangement, if it ever existed, did not long continue. James was on the throne ; Bacon had his professional career opened up ; Jonson took to writing masques, and Shakespeare, I believe, ceased to act with Bacon.

The Folio of 1623.—The last and closing scene of any relationship which may have existed between Bacon and Shakespeare was the publication of the Folio of 1623. If we are satisfied that Bacon assisted Shakespeare, then, I think, there are a great number of circumstances connected with the publication of the folio to show that it was brought about by Bacon and Jonson—that probably Jonson assisted Bacon in the production of " Henry VIII.," and that, lying with the manuscript of that history, were some of the manuscripts of which Bacon had been the part author ; and from this and other sources Jonson gathered together the plays as we find them in the folio. I now propose to state very shortly my reasons for these suggestions. It has often been pointed out that in 1623 Shakespeare had been dead seven years, and that no attempt to collect and gather his works together had been made till the time of Bacon's fall, when he was greatly in want of money. This folio we only know was published in 1623—no month is mentioned, so that we cannot exactly determine when it was published. It purports to have been published by Hemming and Condell.

These men were now growing old, and one of them, Hemming, was, as we know from the papers of 1632 published by Halliwell, in serious pecuniary difficulties. Shakespeare had been dead seven years, and no attempt, as far as we know, had been made to collect his plays, though many of them had been published in quartos. There is a dedication by Hemming and Condell of the work to the Earl of Pembroke and the Earl of Montgomery, which concludes with the remarkable words, speaking of the plays:—

"That what delights in them may ever be, your lordships, the reputation his and the faults our own, if any be committed by a pair so careful to show their gratitude both to the *living and the dead*."

This dedication is believed by many, as well as the address to the readers, to have been written by Jonson. Be that as it may, Jonson wrote the lines facing the portrait and those addressed to Shakespeare's memory, and, I think we may assume, took an active part in the publication of the work. Hemming and Condell also say they have only collected the plays, and the title page says they were published according to the true original copies. I propose to consider presently the question where those original copies were found.

The work seems to have been put through the press in some haste; this, I think, is shown by two facts: the first is, that the copy seems to have been first divided into three general heads of Comedies, Histories, Tragedies, and each commences with page 1, &c., as if they were being set up simultaneously. More than this, we find that in the last two of the three divisions, the Comedies being properly paged, the copy has been again sub-divided, and the number of the page for the second sub-division guessed at, so that the pages do not follow on; but there is either an overlapping of the numbers or a gap. This seems to be a reasonable explanation of this want of consecutiveness in the paging. Thus, in the Histories, we commence with page 1, and the pages run on continuously to 100, which brings us to the end of "Henry IV." But "Henry V." commences with page 69, and the numbers there go on, 70, 71, up to 232 (the end of "Henry VIII."), showing, in my view, that up to "Henry IV." the type was set up in one place, and at the same time the rest of the Histories, which were estimated to commence at 69, were being set up at another.

When we come to the Tragedies, there is another curious fact which shows that the first, viz. "Troilus and Cressida," was interpolated, after the others, beginning with "Coriolanus," had been put in type. For the play of "Troilus and Cressida" commences at page 78; we then have 79 and 80 properly printed, 81 is put in as 18, 82 is correct, 83 is printed £8 at the wrong corner, and so is 84 put 48, and after that the play is not paged; and when we come to the Table of Contents we find this play is not there, the Tragedies commencing with "Coriolanus," page 1. The paging goes on to 98, the end of "Timon of Athens." But "Julius Cæsar," the next play, commences at 109, showing this time the printers over-estimated the space required. From thence the paging is correct, except printer's errors, of which there is a very curious one in the middle of "Hamlet," where page 156 is succeeded by page 257, and thence to the end this error of 100 is continued, the last page but one being 398 instead of 298, and the last page of all is put as 993, a misprint for 399, that being an error for 299. This error of 100 is copied in the Table of Contents. Thus, "Hamlet" is put at 152, and

"Lear," the next play, at 283. Some of the plays are not divided into acts and scenes; some of which, as, for example, "Hamlet," are supposed to be printed from the acting or play-house copies, to which, it is presumed, Hemming and Condell would readily have access. But it seems that this can hardly be the case, for one would expect the acting copy would show the beginning and ending of the different scenes. In the Quartos these divisions are not given; but in the Folio some are and some are not. The most curious example, perhaps, is that of "Hamlet," where at starting the play is properly divided, as we have—

Actus primus. Scœna prima, scena secunda follows, then *scena tertia*, as we have them in the modern editions. But the rest of the act is not divided, scene four, on the platform, and the second scene with the ghost, where he imparts his story to Hamlet, not being separated from the scene between Laertes and his father. We then have *actus secundus*, when Polonius and Reynaldo enter, but no mention is made of the scene, and then follows *scena secunda*, but there are no subdivisions either of acts or scenes afterwards for the remainder of the play. Most of the plays are headed at the beginning *Actus primus, Scœna prima—scœna* being spelt with a diphthong, but subsequently with the e only—*scena*. "Julius Cæsar" is divided in acts, but not scenes. "Anthony and Cleopatra" into neither. Some, as "Macbeth," are divided into both acts and scenes.

The next important thing to be considered is, where do the manuscripts come from? Various accounts have been given by different authors as to this; but it seems to me they have all overlooked this difficulty, that if, as they suppose in many cases, the publishers obtained an acting copy from the playhouses, that we should at least find such acting-copy properly divided into acts and scenes, and that the text would be free from such topical allusions as the quarrel between Shakespeare and Jonson and other incidents connected with the Blackfriars Theatre, as we find in "Hamlet"; and more particularly, I think, we must ask ourselves how it is that, in the play of "Henry V.," we have the choruses given to us, which are not to be found in the Quartos. Now, the chorus to the 5th Act contains one of those compliments I think so characteristic of Bacon addressed to Essex, when he was in Ireland, in these terms :—

> How London doth powre out her Citizens,
> The Maior and all his Brethren in best sort,
> Like to the Senatours of th' antique Rome,
> With the Plebeians swarming at their heeles,
> Goe forth and fetch their conqu'ring Cæsar in :
> As by a lower, but by loving likelyhood,
> *Were now the Generall of our gracious Empresse,*
> *As in good time he may, from Ireland comming,*
> *Bringing Rebellion broached on his sword;*
> *How many would the peacefull Citie quit,*
> *To welcome him?* much more, and much more cause,
> Did they this, Harry.

Essex was in Ireland between the months of March and September, 1599, when he suddenly returned and surprised the Queen in her palace of Nonsuch. He was executed shortly afterwards under circumstances which would prevent any reference to him being made upon the stage. The choruses, as stated, are not in the Quartos. I think, therefore, we may fairly conclude that the play, as we have it in the Folio of 1623, was printed from a manuscript which had not seen the light or been subject to revision for about twenty-four years. No one supposes that Bacon, after his treatment of Essex, would have willingly allowed this allusion to be published. My view is, that he was too engaged with the play of "Henry VIII." to trouble about the matter.

One more thing to be pointed out is, that Jonson, both in his lines to the portrait and those on Shakespeare himself, has written words which, like the Delphic Oracles, can be read either way. This, again, may be a coincidence—one of the very many which we come across in considering the facts, which have come down to us concerning Shakespeare, Bacon, and Jonson.

THE END.

R